Famous Last Words

Chris Wood

PEN & SWORD HISTORY

First published in Great Britain in 2021 by
Pen & Sword History
An imprint of
Pen & Sword Books Ltd
Yorkshire – Philadelphia

ISBN 978 1 52677 089 9

Typeset by Mac Style
Printed and bound by CPI Group (UK) Ltd, Croydon, CR0 4YY

Pen & Sword Books Limited incorporates the imprints of Atlas,
Archaeology, Aviation, Discovery, Family History, Fiction, History,
Maritime, Military, Military Classics, Politics, Select, Transport,
True Crime, Air World, Frontline Publishing, Leo Cooper, Remember
When, Seaforth Publishing, The Praetorian Press, Wharncliffe
Local History, Wharncliffe Transport, Wharncliffe True Crime
and White Owl.

For a complete list of Pen & Sword titles please contact

PEN & SWORD BOOKS LIMITED
47 Church Street, Barnsley, South Yorkshire, S70 2AS, England
E-mail: enquiries@pen-and-sword.co.uk
Website: www.pen-and-sword.co.uk

Or

PEN AND SWORD BOOKS
1950 Lawrence Rd, Havertown, PA 19083, USA
E-mail: Uspen-and-sword@casematepublishers.com
Website: www.penandswordbooks.com

Contents

Acknowledgements

An incredible amount of support and encouragement goes into the writing of a book. Before this, my first foray into such endeavours, I could never have known quite how much, on a professional level and, of course, personally.

In these rather inadequate efforts to express my thanks, however, there can be no other way for me to begin these pages than by bestowing the most emphatic and heartfelt gratitude upon my wife Charlotte and daughter Emma. Without their unconditional love and unrelenting support, this book would have remained an impossible dream. It has certainly been an eventful journey – and one which could not have been travelled without you both at my side.

Emma: in your own inimitable toddler fashion you have provided me with countless sleepless nights to allow me to work on the book, and for this, I thank you. Although now it's written, I very much hope you might now consider the odd 'lie-in'. During the more difficult moments, you have both been the constants which have enabled me to smile and to continue writing with renewed vigour. Thank you, both.

To my parents: your continued support is, and has always been, boundless and so very much appreciated, particularly in allowing me to descend upon you at all hours and attach myself to the kitchen table for hours on end whilst you both suffered hungrily in the lounge. But for everything you have both done for me, and the rest of us, thank you – we are blessed to have you both.

I must also extend my warmest thanks to the rest of my family and incredible friends, all of whom have provided their unwavering support and constant kindness throughout this venture. I had immersed myself in a state of self-isolation long before it was ordered for everyone in response to a global pandemic, and finally being able to socialise once more with you all is a prospect I am very much looking forward to!

In regards to the creation of the book itself, there are, of course, many people to whom I need to express huge gratitude. I begin here by thanking Kate Bohdanowicz, for initiating things in the first instance in respect of the book and for always being on hand to help with my many queries.

Aileen Pringle, my delivery contact with Pen and Sword: I cannot thank you enough. You have without fail responded to my incessant emails and endless questions with nothing but kindness and care, and have been an absolute pleasure to deal with. I realise you may not be as willing, but I very much hope to continue working with you lots more in the future, whereby hopefully my quizzing of you will at least become less and less!

I am also hugely grateful to my copy-editor, Michelle Higgs, who has with much patience helped me through the final stages of the book. Your willingness to help and readiness with insightful suggestions wherever possible has been utterly peerless and I am very grateful to you.

There is an endless wealth of wonderful research facilities in this country, many of which have been vital in the writing of this book. To all of the amazingly kind and helpful people in our archives across the land, I am indebted to you all. I must, however, deliver a special mention here for Cheshire Archives and Local Studies, and Wiltshire and Swindon History Centre, the staff of which regularly went above and beyond regular duty for me; our documented history lies in safe hands indeed. These thanks I must extend further to The Wellcome Collection, The British Newspaper Archive, The British Library, Newcastle City Library, Northumbria University Library and The National Records of Scotland. Working with you all has been a lovely 'by-product' of this book, and something which I would love to do again. I am grateful for the guidance offered by the coroners of Lancashire and Southampton, and though further afield, but of no less importance, I convey immense thanks to the wonderful Historical and Special Collections Library of the Harvard Law School for their kind assistance.

I offer my sincere gratitude also to Mark Wylie, the curator of Manchester United's museum, and to Amy Mechowski of London's fabulous Garrick Club, another two whose efforts knew no limits. Livia Scott, Jenny Harrison and Fiona Harwood – students of Newcastle University's History department – thank you for all of your hard work on my behalf; it will always be hugely appreciated.

These words alone do not seem adequate in comparison to what each and every one of you have done for me. Nonetheless, I hope that they do offer some realisation of how important you have all been to me during this adventure – I am forever beholden to you all.

In the context of this book, it is perhaps fitting to impart some final words which, to my mind, encapsulates you all perfectly. Upon his deathbed, shortly before his worldly departure, Sir Arthur Conan Doyle whispered to his wife: 'To me, you are wonderful!'

And you lot truly are.

Sources and Illustrations

Every effort has been made to contact copyright holders of sources and illustrations in this book. If the publishers are made aware of any oversights, these will be corrected in future editions.

Introduction

The almighty taboo of death. A final journey we must all travel, the one aspect of life that truly does not discriminate, its foreboding shackles ultimately gripping us all. Yet still, even in our own enlightened times, its very concept is still something that we very often struggle to embrace. Our ancestors it seems, less so. The witnessing of an executed felon 'dancing the hangman's jig' was viewed as roaring entertainment; the chance to observe the last actions and words of somebody was an intriguing prospect and, as you will see within these pages, was often regarded as unmissable. The idea of attending such an event nowadays seems barely thinkable, but I often wonder how many of us today – if offered the chance to attend a bygone spectacle of that wincing nature – would, out of the morbid curiosity that seems to dwell within so many of us, follow the crowds and observe the event ourselves? It is an interesting thought and if, incidentally, you are one of these people, some of your curiosities will certainly be satisfied in this book.

Some of the individuals detailed within, you may have prior knowledge of. Included also, however, are a host of souls that will be introduced to you for the first time. Learn of the fates which culminate in that inevitable finality, as you glimpse into their preparations for an entry into eternity.

You will encounter an eclectic array of subjects which occupy the thoughts and minds of the dying, from those who use their final utterances to poke fun at the grisly king himself, slipping away with a jest upon their lips, or perhaps a miserable protestation of innocence, to others who, more conventionally, choose to emit words of love, courage, wisdom or perhaps sorrow. Restraint has been adopted, however, so as not to include the vast array of such accounts which exist from warfare and the trenches, as these are rightfully covered more comprehensively in other genre-specific works.

Included are portrayals from varying eras and locations, some who are entrenched in pauperism, others in the palace, for status and prestige does not equate to an exemption from the reaper's relentless tenacity.

Each case carried its own appeal, but rather than compiling a mere list of final words, the context of each individual is considered in terms of their arrival at their concluding moments, and ultimately their final words. Some are short and succinct, while others are lengthier, but all are nonetheless filled with intrigue and often mystery.

As the one thing which connects us all, I invite you to witness some of the final throes of those that have gone before us, from criminally infused minds, to those who wish to confess, and to those who chose to master their own destiny – each one has a story to tell.

Now it is time to hear them.

Chapter 1

Frank Franklin

The hamlet of Kingsdown in Upper Stratton, Swindon, boasts a picture postcard setting. There are green spaces and a delightful village pub engrained with a rich history serviced by its very own brewery immediately next door. The brewery has the proud distinction of being Swindon's oldest company and one of the oldest traditional breweries still in operation in Britain today. The beer, having made merry its local residents since 1843, is still brewed today in much the same way as it was when it was first created by John Arkell more than 175 years ago. The Arkell name remains much acclaimed in the locality, the family still proudly at the helm of the Wiltshire institution. Indeed, perhaps this longevity best reflects the village feeling where community spirit and comforting familiarity bind its residents together.

In the latter part of the nineteenth century, however, the community would endure two shocking occurrences which would initiate a feeling of abhorrence and distress throughout this routinely serene area. Kingsdown bore witness to a most sensational double tragedy. The initial events were as tragic and shocking as one could imagine. Yet the happenings that would later unfold completed a truly sinister episode, and would ultimately help unravel an enduring mystery of child murder.

Katie Reeves was born on 1 June 1885 in Stratton St Margaret. Katie's mother was a domestic servant named Emily Reeves. The young girl was born into a difficult early family life. Emily was unmarried and did not reside with the father, Walter Nicholls, who was steadfastly disinterested in helping to provide for his young child. Such was his resolve, in fact, that Nicholls was even prepared to serve a short jail sentence for the non-compliance of an order he received from Swindon Police Court in 1885, which had instructed him to provide financial help for the upkeep of his daughter. Several months elapsed without any form of payment and so Nicholls was forced to serve one month's imprisonment as punishment.

Despite this conflict, life was becoming a happier affair for Emily, and in 1888 she married William Speck, a blacksmiths' striker with whom she subsequently lived, along with his children, at 21 Carr Street, Kingsdown. Perhaps this arrangement, though, was a strain on capacity at Carr Street as young Katie was subsequently adopted by her maternal grandmother, Hannah Reeves, and they both lived together at nearby Flower Cottage.

In early 1890, Emily's marriage to William had sadly run its course and the pair separated. The split did, however, reunite Emily and her young daughter Katie, as Emily was forced to move back into her mother's home at Flower Cottage. But if a failed marriage was cause for any sadness within the family, what happened less than a year later would pale this into insignificance, as a parent's most crushing nightmare morphed into a devastating and mystifying reality.

On Sunday, 1 March 1891, 5-year-old Katie had enjoyed her afternoon Sunday school session before returning home for tea at five o'clock. Katie did not attend day school, so the chance to join up and play with other children was a keen highlight for the young girl. Indeed, on this particular day, she had gone outside to play immediately after her tea, before conscientiously returning to Flower Cottage to ask her grandmother if she could stay out a little longer. Permission was granted, on the condition that she did not stay out too long, as the night was drawing in and a cold damp air was beginning to envelop Kingsdown.

Katie was seen playing in the street close to her home with four friends. Sometime around twenty past six, the other children had made their way home, unwilling to irk their parents by baying for extra playtime. Katie, though, remained outside, alone. This would not ordinarily be a cause for concern, however. Youngsters frolicking without care upon the cobbles has, after all, developed into a symbol of an apparent worriless age, one where communities were tightly entwined and locals' watchful eyes would never be too far from the spirited children of the neighbourhood.

As the afternoon passed through to evening, the day's remaining light gave way to the inevitable darkness and dimly-lit streets. The dwellers of sedate and sleepy Kingsdown could never have thought that anyone amongst them could be harnessing the shadows to carry out an act of sinister wickedness.

Sometime after half past six, Katie Reeves vanished from the hushed streets, which had formerly been her playground. Initially, there was no understanding that the child was even missing; Katie's grandmother had ill-fatedly assumed that she had walked towards Gorse Hill, where her mother had been visiting her brother, George. Upon Emily's return home shortly before ten o'clock, it became clear that wires had been crossed, and a frenzied realisation that young Katie was missing prompted a desperate search of the local area.

Brooks, ditches and hedgerows were frantically searched, but without any success. As such, the police were belatedly alerted just after midnight, when PC Lodge, who was stationed at nearby Stratton, was tasked with heading the search. He spent the rest of the night diligently looking for Katie, but the efforts would prove to be in vain with no trace forthcoming.

Sadly, at half past ten on Monday morning, a gruesome discovery was finally made which plunged Kingsdown into desolate disbelief. The find ensured that police were now investigating a 'shocking child murder' as the local press announced. Frank Franklin was the local lad, only 16 years old himself, who made the grim discovery in a brook which was filled with shallow water. The brook lay at the bottom of a set of allotments owned by Thomas Arkell.

The police, in contrast to the search, were called immediately and initial assumptions were formed. The little body of Katie Reeves was transported the short distance to the Kingsdown Inn, which would host the inquest to be opened the following day.

The coroner for North Wiltshire was Mr William Browne, who duly opened inquest proceedings on Tuesday, 3 March. Great interest had manifested itself in the local area since the discovery of Katie's body and was, understandably, the only thing on local minds. A jury was rapidly assembled, fronted by Mr S Colborne as foreman. Juries of this time were required to visit the spot where a body had been found, before also having to view the body itself. These disturbing visual directives preceded the witness statements from all individuals that were in some way enmeshed in the tragedy.

The first witness called was Katie's grandmother, Hannah Reeves, who principally confirmed that the misunderstanding concerning her granddaughter's whereabouts resulted in the delayed search for the missing child. The primary witness, however, was the young man who found Katie's body, Frank Franklin. Franklin was a baker's assistant employed at George Hale's bakery. He was the last person known to have seen Katie before she disappeared. Franklin reported that he saw the young girl on Sunday evening at half past six, near her home. He did not speak to her, but continued past her towards Blunsdon, a mere short walk away.

Franklin's evidence continued, as he then relived to the jury the events of how he discovered Katie's body. On the Monday morning, he rose typically early for work, arriving at Hale's bakery just after five o'clock, and it was at this point that he heard about the missing child. Franklin worked for a few hours before returning home for breakfast at quarter past eight, then stated that upon his return to work, Mrs Hale sent him to the allotments to 'gather some greens'. As he busily bagged up vegetables for Mrs Hale, Franklin saw Lucy Durham, another local resident, in the adjacent plot. The pair struck up a conversation about the missing child, before Franklin quizzically called out to her, 'I wonder whether the child has got in the brook?' Upon this intriguing deduction, Franklin curiously wandered towards the bottom of the allotments where a series of small ditches lay. His fortuitous hunch quickly reaped its reward as he was soon heard calling out: 'Here it is!' He had located Katie's body, lying stiffly on her back in an apparent shallow grave.

PC Lodge then provided his evidence to the inquest. Following news of the discovery of Katie Reeves, he immediately proceeded to the spot where her body lay prone, in a ditch of 'about three inches of running water'. PC Lodge asserted that her clothes were disarranged and blood stains were visible on her under-garments. Katie's hat was found a few yards from the body, but PC Lodge could see no sign of a struggle having taken place on the bank and so naturally concluded that she had probably been injured elsewhere prior to being placed in the brook, an opinion with which several of the jurymen who had also seen the body in situ had concurred. PC Lodge concluded his evidence stating that having examined the murder scene, he promptly called Dr Fernie to view the body.

Following the constable's evidence, the inquest was adjourned until two o'clock on the afternoon of Friday, 6 March. Upon resumption of the inquest, the results from Dr Fernie's post-mortem were to be disclosed.

So it was, in the Kingsdown Inn, before Mr Coroner Browne and the existing jury, the medical evidence was heard. The exhaustive examination of Katie's body had been conducted by Doctors Fernie and Duffet, the pair working in tandem. The duo reported that there was an abrasion over much of her left cheek, ear and nose, with mud nestled in her right ear, similar to the mud found in the stream where she was discovered. The tongue protruded between her teeth and there was a small wound on the lower part of her body. Her internal organs were described as being generally healthy, though her 'left lung was bad.' After these disclosures, Dr Fernie confirmed that he had sought guidance from several 'medical men' to help ascertain the cause of Katie's death. Dr Fernie was firmly of the belief that she had died from suffocation and not drowning, as had been an early suggestion.

Mercifully, there was no evidence of rape having been committed, and it was deduced that Katie had likely been dead before being dumped in the stream. The coroner then reiterated to the two doctors all of the evidence that had been heard a few days previously, and provided a brief summing up of the case so far as was known, before the jury considered their verdict. The jury, of course, could not seek to convict or mete out guilt upon an individual at this point, with no suspects uncovered; rather, their role was simply to conclude the manner of fate that had befallen Katie Reeves. Having considered their verdict, the members of the jury confirmed that Katie had come to her death 'through suffocation, caused by some person or persons unknown' and to this end, murder had been committed. To try and coax any information that might lead to the killer, the jury took a step which was unusual at the time, recommending that a reward should be offered, so the sum of between £50 and £100 was suggested for the detection of the murderer.

On Sunday, 8 March 1891, the small body of Katie Reeves was laid to rest at St Margaret's Church, Stratton. The funeral was attended in huge numbers as relatives, friends from Katie's Sunday school, villagers, and hordes of people from Swindon came together, engulfed in united grief and linked by their desires to pay their final respects. Hundreds were unable to gain admission, as estimates of between 1,200 and 1,500 persons were present. The *Swindon Advertiser* reported at the time that the coffin was 'covered with wreaths and crosses from sorrowing relatives,' and the small coffin was 'carried into the church by four young women.'

Following Katie's committal to the earth, it was also reported that scores of people rather ghoulishly visited the site where the young child's body had been found, out of apparent curiosity and the need to feed a macabre thirst and attempt to understand her death.

As police tried to enhance their understanding of just who had murdered Katie, very little progress was made regarding the identification of any suspects for the killing. Police appeared to know very little, and although they favoured the idea that the killer was not a stranger, this still failed to herald any potential suspects.

However, as the second anniversary of Katie's murder approached, the final words of a young man would unveil Katie's killer and in doing so, unravel the most sensational chapter in Kingsdown's history.

Kingsdown's baker, Mr George Hale, employed three young men as his assistants, including Frank Franklin, the unfortunate finder of Katie Reeves' body. The three shared a bedroom within Hale's residence, and on Friday, 16 December 1892 they had all retired to bed shortly before nine o'clock. Whilst his colleagues slept, Frank Franklin rose quietly and crept out into the darkness of the night. Just after midnight, he encountered PC Lodge in Lower Stratton. The pair briefly spoke before bidding each other goodnight. PC Lodge could not have known it then, but Franklin was about to solve the very mystery that the constable had so vainly attempted to fathom months earlier.

The young man wandered down to the Great Western Railway main line near Stratton Cross Roads Bridge, and placed his head on the railway track before an oncoming goods train. He was killed instantly. The driver of another train passing the spot saw the sickening sight and immediately reported the incident to the police. Upon attending the scene, the police were met with a most horrendous sight, with local press reporting that the head was 'horribly disfigured and some of the brains were found scattered as far as twenty-five yards away' from where Franklin had been struck. His body was removed from the tracks and taken to Swindon Police Station.

The same afternoon, an inquest was heard at the Great Western Railway Station, with Coroner Browne once again leading matters. Dr Edward Covey provided the rather frightful medical evidence, stating that the deceased's body bore no fractures whatsoever, but the 'whole of the skull was missing, and nearly all of the brains.' If these descriptions were to be expected in the horrifying circumstances, the revelation that was next to be uncovered astounded everybody. Dr Covey informed the congregated inquest that he had discovered a small black notebook in one of Franklin's pockets. This little book caused much consternation amongst the jury as it was handed around for collective viewing. It contained numerous recipes for baking cakes, texts of scripture and the alphabet written in Pitman's shorthand. But alongside these haphazard scribblings came two verses. Both written in ink, they appeared to prophesise the young man's preferred impending destination:

> Heaven's a beautiful city,
> The streets are of pure gold;
> I'm going there to see Jesus,
> And all the Apostles of old.

> Heaven's a beautiful city,
> And God will sit on His throne;
> I'm going there to see Jesus,
> And will you let me go alone?

Franklin had clearly decided upon his fate, and with his final words – addressed solely to his mother – made the following breath-taking admission:

> Dear Mother, – Don't trouble about me. I am the murderer of Katie Reeves. I am so miserable I can't stand it. When you see this I shall be dead. So good-bye. Give my love to all. F. Franklin.

Franklin's last words clearly portray an individual immersed in unliveable guilt. But it appears that whilst he could no longer cope with the unbearable pressure of his actions, he was generally able to live normally and not outwardly convey any panic that he had been feeling. This was confirmed with the coroner's cross-examination of Franklin's friend and fellow lodger, 17-year-old Ernest Tom Hacker. Upon being asked if 'the deceased had ever expressed a wish to destroy himself,' Hacker simply replied, 'No, sir.' When a juryman questioned if Franklin had 'been in a strange mood yesterday,' Hacker again retorted in the negative, adding that Franklin was actually brighter than usual, and that he was 'full of fun'.

Hacker did, however, reveal an instance where his deceased friend did demonstrate an insight into his thinking at the time of the suicide. Hacker revealed that Franklin had once asked if there would be forgiveness for anyone who committed suicide. A staunch teetotaller, Franklin was also of strong faith, and the idea of forgiveness would have been paramount to him. Less so, it seems, the need to be forgiven for the snuffing out of an innocent child's life.

Foreman of the jury, Harry Thomas, returned a verdict that Franklin had 'committed suicide whilst temporarily insane.' It was considered that his final words proved beyond any doubt that his mind was in a 'very deranged state'. Whatever the truth in this respect, his words unequivocally unmasked himself as a most unlikely child killer; one that robbed an innocent young girl of her life and hurled a sedate community into stricken despair.

Chapter 2

Mary Blandy

It is difficult to imagine a more sorrowful tale than the eighteenth-century case of Mary Blandy; it was one of love and adoration, much of it misplaced, and through some naïve and ill-judged desires, she would be catalogued in the annals of female criminality forever.

Not that the upbringing of Mary Blandy was typical of such perpetrators. She was the daughter of Francis Blandy, a prosperous lawyer greatly esteemed for many years as the town clerk of Henley-on-Thames, Oxfordshire. Francis was a buoyant figure steeped in respect and recognition throughout the local parish, and his professional skill ensured that he acted for much of the neighbouring gentry and was indeed a person of some importance. His wife, Mary, née Stevens, was held with equal adoration, described as 'an emblem of chastity and virtue; graceful in person, in mind elevated'. It was thought these amiable qualities had been instilled in the couple's only child, their daughter Mary.

Francis Blandy relished his swelling reputation as a man of considerable wealth and elevated social standing. The family home was a comfortable property in Hart Street, which afforded a most flamboyant level of hospitality to any visitors. The Blandys' cherished daughter Mary revelled in such surroundings and was doted on by her parents, even home-schooled by her mother, developing a keen interest in reading, a pursuit many children would not have had the fortune to sample in eighteenth-century Britain. Mary was advanced beyond her years, achieving attainment long before peers of her age. Physically she was slight and petite, and when the combination of her gifted brain and charm of manner was supplemented by the prospect of an advertised dowry of £10,000 for the man who married her, an inevitable stream of suitors promptly pursued her. Considered a 'catch' by much of the grandiose Henley society, a host of cavaliering admirers shadowed Mary in hope.

Any optimism, however, turned for the most part to dismayed rejection, as one by one their attempts were staunchly rebuffed. Mr Blandy was proving himself most business-like in all things, including the dealings with his only daughter's potential husband. Full value for money was required and should it not be forthcoming, neither too it seemed would be Mary's hand in marriage.

Cupid's unwavering arrow, though, finally appeared to strike with success in the summer of 1746. The aristocratic circles in which Mary was so naturally captivating would ironically prove to be the desolate unravelling of the young girl, rather than the commencement of a fruitful and joyous relationship.

General Lord Mark Kerr was one of Mr Blandy's more esteemed acquaintances. Upon dining with her parents at Lord Mark's home – aptly named 'Paradise' – Mary first encountered one Captain William Henry Cranstoun, also a guest of Lord Mark. A Scottish soldier with an apparent uninviting appearance and demeanour, he was not at first glance a satisfactory companion for the effervescent Mary. Described as small, freckled and 'pitted with the smallpox,' he lacked all of the elegance that Mary radiated so abundantly. Any deficiencies in these respects though were gladly overlooked, particularly when Mr Blandy discovered that the captain was actually the fifth son of a Scots peer, William, fifth Lord Cranstoun. This rapturous news thrilled Mary's father: the desire to marry his daughter to such an honourable gentleman usurping all else, whilst enabling him to obtain kinship to much of the Scottish aristocracy.

According to Mary Blandy's own account of proceedings, it was not until the following summer of 1747 that this small, ungainly chap Cranstoun declared his passion for her, and his wish to take her hand in marriage. He asserted his intentions to Mr and Mrs Blandy, a proposal which was greatly welcomed. In the proposal Cranstoun helped allay any fears that he was in fact already married, a suggestion that had been circulated previously and been a cause for some concern. These fears quashed, the captain began to enjoy hospitality the Blandy way, and likewise, Mrs Blandy enjoyed his company, whilst a proud father took much pleasure in boastfully broadcasting his daughter's acquaintance with nobility.

The scene of domestic bliss, though, would not last and Mr Blandy would be catapulted into a rage and fury reserved for the likes of a wrongdoing against a daughter. Upon receipt of a written letter from Lord Mark, Mary's father learnt the painful and ignominious truth that his much-coveted son-in-law-to-be was indeed already a married gentleman, with a wife and child living in Scotland. Quite how much of old Mr Blandy's irk and ire was conceived through the upset caused to his only child, as opposed to his own personal humiliation, we can only speculate, but the capitulation in the proposed kinship was definite.

It transpired that Cranstoun was privately wed to an Anne Murray at Edinburgh on 22 May 1744. Anne and her family were of Jacobite and Roman Catholic faith, so the marriage was not published for fear of jeopardising the 'gallant' Cranstoun's chances of occupational promotion. The pair lived together for some months clandestinely before she returned to her family and the captain resumed his regimental duties in London. The newlyweds corresponded regularly by letter throughout their uncoupling and in February 1745, the newest Mrs Cranstoun gave birth to a daughter. This did nothing to evoke any paternal instincts within Cranstoun, instead adopting the position that Anne had merely been his mistress and as gallantly as ever, had promised her marriage if she would change her religion to his own perceived 'loftier' Presbyterian faith. As she refused to do so, he believed this entirely freed him from their engagement. Anne, however, was not as willing to adhere to his deceit as he was in contriving it. In October 1746 and in accordance with Scots practice, she raised an action of 'declarator of marriage' against her insidious spouse in the Commissary Court at Edinburgh.

Incensed at the way in which he had fallen victim to Cranstoun's craft, a belligerent Blandy demanded a rendezvous with his treacherous and roguish guest. In contradiction to much of Cranstoun's behaviour, he agreed to the difficult grilling he was sure to receive from his prospective father-in-law. Of course, his attendance was undoubtedly fuelled by his unrelenting desire to lay claim to the dowry, rather than to appease any transgression on his part.

'I am not, nor ever was!' was the declaration from Cranstoun in reference to his apparent marriage. In Mrs Blandy, Cranstoun had an unlikely ally, a blinkered lady who clutched at any explanation Cranstoun would offer. She had desperately enjoyed the captain's company, and eventually would have her husband accepting Cranstoun's word too and he – albeit reluctantly – allowed the engagement to continue, at least until the result of the legal proceedings became clear. Blandy was, after all, loathe to relinquish his newly-claimed aristocratic connections, regardless of the ignominy he had endured at Cranstoun's hands.

Mrs Blandy's ill-judged adoration for the captain, riddled with his curious imperfections, was to be demonstrated most vividly in May 1748. Mary and her mother made a visit to Turville Court, a grand property owned by a family friend, Mrs Pocock. During their stay, Mrs Blandy became gravely ill, indeed for a time, it was feared fatally so. During her bouts of prolonged suffering, she was heard to demand the attentions of her daughter's lover, crying, 'Let Cranstoun be sent for!' Clearly her faith in Cranstoun to expedite an unlikely recovery was far greater than most would place upon him. Nevertheless, by fortune or by design, the captain's attendance did, indeed, herald a most improbable recovery of the stricken patient. Mrs Blandy now refused to take medicine from any hand that was not Cranstoun's, and declared that with his presence at her side she would only continue to heal. This episode did nothing for relations between Cranstoun and Mr Blandy, who, having also been summoned by his sick wife, was now also especially crotchety at the 'great expense' incurred by the hastily arranged excursion to Turville Court. When she was deemed fit and able to travel again, Mrs Blandy – with the 'indispensable' captain in tow – made her return to Henley with her family. Owing to the continued illness she was enduring, Cranstoun lodged once more under the Blandys' hospitable roof, the lady of the house believing that his presence was curing her ailments in some way.

If Cranstoun was revelling in his free lodgings, any knowing smirk would be wiped clean from his face when, on 1 March 1748, the Commissary Court decreed Cranstoun and Anne Murray to be man and wife and ordered the captain to pay an annuity to Anne and their daughter. Cranstoun's scheming and persuasive nature, however, now came to the fore. A short time after leaving his wife, he wrote to Anne claiming that his sole chance of army promotion depended upon him being unmarried. This being the case, he persuaded her to write a letter claiming that she had never been his wife. Obligingly, and perhaps foolishly, she adhered to his wishes, and upon receipt, Cranstoun was soon administering copies of her letter to his and his wife's relatives in Scotland, who in turn shunned and neglected Anne.

Mr and Mrs Blandy were now also aware of the Court's decision on Cranstoun's previous nuptials – but still Cranstoun dismissed this, claiming that the Court had made errors and he had been encouraged to appeal the decision, with apparent excellent hope of success. This appeal, of course, never did progress and the marriage remained as valid as Scots Law could make it.

In the springtime of 1749, Mrs Blandy's health was still suffering. It was decided that with Mary, they should attend London in the hope of gleaning medical advice to help with her prolonged afflictions. Mrs Blandy's brother resided in the metropolis and both Mary and her poorly mother enjoyed their medicinal sojourn, and for a time, her condition steadied.

Sadly, however, upon Mrs Blandy's subsequent return to Henley, her state worsened dramatically. On Thursday, 28 September, the outlook was imminently bleak, thus the Henley doctor and her two brothers were sent for. During the night of 30 September, with her family around her, Mrs Blandy's end drew near. Even then, her unwavering belief in the good faith of Cranstoun was expressed. Her last words to her husband confirmed this conclusively: 'Mary has set her heart upon Cranstoun; when I am gone, let no one set you against the match,' she told him. These dying comments would doubtless have been a source of much irritation to Mr Blandy. Perhaps he would feel a dutiful inclination to honour his wife's passing words, or, with Cranstoun's most loyal supporter now committed to the earth, could he now convince his daughter of her lover's conniving ways? The belief in the union between his daughter and aristocracy, and all the splendour that could bring, was diminishing almost daily for old Mr Blandy. With a dream that was turning into a delusion, coupled with the pain of losing his wife, Mr Blandy now cut a pale resemblance to the ebullient figure that Henley had once embraced.

Well aware of Blandy's disdain towards him, Cranstoun needed to reverse his hostilities – £10,000 depended on it. What he did next would implicate his lover in a murderous entanglement that she would never escape.

Cranstoun was acquainted with a Mrs Morgan: 'A cunning woman known to him from Scotland.' She had given him a so-called 'love powder'; a love philtre which, if ingested, could transform the most bitter hatred to feelings of love and warmth towards an individual. In

Mary's written account, she claimed that if her father took some of this powder, Cranstoun asserted they would 'make him love me,' referring to Mr Blandy. The 'educated' Mary poured scorn on this idealistic notion of the captain. 'Are you weak enough to think that there is such a power in any powders?' she asked him. Cranstoun replied in the affirmative, insisting that he himself had taken some, and had soon after forgiven a friend, which he had initially no desire or intention to do. One evening, with Mr Blandy in a particularly cantankerous mood, Cranstoun declared that if he had had any of these powders, he would 'put them into something that Mr Blandy should drink.'

In late summer 1750, Cranstoun seized his opportunity to lace Mr Blandy's tea with these 'miraculous' powders. The old lawyer, who at breakfast had been in a particularly foul mood, appeared later at dinner much improved – in the best of humours – something which would continue for the duration of Cranstoun's stay. Surely now any modicum of doubt as to the merit of these mysterious powders had been vanquished?

As Henley's autumn withered away and the onset of winter began, Cranstoun left the pretty parish for what would be the final time. Mr Blandy was certainly insistent that this would be the case. He ordered his daughter to write to her lover that he should not trouble the Blandy family again, or at least until his matrimonial difficulties were 'quite decided'. The couple, already aware that the appeal had long since been dismissed, knew that as long as Cranstoun's wife Anne lived, he could never marry Mary. More worryingly still, Cranstoun knew that should the wily old lawyer discover the truth, he could, and most certainly would, revise the distribution of his fortune.

In late April or early May 1751 – in Mary's own account she is not certain of dates – Mary received a letter from Cranstoun advising her that he had seen Mrs Morgan and she was happy to oblige him with a fresh supply of the powders. He instructed Mary to merely 'mix the powder in tea.' Despite continually declaring her doubts over such apparent folly, at this point, Mary's resolve wavered and she finally agreed to use the philtre. Quite what she expected to achieve, we can only speculate, but what is certain is that old Francis Blandy, from that point onwards, began to suffer the most horrendous internal pain coupled with numerous bouts of sickness. That Mr Blandy was personally targeted here seems certain;

nobody else within the house fell sick, other than those who drank from his own cup – he had to have his tea served in 'a different dish from the rest of the family'. Two housemaids, Susannah Gunnell and Ann Emmet, however, did drink from his cup, and both were seized by crippling pain so severe that they almost died.

In mid-July, Cranstoun wrote Mary several letters suggesting that she ought to put the powder in gruel rather than tea, as tea was apparently not an effective enough vehicle for conveying the powders and drawing the best from them. On Sunday, 4 August, Mary ordered Gunnell, who had since recovered from her sickness, to make a pan of gruel. The following day, Mary was seen to stir something into the pan. In the evening, a quantity was taken up to Mr Blandy in a half-pint mug. The following morning, the house was thrown into disarray as Mr Blandy became dreadfully ill. The Henley apothecary, Mr Norton, was summoned, who at this point had no reason to suspect poison; indeed, his initial diagnosis was colic.

Something altogether more sinister, though, was about to be uncovered. The gruel and its brutal side-effects had aroused suspicions from the housemaids. Gunnell examined the contents of the pan and found a white gritty sediment at the bottom. She discreetly locked the pan away overnight before presenting it the next morning to a neighbour, long-standing family friend Mrs Mounteney. She wisely sent for Mr Norton once more and the contents of the pan were removed for examination. It should be remembered that unlike today's forensic inevitabilities which lay the basis for so many criminal cases, forensic workings in the eighteenth century were not just in their infancy, they were at a truly embryonic stage. Indeed, Mary's case is considered the first to have involved the use of medical evidence being presented within the theatre of the courtroom.

The following morning, Friday, 9 August, Mary's uncle, the Reverend Stevens, visited Hart Street having heard of his brother-in-law's illness. Gunnell relayed to him the suspicious circumstances which appeared to have floored the master of the house. The reverend, with conventional sincerity, urged the maid to inform Mr Blandy of all that she knew. Thus, amid doubtless unease and distress, at seven o'clock the next morning, Gunnell entered old Mr Blandy's bedroom and passed to him the news that would pain him more excruciatingly than any poison could – that his own affable and genteel daughter was the catalyst for his crippling pain.

His initial disbelief soon dissipated as he chose to focus not upon his daughter's actions, but instead sought an answer as to who had *given* her the poison. This suggests that Blandy could not comprehend the notion that Mary could be capable of such a deed. Why would he? His daughter had, to this point, been the archetypal model daughter who appeared certain to become ingrained within aristocratic circles. The question of who had given Mary the poison was emphatically answered by Susannah Gunnell, the housemaid: Cranstoun. 'Oh, that villain!' cried Blandy, hit by the realisation that he had become the stricken victim within a rebellious plot in his own home.

Despite being in the throes of immense pain, Blandy roused himself to confront his daughter, who was breakfasting and unaware that her father had been acquainted with the horrible truth. Mary handed her father his tea, it was tasted, and with his eyes trained firmly upon his daughter, he remarked that it had a 'bad, gritty taste' and asked if she had put anything in it. Startled, Mary meekly replied that it had been made as usual before hastily retreating from the room. Clearly embroiled in a state of panic and fear, Mary bolted to her room, apparently to carry out measures of self-preservation. She gathered together the bundles of letters and any remaining powders that her lover had sent her previously, and threw them all into the fire grate. Mary's aim here of obliterating any evidence partially worked; the letters were reduced to ash, but when their mistress had left the kitchen, the vigilant maids were able to rescue a small paper packet containing an amount of powder, which they delivered to Mr Norton when he made his call to the house later in the day. Norton found Blandy's condition had deteriorated vastly and, as such, suggested that the much-esteemed Dr Addington be called from Reading.

Addington arrived at Hart Street at midnight. From examining the patient and from information gleaned from Norton, the doctor had no doubt Mr Blandy was riddled with the effects of poison. He immediately conveyed this to Mary and sought to establish if her father had any enemies that may have had a desire to inflict such misery upon the man. 'It is impossible! He is at peace with all the world and all the world is at peace with him,' she replied. Dr Addington remained at Hart Street until the following morning whereupon leaving, he covertly took with him the sediment from the pan and the rescued packet from the fire. Chillingly for Mary, before he left the house, he warned her that if her father were to die, she would 'inevitably be ruined'.

At this point, Mary must surely have had an awareness of how precarious her position had become. This did not stop her from trying to warn her lover of their joint predicament though, writing to Cranstoun with a stark warning. Mr Blandy's clerk, Robert Littleton, had up to this point directed Mary's letters to Cranstoun, but now, with vast suspicion swirling around Mary, he opened the letter and at once read it aloud to Mr Blandy: 'Dear Willy, – My father is so bad that I have only time to tell you that if you do not hear from me soon, don't be frightened. I am better myself. Lest any accident should happen to your letters, take care what you write. My sincere compliments. I am ever yours.' The letter proves that Mary was more than aware of the graveness of the situation, yet it also illuminates just how unwavering her feelings were towards the crafty Cranstoun.

Despite the disturbing and unsettling tone of the letter, the sick man still could not find it within himself to apportion any blame to Mary, proclaiming her to be a 'Poor love-sick girl!' He also announced, through doleful tears, that he forgave his daughter. The old lawyer, who had always bristled with intelligence, was acutely aware that his demise was near. His dying wish, transmitted through Susannah Gunnell, was to have Mary visit him one last time. She was admitted to his room, under the watchful eyes of both Gunnell and Norton. Those eyes would witness a heartrending show of captivating theatre as Mary, the most unlikely of poisoners, was finally made aware of the damning discoveries which implicated her so fully in her father's imminent death. The unveiling of these revelations slumped Mary to her knees, begging forgiveness and pledging to never again see or write to Cranstoun. Was Mary's show of emotion a mere theatrical ensemble revealing genuine remorse and regret, or was it a reaction to the proverbial net closing in around her? To this end we cannot be certain, though it is clear Mr Blandy forgave his daughter for her actions. 'I forgive thee, my dear,' though he was less certain that God would afford her similar exoneration. 'Sir,' implored Mary, 'for your illness, I am entirely innocent,' and whilst admitting to adding the powder to the gruel, she was adamant that 'it was given me with another intent.' Upon these words the decrepit lawyer squirmed uneasily in his bed exclaiming, 'Oh, such a villain!' Clearly any blame from Mr Blandy was levelled towards Cranstoun. From this point on, Francis Blandy's final efforts in life centred around minimising any repercussions that his daughter may have to endure after his passing. The ever-diligent lawyer to the last, and a dying father, insisted that Mary leave his sickroom and 'say no more,' for fear she may incriminate herself with a misguided comment. These preventative efforts from Blandy were commendable indeed, though whether or not a man of such legal distinction could have ever really believed his efforts would help Mary seems unlikely.

By now, Dr Addington had adopted the scientific methods of the time and concluded that the mysterious powder that he had examined was not the innocuous 'love philtre' as claimed. Rather, it was that most potent of poisons – arsenic – thus confirming the sinister suggestions that had been rife amongst the maids within Hart Street's kitchen and washrooms. Mr Blandy's state deteriorated to such a place that prominent Oxford chemist and physician Dr Lewis was called, who swiftly confirmed the diagnosis of poisoning and insisted that Mary be confined to her room, warning her that 'the affair might come before a court of judicature', and as such a guard was assigned to her door. This would not be the last time that Mary endured such ignominy. As she forlornly pondered the bleakness of her predicament, across the hallway her father was entwined in his own struggle – for life itself – which, on Wednesday, 14 August 1751, he would finally lose.

With both of her parents now dead, Mary declared herself 'one of the most wretched orphans that ever lived'. She appeared though to exhibit little in the way of remorse over her father's death, but demonstrated much despair regarding her own situation, entirely understanding its graveness – even pleading with the footman and cook of the house to escape with her. These intentions do not convey the ideals of an innocent woman, but whilst her two initial propositions were both refuted, one of Henley's most polished and courteous of ladies was finally able to make her escape when the guard charged with watching over Mary relaxed his duties – absenting himself while ironically digging Mr Blandy's grave. Mary saw her opportunity and bolted for her freedom.

Dashing through Hart Street, she had already attracted unwanted attention; word of the apparent dastardly plot waged against one of

Henley's most virtuous of gentlemen had circulated fast, and been received with palpable anger. Indeed, initial cries of 'Murderess!' echoed from a small group of children, soon attracting a more ravenous rabble, and shortly the fugitive was engulfed by a baying crowd. Managing to break free from the incensed swarm of townsfolk, she rushed over the Henley Bridge towards the Little Angel Inn, where she sought refuge. The obliging landlady, Mrs Davis, slammed the door shut behind Mary, leaving the enraged mob outside.

Of course, Mary could not hide indefinitely, however appealing the idea had become. Richard Fisher, a friend of the recently-departed Mr Blandy, was tasked with retrieving the fleeing maiden and returning her home in an enclosed carriage to 'preserve her from the resentment of the populace'. Fisher was a prominent figurehead of Henley's town council and would later the same day appear as a jury member summoned to the hastily arranged inquest. Such was the rapidity of eighteenth-century justice, Mr Blandy's body had already been opened for autopsy with incriminating results for Mary having emerged.

Henley's surgeon, Mr Edward Nicholas, and Dr Addington performed the post-mortem. Though a standard grim affair, this examination was exceptional in its findings; Addington remarked that he had 'never found or beheld a body in which the viscera were so universally inflamed and mortified'. The stomach was dreadfully discoloured and inflamed, the intestines pale and flabby, the lungs peppered with black spots, and the liver and spleen were in an equally appalling deformed state. The outcome of all of this was not revelatory; it simply concurred with Dr Addington's initial findings that Francis Blandy had indeed suffered a grotesquely painful death induced by arsenic poisoning. With a cause of death now confirmed, it was now the turn of the inquest to seek to establish the facts in respect of just *how* Mr Blandy had befallen his excruciating expiration.

Henley's mayor and coroner, Richard Miles, presided over the inquest. A curious scene to the contemporary eye, yet historically commonplace, the inquest was held in a private home, that of Mr John Gale, who, on the afternoon of Thursday, 15 August, accommodated thirteen 'good and lawful men' as the jury that would go some way to deciding Mary Blandy's fate. This was a fate that was perhaps sealed even prior to evidence provided by the Blandy household servants, but one which had now officially befallen Mary Blandy after the verdict declared she was guilty of poisoning and thus of murdering her own father.

The following day, Richard Miles efficiently conducted his duties and issued the warrant permitting the conveyance of Mary to the county gaol at Oxford. Mary was to be a prisoner therein and set to be detained until 'discharged by due course of law'. On the same evening, Francis Blandy's affliction-ridden body was buried next to his wife in Henley's parish church. Mary was transported to the gaol under the cover of darkness – undoubtedly a wise move following the public consternation that her wanderings of Henley's streets had previously created.

Mary's arrival at the gaol must surely have brought home the gravity of her situation, and the contrast of her serene life on Hart Street to her imminent confinement within an imposing and unforgiving prison could not be starker. However, despite her most foreboding of fears, Mary's reality would not be so frightful. Described as more akin to being 'like a retirement from the world than the confinement of a criminal', her imprisonment included the dutiful attentions of her own maid and the best rooms available to her. Tea was taken twice daily with the evenings wiled away playing cards; hardly the traumatic and punishing regime many others had previously endured within its monumental walls.

If Mary's initial period of incarceration had been gentle, a brutal realisation was delivered when on 25 October, the sheriff of the county was instructed by the Secretary of State to 'take more particular care of her'. The instruction led to an immediate fettering of Mary, the restraining of her slender ankles being something she had greatly feared. Such a physical intrusion of Mary's person was a new experience for her and a stark reminder, if she needed it, of her position, one that would weaken further following news from a visitor Mary received at the gaol. Mary's father had not penned a will prior to his passing and so Mary was the sole heiress to his fortune. As we know, this had been largely purported to have been £10,000 – the reality though was substantially different, amounting to less than £4,000. The harrowing irony was, of course, that the inflated sum had been the catalyst for Cranstoun's manufacturing of old Mr Blandy's demise – and ultimately, Mary's now terrifying position. The realisation of her plight induced a renewed demeanour within the lonesome girl; gone were the pleasantries of tea and card-playing, replaced instead by frequent prayer services in the prison chapel.

Attempts were made to apprehend the coordinator of the situation, but Cranstoun, now showing as powerful perception as he had persuasion, was long gone, to the shores of France no less, and leaving his 'lover' to face the morose music he had so craftily written.

As the furtive fugitive basked in his French liberty, in her gaol cell Mary Blandy was readying herself for an impending trial, consumed in the knowledge that the direst of consequences could be meted out to her. In efforts to avoid such a fate, Mary sought out a Mr Newell to defend her, a man of high standing who had succeeded her own father as town clerk. She did, however, take umbrage to rather insensitive comments made at an early consultation, with Newell openly expressing his bewilderment that she had managed to become embroiled in affairs over such a 'mean-looking little ugly fellow' as Cranstoun. Belittled by Newell's observation on her taste in lovers, Mary instead employed the services of an attorney from Woodstock, Mr Rivers.

It is doubtful that Newell would be particularly perturbed by his dismissal; Mary's case was bleak indeed, and furthermore, rumours of her guilt abounded almost by the day, hence weakening the chances of a positive outcome. Mary herself complained that 'it has been said that I am a wretched drunkard, a prophane [sic] swearer, that I never went to chapel, contemned [sic] all holy ordinances, and in short gave myself up to all kinds of immorality.' The busyness of the rumour mill indicated just how anticipated this trial was, and coupled with the zeal and animation that it incited within the presses of the time, nobody was left in any doubt as to the levels of interest shown in Mary's trial.

So it was that on Tuesday, 3 March 1752, Mary's trial would begin. The Assizes were usually held within the Town Hall, but owing to refurbishment, the official ceremonial hall – the Divinity Hall – of Oxford University would instead accommodate this most eagerly awaited trial. On the first morning, the long chamber of the Hall was packed to the brim, and even open windows were an avenue for some determined souls to catch a glimpse of the accused. Immaculately presented, Mary was ushered to the bar and provided with a chair for the proceedings should she fatigue, with her maid still loyally at her side to attend her if required.

The judges overseeing Mary's ultimate fate were the Honourable Heneage Legge and Sir Sidney Stafford Smythe. For the Crown, the Honourable Mr Bathurst and Mr Serjeant Hayward were appointed with

Mary's defence conducted by Mr Ford. As Mary listened intently to the indictment against her, it was noted by many that she remained 'sedate and composed.' To the indictment, Mary entered a plea of 'not guilty', and a jury was obediently sworn in.

The Crown case opened with the medical witnesses, Doctors Addington and Lewis, and Mr Norton, the Henley apothecary. They were able to clearly establish that arsenic was the cause of Mr Blandy's death, that it was in the remains of his gruel and also that arsenic was the powder which the prisoner had attempted to destroy in the fire grate. Despite the damning nature of the evidence, Mary remained the image of composure at the bar for the most part: her unflappable conduct disturbed only once following the evidence given by witness Mrs Mounteney. She was Mary's godmother and upon departing the arena, she clasped Mary by the hand and exclaimed, 'God bless you!' In this moment, a small epoch of time where she must have felt not completely alone, Mary's eyes welled before shortly resuming her stoical stance once more.

Her resolve would be tested further upon the deliverance of subsequent witness declarations. One of the cooks, Betty Binfield, claimed that she had heard Mary irately remarking, 'Who would grudge to send an old father to hell for £10,000?' Susannah Gunnell also provided a reflective insight into Mary's polarised relationship with her father. 'Sometimes,' said the maid, 'she wished for him long life, sometimes for his death.'

Following these rather revealing testimonies, the contents of the intercepted letter Mary wrote intended for Cranstoun, were then disclosed. Mary's incriminating position had been exacerbated. And so now the Crown's case was rested.

Mary's defence counsel had an unenviable task, but for the moment their efforts were shelved: Mary was first permitted to make a speech. Whether prepared by her counsel or written by Mary – for she was eminently capable – it is not certain. She spoke with eloquence and did not go so far as to refute the evidence which had gone before, but maintained she was 'as innocent as the child unborn of the death of my father'. Furthermore, Mary resolutely asserted that she 'really thought the powder an innocent, inoffensive thing.' There was no doubt that Mary had added the powder, but the jury would have to decide whether she did it knowingly, or ignorantly. The gravity of the outcome associated with this question was lost on nobody in the Divinity Hall.

Having concluded her own address to the court, Mary now listened intently to the witnesses called by her defence counsel. Eight had been selected, and several offered most favourable character references for her. Perhaps these nuggets of positivity offered Mary some glimmer of hope, confined at the bar as she was, heavily burdened by her sense of injustice, but she needed more. Mr Ford sought an appearance from the Reverend Swinton, the prison chaplain, with the hope he could highlight Mary's excellent conduct whilst in gaol. Alas, the honourable judges declined the request: no further testimony to Mary's character was necessary.

The trial, which had by now lasted thirteen hours, had enthralled the public. Now was the moment that the jury would feel the enormity of their part in the theatre they had witnessed. They were the leading actors in the procession, and their role was imparted to the audience thus:

> If, upon that evidence, she appears to be innocent, in God's name let her be acquitted; but if, upon that evidence, she appears to be guilty, I am sure you will do justice to the public, and acquit your own consciences.

Mr Baron Legge's review of the evidence and his overall disposition throughout the trial was a stately demonstration of his 'ability, impartiality, and humanity'. Observing that Mr Blandy was poisoned by the prisoner at the bar – and this was undeniable – he reiterated to the jury their impending role: 'What you are to try is reduced to this single question, whether the prisoner, at the time she gave it to her father, knew that it was poison, and what effect it would have?'

Ultimately the judge's question was not a difficult one for the jury, indeed, barely ponderable. Without retiring, a brief five-minute consultation returned a verdict of guilty. Mary remained unmoved. Solemnly, Judge Legge, well-versed under such acute pressures, calmly placed the black sentencing cap over his ceremonious wig and passed those shudderingly inevitable words:

> 'That you are to be carried to the place of execution and there hanged by the neck until you are dead; and may God, of His infinite mercy, receive your soul.'

It was now nine o'clock in the evening. For thirteen unrelenting hours, Mary had unflinchingly watched this most curious of spectacles unfold. It had drawn to the conclusion she feared most; yet still no signs of fear or agitation manifested from the young woman. Instead, this image of serenity amidst unimaginable trauma rose from the bar and pleaded to her judge: 'My Lord, as your lordship has been so good to show so much candour and impartiality in the course of my trial, I have one more favour to beg; which is, that your lordship would please allow me a little time till I can settle my affairs and make my peace with God.'

Judge Legge replied with a tenderness that belied the day's events, 'To be sure, you shall have a proper time allowed you.'

And so, the curtain fell upon the great tragedy that had so captivated Henley and beyond. The tense and bustling court room was now replaced with a hushed stillness.

But the final act was still to follow.

Mary had been afforded almost five weeks between the evening of her conviction and execution. Within this sorrowful time, she achieved her wishes of settling any outstanding affairs and indeed making her peace with God. From her cell she also penned numerous letters, perhaps most interestingly to a fellow prisoner who was also awaiting her execution. Mary and Elizabeth Jefferies corresponded from 7 January to 19 March 1752, the former protesting her innocence throughout their communications, whilst Jefferies admitted her guilt to Mary in murdering her uncle. Elizabeth Jefferies would hang at Epping Forest, Essex, on 28 March 1752. Horribly, she took over fifteen minutes to die, struggling agonisingly to the end.

Only days later, Mary Blandy would herself become an instalment within the pantheon of murderesses throughout the annals of crime and punishment. The initial date of execution had been set for Saturday, 4 April, but at the request of University authorities, who claimed that a hanging during Holy Week would be ungodly, she was given a quite literal – albeit short – stay of execution. Thus, Mary would now meet her maker on Monday, 6 April, though there is conjecture as to where this occurred. Accounts vary, but evidence suggests Oxford's Castle-yard had the dubious 'honour' of witnessing the demise of Miss Blandy.

The evening prior to her execution, Mary spent in quiet prayer. Following an understandably restless night, at half past eight on the morning of

Monday, 6 April, the sombre formalities began. The sheriff, Mary's attorney, Mr Rivers, and the chaplain, the Reverend Swinton, arrived at the gaol. The chaplain afforded Mary a brief contemplation period before being escorted out into the castle yard to be received by the sheriff's men and her executioner. Solemnly attired in a 'black crape sack', she was led to her death. To this point, Mary had flaunted a staunch bravery and indomitable spirit. But, a 'stern test of artistry is the gallows' and yet, on seeing the ominous hefty wooden beam crudely placed between two trees before an assembled group of silent spectators upon the Castle Green, she still did not falter. With all of the fortitude she had shown previously, she addressed the curious onlookers and reasserted her testimony that she was 'perfectly innocent as to any intention to destroy or even hurt my dear father; that I did not know, or even suspect, that there was any poisonous quality in the fatal powder I gave him.'

As customary for the time, Mary paid the hangman two guineas – a dark and foreboding irony that she should pay for his 'service' – but this was to ensure that a 'professional' service would be accomplished. The alternative could be a slow and agonising death by strangulation, akin to that endured by Elizabeth Jefferies only nine days prior. To reach the vacant and expectant noose that dangled from the temporary gallows, Mary had to climb a ladder, upon which she admitted, 'I am afraid I shall fall.' As she reached the fifth rung of the ladder, with typical composure, Mary Blandy spoke her final words: 'For the sake of decency, gentlemen, don't hang me high.'

In the immediate throes before death, this nod to her modesty and reticence was remarkable. Any fears of the impending launch into eternity appeared secondary to the worry that any young men in the assembled contingent might see up her skirt. The halter was then placed over her neck and she pulled down her handkerchief over her face. Her hands were tied at the front of her body so that she could hold her prayer book: a prior arrangement had been made that when Mary dropped the prayer book, this would be the signal to the hangman that she was ready. As she released the book, the ladder was turned over and Mary dropped, falling into immediate unconsciousness and dying 'without a struggle' – the guineas paid to the hangman apparently worthwhile indeed.

Perhaps it was her gallantry and courage that so affected those in attendance, or merely the notion that she was, in fact, innocent of wrongdoing, but contrary to the usual raucous etiquette at such spectacles, the multitude – estimated 'at 5,000 strong' – sobbed and wept amidst the palpable air of hush. Whilst such gruesome displays were intended as deterrents to crime and proof that justice had prevailed, spectators would generally exhibit jubilation and bellow hearty roars of approval as the felon was suspended on the end of the noose. On this day though, the spectacle induced a sombre ambience, a melancholy scene which even a blackbird shared in, perched atop of Mary's beam as her life ebbed away; according to common folklore, the site has not since heard a blackbird sing its tune there.

With her feet almost touching the ground, Mary's body remained hanging for thirty minutes, as was the accustomed procedure. If the execution of Mary had been grounded in decorum, arrangements following her death were in sharp contrast. When her body was cut down there was 'neither coffin to put her body in, nor hearse to carry it away'. Instead, she was unceremoniously slung over the shoulder of one of the Sheriff's men and carried 'in the most beastly manner', her legs indecently exposed, through the throngs of spectators. It is with grim irony that whilst her final words were a poignant appeal to preserve modesty, upon her death she was subjected to precisely what she had feared: a graceless and deplorable exhibition of indignity witnessed by thousands.

Mary's burial was officiated by the Reverend William Stockwood on 7 April at Henley's Parish Church. Interred between the graves of her mother and father, she was afforded more than most convicted criminals, who would not ordinarily be buried within church confines. A mere eight months beyond Mary's laying to rest, however, a far more pretentious and grandiose funeral would be held for the inciter of this entire tale – Cranstoun.

Having exiled himself with the intention of so ungallantly allowing Mary to face trial alone, he outlived his fallen 'lover' by a meagre eight months. These months were a world away from the restful ones he may have envisaged; instead, tiptoeing his way across the French countryside wishful of evading attention and ultimately, arrest. Those affiliated in such ideas may well view divine retribution in playing its hand here, for Cranstoun was taken with a severe 'fit of illness'. His suffering lasted for nine days, whereupon his afflictions became so excruciating that on 30

November 1752, he 'expired in great agonies,' and was deemed to have been 'raving mad'. On 2 December, Cranstoun's funeral was attended by the town's dignitaries amid much pomp. Had they been fully aligned with the truths of the honourable captain's past, then his body may very well have endured a far less ceremonial finale.

Whilst Mary Blandy's final words and moments have passed into legend, it is claimed that her spirit has yet to find peace. Accounts of her apparition haunting her hometown of Henley are plentiful and add another dramatic strand of interest to this most intriguing of narratives. Whatever the truth in such 'beyond the grave' appearances though, what remains certain is that Mary Blandy's story continues to enthrall and incite debate. Was she a modest murderess or was she quite simply a gullible soul, guilty of a boundless faith towards the wrong man?

Chapter 3

Sir Henry Irving

John Henry Brodribb first saw the light of day on 6 February 1838 in the charming Somerset village of Keinton Mandeville. The village is a small one, even today its population remains diminutive by the standards of modern life. Regardless of its size, however, it nonetheless boasts the impressive honour of being the birthplace of one of Britain's most esteemed actors.

Brodribb's beginnings began humbly indeed. An only child, he lived with his mother, Mary, and his father, Samuel, who was employed as a tailor's travelling salesman for the local general store. In 1842, the family moved to Bristol but, fearful of any implications to their young son's health by settling in a major city, his parents decided to move John to Halsetown near St Ives in Cornwall. He was sent to live with his maternal aunt Sarah Penberthy and his cousins where they all received a basic education, but when, in 1849, his parents moved to London, the young Brodribb rejoined them, attending the City Commercial School. The school first opened its doors in 1830 and was competently kept by William Pinches, flourishing swiftly despite the inadequate curriculum that burdened Victorian England. The school provided 'the essentials for a good English education, soundly taught'. The additional frills of Greek learning were unserved, and Latin provided merely a fraction of the educational mandate. Instead, the school aimed to equip its pupils with the function of writing clearly and reading aloud with 'intelligent emphasis' – something that would ultimately prove crucial in the forthcoming years and ensure that the fees of £6 per annum were well spent.

As Brodribb entered his teenage years, the many recitations he had given at school had already irresistibly drawn him to theatrical life and he began to attend evening elocution classes. Brodribb was not born into any theatrical hinterland, but the foundations that would see him revered throughout the land had now been firmly anchored. Repeated visits to

Sadler's Wells Theatre to behold the acting talents of Samuel Phelps was a favoured pastime. Phelps was by this time the actor-manager of the theatre, succeeding in altering its perception in the eyes of the public almost single-handedly. In the 1830s, Charles Dickens had described the theatre as having 'as ruffianly an audience as London could shake together' – yet against this anarchic grain, Phelps made a commercial success of a lengthy run of Shakespeare productions, bringing a myriad of the great playwright's works to Sadler's Wells.

As a 17-year-old, Brodribb, as familiar a face as Phelps would see at Sadler's Wells, secured an interview with the great tragedian. Despite Phelps's success in the world of theatre, however, he discouraged the young man from following suit, perhaps a revealing indictment into the difficulties he had experienced throughout his own career. Nevertheless, Brodribb demonstrated great persistence in his theatrical designs and following an amateur performance as Romeo at the Soho Theatre in 1856, he received a timely legacy of £100 from an uncle which was used to equip himself with all of the essentials a Victorian actor would need: props, costumes, and an array of wigs. Brodribb's professional career may have been in its embryonic stages, but after the leading man fell ill in a production of *Richelieu* at Sunderland's Royal Lyceum Theatre, the name Henry Irving was added to the playbill. This was to be the stage name of Brodribb, and it would become forever synonymous with British theatre.

Monday, 29 September 1856 was a momentous day, not only for the fresh-faced Irving but also for Sunderland's Royal Lyceum Theatre itself. The building had been destroyed by fire only a year before, and as the curtain rose on Irving's burgeoning career, so too did it upon the resurrection of the town's cultural hub in Lambton Street. Irving's initial stage job at Sunderland was without remuneration, and in many respects was the beginning of several years of grinding toil, but equally, it offered a comprehensive grounding and a multitude of arenas in which to hone his considerable talents.

'Here is to our enterprise,' were the first words that Irving bellowed on that untrodden stage – how prescient these words would turn out to be. Assignments followed in Edinburgh, Glasgow and Manchester, followed by short-term engagements in the provinces and Ireland. At this time, Irving was predominantly supporting many of the eminent actors of the day; Walter Montgomery, Barry Sullivan and Ira Aldridge all unknowingly helped to mould Irving into the impressive player with the unique ability of 'carrying' his audiences.

Eventually, his unquenchable thirst for theatre combined with his passion for learning ensured that his supporting roles became leading parts. Punctuated between his flourishing successes, Irving experienced great pain shortly before one of his most prominent stage triumphs, as, in 1869, his mother died, which subsequently tempted his father to move back to Bristol to live with his remaining family.

In the same year, however, Irving was to marry Florence O'Callaghan on 15 July 1869 in St Marylebone in London. The pair had met in 1866 but the marriage appeared rather doomed from the beginning, Florence having little understanding of actors' lives and the demands placed upon them. In spite of this, they did have two sons, Harry and Laurence, who would both later follow their father into the theatre.

The winter of 1871 would enduringly change Henry Irving's life. He gave a stunning performance as the haunted burgomaster, Mathias, in the French melodrama *The Bells*. The play ran for 150 nights and firmly established Irving at the forefront of British drama. His electrifying personality had turned him into an overnight star revered by the literati. Irving's wife, Florence, however, was not quite as impressed with her husband's latest role when, whilst travelling home on the opening night of 25 November with the applause freshly ringing in his ears, Florence queried her husband with the legendary question: 'Are you going on making a fool of yourself like this all your life?' Irving – perhaps grateful for the opportunity – exited the carriage and walked off into the London night, choosing to never again see his wife. The separation inevitably hindered Irving's relationship with his boys, both of whom had obtained a rather 'jaundiced' view of their father through Florence.

The Lyceum Theatre in London had originally been built in 1771, but throughout the nineteenth century it had suffered much misfortune, including its decimation by fire and a host of its managers plunging it into bankruptcy. In 1871, however, this site of previous misadventure would provide the opposite for Irving, with American actor and manager Hezekiah Bateman assembling a company, to be headed by Irving, that would run the theatre. The audiences began to swell as Irving excelled in various title roles including *Charles I, Hamlet, Othello, Macbeth* and *Richard III*. Many observers were left dumbfounded by the visionary intellectuality of his work. After Bateman's death in 1875, his widow offered the Lyceum's lease to Irving after she found it too onerous a task to run the theatre. Irving was now the Lyceum's manager as well as thrilling the throngs as its leading actor.

The timing of Irving's new venture coincided happily with a revival in British theatre. The popular appeal of theatre had been growing for several reasons; since 1660, plays in the metropolis had been restricted merely to Covent Garden and Drury Lane, but with the passage of the Theatre Regulation Act (1843), this monopoly was justly abolished and as a result, a swathe of new theatres opened across London and, indeed, the rest of the country. Queen Victoria was also an ardent theatre enthusiast and other members of the Royal Family merrily shared in her gusto. So, too, it would seem, did the new urban populations of the expanding industrial cities in Britain.

In December 1878, Irving opened his first season as manager with a revival of *Hamlet*. Irving recruited Ellen Terry as his stage partner and the pair began launching an itinerary of lavish productions which attained both critical acclaim and box-office prosperity. Terry was one of the few actresses of the time who could match Irving's stage presence and the perfect pairing transformed the Lyceum into the theatrical capital, not only of Britain, but also the world. Such a success story could never have seen fruition without a solid infrastructure; Henry Loveday was recruited as stage manager, and crucially, Irving drafted in Bram Stoker to the operation as business manager and personal assistant for a full twenty-seven years. Stoker would, of course, later make his own indentation upon classic literature with his Gothic novel of 1897, *Dracula*.

Indeed, it is believed that Irving himself unwittingly provided Stoker with the real-life inspiration for the vampire count. There is virtual unanimity on this point and certainly physically, this notion is surely plausible; Irving stood as a slender and tall man at over six feet with hollow cheeks and thin lips – an unerringly accurate caricature of the bloodthirsty character.

Stoker, as was much of Britain at this time, was fully hypnotised by Irving's charisma and charm. Fellow actor-manager John Lawrence Toole judged that Irving was somebody who 'every right-minded actor was proud of'. Like all of Irving's staff, Stoker beheld the 'Governor' with abundant adoration and steadfast devotion. In Stoker's *Personal Reminiscences of Henry Irving*, he proudly states that: 'For nearly thirty years I was an intimate friend of Irving; in certain ways the most intimate friend of his life. I knew him as well as it is given to any man to know another.'

Upon such a tide of overwhelming positivity, Irving used his privileged position as a force for initiating much evolution in Victorian theatre and how it was viewed. Irving had always believed that drama ought only to be regarded as a force for good, and that its position and status required elevating to that of the other arts. With his impassioned zeal for theatrics as a civilising and enriching aspect of cultural life, Irving was the perfect advocate to deliver such a directive. Irving's ultimate goal was to improve the standard of productions, gain approval of the clergy (church leaders having held a long-standing opposition to the theatre), and to elevate the stage onto an equal level of respectability and standing as the other arts. His foresight and meticulous nature demanded his productions were designed by the best scenic painters, and his music commissioned from the principal composers of the Victorian era. Even the publicity was designed with precise innovation. The results were a plethora of major successes laden with opulent grandeur; *The Merchant of Venice*, *Much Ado About Nothing*, *Henry VIII* and *Othello*. Irving had delivered Shakespeare to the masses and furthermore, he had transformed the theatre into an attractive proposition for all classes. From Queen Victoria to the galleryites, he reciprocated the very respect they demonstrated to him, enhancing his appeal all the while.

Following each season exhilarating the London crowds, Irving would tour his company around the British Isles and from 1883, embarked on the beginning of a host of transatlantic tours. Displaying his customary precision, the preparations were as meticulous as ever, travelling across America with trains loaded with scenery, props and the full company. A lamentably arduous task it is to conquer 'the land of opportunity', yet audiences were as enthralled as those he had left behind in Britain. Eight successful tours ensured that his legacy across the pond would never waver, Irving's popularity was incalculable.

In 1895, the climax of a lifetime's tireless endeavours resulted in Henry Irving's knighthood from Queen Victoria – the first ever to be bestowed upon an actor. He had transformed British theatre beyond all recognition, striving endlessly to enhance the standard of the art to which he was devoted.

Regretfully, Irving's final years were characterised by a host of irretrievable reverses. In February 1898, much of the scenery and costumes for a variety of productions in the company's repertoire were lost to a disastrous fire at Irving's off-site store. In 1902, Ellen Terry left the Lyceum Company, his mainstay's departure heralding more problems behind the curtain. Irving's health was by now beginning to fail, and following bouts of pneumonia and pleurisy, his physical decline was evident. An ebbing financial situation appeared to mirror his physical downturn. Following the fire and a falling box-office revenue, Irving decided to hand the management of the Lyceum to a limited company, thus severing his long-standing association with theatre management.

Irving continued in his own inimitable fashion, surviving on tour interspersed with seasons at Drury Lane. Sir Henry Irving's final performance was the lead role in Tennyson's *Becket* at Bradford's Theatre Royal in 1905. His health concerns had caused much consternation among Irving's intimates, Stoker particularly fearful of the strain placed upon his already fragile companion.

On the evening of Friday, 13 October 1905, Irving – playing Becket – had just been 'wounded' on stage by the murderous De Tracy. Prior to falling prone before the altar, Irving gave utterance to the following passage:

'At the right hand of Power,
Power and Great Glory,
For Thy Church, O Lord -
Into Thy hands, O Lord,
Into Thy hands!'

With unnerving irony, having announced his final prose, Irving was seized with syncope. As the curtain descended, few could have possibly imagined that these words, his last spoken upon his beloved stage, would also become the great man's final words in life itself, for although he lived an hour longer, Sir Henry Irving never spoke again. Having been returned to the Midland Hotel, he collapsed in the foyer. He was helped to a chair but sadly expired ten minutes before midnight. As with his stage debut, so too in his final appearance, his last words were eternally apt, belying a beautifully tragic significance within.

The land was united in collective grief for the 'foremost actor of our time', reported the British press: 'His loss will be keenly felt throughout the English-speaking world. His death is a national loss and his memory a national possession.' It was apparent that Irving's death had generated a huge outpouring of anguish; a clear indication was the petitioning by several noted members of society upon Irving's death that he be buried at Westminster Abbey. The clamour was continued with 50,000 applications received for the meagre 1,200 places available at the service within the Abbey.

At noon on 20 October 1905, the funeral took place. The procession of Irving's coffin was watched by over 40,000 people. The teeming pews in Westminster Abbey held many distinguished peers and members of the acting profession, overcome with sorrowful emotion. Outside, hordes of mourners stood in respectful silence. Inside, Irving's ashes were buried in the south transept beside the grave of the eighteenth-century Shakespearian actor David Garrick, and with impeccable appropriateness, in front of Shakespeare's memorial statue.

The chair in which Britain's first actor-knight died is today housed in London's splendid Garrick Club, owing to a mindful observer of Irving's final moments realising, perhaps rather ghoulishly, that the chair would hold sentimental and historical significance; it was kept separate from the other chairs in the lobby. That it should be in the Garrick Club serves as further appropriate homage because Irving, as a keen member, joyously frequented the establishment whenever possible.

Hints of Irving's influence remain strong. Every February a wreath is laid at the foot of Irving's statue in Charing Cross Road, which tellingly remains the only statue of an actor in the capital. He chose the stage and with his iron-like will, he ascended unprecedented heights. As the *Bath Chronicle* noted following his death: 'He has earned his rest and to it, with our gratitude and our affection, we leave him.'

Chapter 4

Lady Jane Grey

L ady Jane Grey is perhaps the least celebrated English queen of the sixteenth century. The very fact Jane's royal title is seldom associated with her name, usurped instead by the more recognisable honorific prefix of 'lady', is evidence of this. Her brief reign over a nine-day period in the summer of 1553 concluded the tenure of England's first queen. From the moment of her proclamation, Jane's sovereignty was vehemently contested, which would ultimately lead to the grisly demise of the 'nine day queen' ensuring her place as one of the most compelling and tragic figures in Tudor history.

The character of Jane Grey is a relatively obscure one in terms of our depth of knowledge; she was not a king's daughter so the glare of the spotlight was relatively dim. Moreover, as a Tudor teenager who died so young, she is unlikely to have greatly indented the historical record, even less so with her being female. Her precise birth date cannot be ascertained with any great certainty, though it is probable she was born in 1537 at Bradgate, Leicestershire.

It is said with some conviction, though, that of prominent centrality to Jane's character was a quick and articulate intelligence. She possessed a great appetite for learning and this, paired with a remarkable capacity for such acumen, created a most formidable brain in one so young. This was accompanied with a fiery and resolute will of personality, her unwavering commitment to her Protestant faith perhaps the clearest evidence of this. Ironically, this fierce allegiance would play a significant role in her eventual fate.

The story of Lady Jane Grey was played out amid the heart of the Tudor family. Henry VIII's reign, notorious for its bloody sea of executions, violence and the Reformation, finally concluded upon his death in 1547. The throne was left to his young son, Edward VI, who at the time of his coronation was only 9 years old. At such a juvenile age, Edward could not, of course, practically rule as king. Instead, a regency council governed the realm until such a time that Edward reached maturity. At the summit of this council was John Dudley, the Duke of Northumberland, a zealous protector of the young king and one with far-reaching, and ultimately tragic, designs of grandeur.

Northumberland had been a leading figure and close advisor to the fledgling king since 1550. The question as to the levels of influence Northumberland held over Edward has been the subject of much scholarly debate and scrutiny, though what is undeniable is the uninhibited commitment to the Protestant faith shared by both. Whether Edward's religious sentiments were of his own design or largely formed through the influence of the duke is in many respects incidental, for what was certain was that Edward was staunchly Protestant, and Northumberland was firmly ingratiated within the king's circle.

In early 1553, Edward was 15 years old and had begun to fall terribly ill. During his long and lingering affliction, he was induced to carefully consider the succession of his throne. Henry had indicated in his dying will that Edward's half-sisters, Mary and Elizabeth, should succeed him, but for several reasons Edward was adamant this should not happen. Largely, his doubts hinged around the apprehension of a return to the previous system of popery, which, if Mary ascended the throne, was a most likely scenario in concurrence with her strict Catholic faith. This would amount to a reversal of seismic proportions in consideration of Henry's erstwhile Reformation of the Church. Furthermore, allegations abounded regarding the illegitimacy of the two sisters, which also presented a major bar to their succession. The prospect of Mary succeeding Edward was not one he or his Privy Council had pleasure in envisaging. The veil of Protestantism was so overwhelmingly dominant within Edward's Privy Council, the idea it should revert back to former Catholic doctrine was an abhorrent one to be entirely avoided.

This raised the problem of Edward's succession to the throne; he himself had not been of age to marry or have an heir of his own, therefore something of an impending crisis loomed large within the monarchy. To this end, Edward had drawn up a draft document entitled 'My Devise for the Succession', a quite remarkable testimony which still exists today, safely deposited in London's Inner Temple Library. The document, in

Edward's own handwriting, lays out a basis for the future inheritance to the throne of England. Edward's intentions are clear: principally his desire to be succeeded by a king of Protestant orientation.

So it was that Edward set about bypassing his half-sisters from the succession. He passed over the claims of Mary and Elizabeth, settling the crown's future position towards the head of his first cousin once removed, 16-year-old Lady Jane Grey – or at least, initially, to one of her male heirs. Jane had recently become married to Lord Guildford Dudley, son of the Duke of Northumberland. The union was proposed by Guildford's father, which has led many to believe the marriage was the result of his manipulation and cajolery of Edward; the fundamental reasoning here being that should Jane indeed be crowned queen, her youth and perceived innocence would make her a malleable 'puppet' who could essentially be controlled by Northumberland. Moreover, if Jane was to become queen, it would allow the continuation of the Protestant beliefs that were so important to Edward, with Jane herself of such a fierce Protestant persuasion. In many ways, she was the ideal representation of Protestant virtue – a monarch in this mould would allow the continuity of a regime already in motion, as well as preserving both the futures of those within the Privy Council, and England, as they had designed it.

The marriage offered some possibility that Jane might produce a male heir who could succeed Edward. This prospect, though, was short-lived and overtaken by the events of June 1553 when it became apparent that Edward's illness was rapidly worsening. The health of the young king became the subject of considerable anxiety, even more so when it became clear that he was terminally ill and had little time remaining. His 'Devise for the Succession' document now heralded huge significance.

At this crisis, Northumberland's ambition burgeoned with great vigour, and whilst the extent to which he manipulated the dying king is undeterminable, it is an oft-cited belief that in his delivery of powerful religious arguments, he persuaded Edward to revise his plan of succession swaying it in favour of Jane, Northumberland's daughter-in-law. In his waning health, the king made a very subtle alteration to his succession document, with the addition of two words: 'and her'. Though small, the words signalled huge ramifications. Evidently added in hindsight, the document now decreed that Lady Jane was next in line to succeed Edward following his approaching death. Edward's alterations directly contravened his father's Third Succession Act of 1543, which had named both of his daughters as successors should Edward die without leaving a male heir. Edward excluded his sisters on the basis of bastardy, Henry having not renounced his daughters' legitimacy prior to his death.

The succession of Mary and Elizabeth, Edward's two half-sisters, was now entirely superseded and ratified by the king's council, chief of nobility and all principal players of the realm, subscribing their names to the regulation – urged on most enthusiastically by Northumberland. The young king addressed his public for the final time on 1 July 1553 from the window of his Greenwich Palace. The crowds were horrified at his impending demise, his appearance gaunt and wasted. It was now clear even to his subjects that King Edward VI would shortly be dead. On the evening of 6 July, Edward sighed, 'I feel faint.' His life almost extinguished, he uttered his final words: 'Lord have mercy upon me and take my spirit.' It was an excruciating end and a tragically premature one, but the boy's suffering was finally over.

The throne of England was now vacant, but the nobles who had conspired to prevent Mary's succession and had been instrumental in prompting and advising Edward, had designs of speedily proclaiming Lady Jane Grey as England's first queen. Jane herself was oblivious to the actions that had been unfolding in her favour. It is generally accepted that she was completely uninformed in regards to the plan as it was being devised. Even the king's death was initially kept secret from the queen-in-waiting. She was ordered to Syon House in West London, where, in Jane's own words, 'they did tell me of the death of the King.' This was not the only news that Jane would receive. The Duke of Northumberland, amid the lavishness of Syon, proceeded to announce that on his deathbed the king had chosen to omit his 'bad sisters' from the line of succession. The duke followed this with the tumultuous news that Jane was to be the heir named by His Majesty, to succeed the crown.

Jane was stunned. She fell to the floor, the enormity of the crown's burden already weighing heavy. She cried out asserting that the crown was not her right and that 'Lady Mary is the rightful heir.' A period of persuasive coaxing from the council and Northumberland followed, and finally the girl submitted to their will. Regardless of how enforced and unwanted the act was, Jane was now the queen of the realm.

London was in a chaotic and uncertain state; the news that the king had expired had not yet been officially announced, though many suspected his demise such had his frailties been. The proclamation announcing Jane as Queen of England was declared on 10 July 1553, thus cementing the confirmation of Edward's death. Due to her relative obscurity in the minds of her public – particularly in comparison to Mary Tudor – the proclamation document is lengthy, requiring some literal explanation to the people of just who England's new monarch was. The document advocates Jane as the rightful – Protestant – heir to the throne, disputing the claims of both Mary and Elizabeth. Jane, however, had little public support; indeed, her proclamation appeared to do little more than disperse confusion on London's streets and create a swell of approval for the shunned Mary, who many considered the rightful heir.

Mary, however, was unprepared to forego what she considered her birthright. Upon learning of Edward's death, she fled to East Anglia where her support was most buoyant and, crucially, there lived many adherents to the Catholic faith. From here, Mary wrote to the Privy Council with orders of her proclamation as Edward's rightful successor, and demanded the council's allegiance. Certainly, Mary had an ardent following, all eager to see her ascend the throne. She had always been popular and even despite the stigma of illegitimacy, she was still considered to be Henry VIII's legitimate daughter and therefore Edward's natural successor. The fact that Northumberland was endeavouring to deprive her of what much of England considered her birthright also garnered Mary further support in retaliation to the perceived injustice.

When Mary's letter reached the Privy Council, it confirmed their worst fears. Mary was not prepared to meekly surrender her crown; worse still, she had been made aware of the 'aristocratic conspiracy aimed at her destruction.' In a matter of days, Mary had assembled a considerable military force at Framlingham Castle, Suffolk. On 14 July, Northumberland proceeded to meet with Mary's forces and was staggered to find his support vastly outnumbered. With this, Northumberland's support collapsed, while Mary's swelled ever further, with any lingering endorsement for Jane dissipating by the hour. Northumberland had majorly miscalculated, and by 18 July, only a handful of the Privy Council remained loyal to Northumberland.

On 19 July, Jane was deposed as queen, a mere nine days following her 'crowning'. Mary was proclaimed queen, riding into London on a tide of popular support and goodwill, accompanied by her sister Elizabeth and a procession in excess of 800 nobles and gentlemen. In the immediate aftermath of the failed coup, and having obtained the sword of authority, Mary was unsparing in its exercise. Any supporters of Lady Jane Grey were destined to feel its full force. The Duke of Northumberland was arrested, and despite his craving for mercy, he was the first to experience her savage resentment. He was brought to the scaffold to suffer as a traitor, and as a result of his sordid misplaced ambition, was executed on 22 August amid little sympathy.

Lady Jane and her husband were both confined to the Tower, rigorously detained in separate apartments to await their trials for treason. Scarcely could she fathom the breakneck speed of her decline; dethroned as queen of the realm to confinement as a state prisoner within the Tower that was so recently her palace and now imprisoned her as a common criminal.

In mid-November, the trial commenced at Guildhall. Led from the Tower to this place of reckoning that had accounted for so many previously, crowds lined the way, eyes fixed curiously upon this young girl who had so recently, if briefly and reluctantly, reigned over them. Jane was the focal point for most of the examining assembly, though she was joined in the mile-long walk by four other prisoners, including Guildford, her husband of mere months, and two of his brothers, all charged with high treason.

Jane pleaded guilty. She rightly protested that she had been the victim of a manipulative scheme but no matter, she also acknowledged that she 'should not have accepted the crown.' She and Guildford had both admitted their guilt, and the resultant outcome was therefore inevitable: 'indictment and execution'.

Guildford and his brothers had their fates revealed first:

Each of them so be dragged, and there hung and each of them hung, and laid out rotting on the ground, and their interior organs should be brought outside their stomachs, and as these rot they should be burned. And their heads should be cut off, and their bodies, and those of any of them, should be divided into four quarters, and their heads and quarters should be placed where the Queen wishes them to be assigned.

Jane's own fate was then disclosed:

The said Jane be led off by the said Constable of the said Tower of London to the prison of the said Queen within the same Tower, and then on the order of the Queen herself led to Tower Hill and there burned, or the head cut off, as it will then please the Queen.

Despite the sickening gratuity of the violence, Jane – a teenager – retained complete composure. Perhaps she harboured hopes of a merciful reprieve from Queen Mary, or perhaps was simply paralysed with shock. What was clear was that the instrument foremost in Northumberland's conspiracy, despite her naivety of the fact, appeared certain to die an ugly, traitor's death.

It was soon apparent, though, that the horrible certainty awaiting Jane was not perhaps as categorical as first thought. Although she had been condemned to die, no date had been fixed for the grisly practicalities, thus appearing that Mary may yet spare her young cousin's life. Mary was ultimately sympathetic to Jane, recognising her to have been little more than a pawn in Northumberland's overly-ambitious doomed crusade.

With Jane safely enclaved within the Tower's almighty walls, Queen Mary was eager to reunite England with the Catholic Church following the preceding Protestant monarchs. Attending Protestant mass quickly became illegal, whilst influential Protestant leaders had immediate cause for concern, for if they would not reconcile themselves to the Catholic faith they were forced into exile or suffered severe punishments, including death. Coupled with this enforced return to the dogma of Catholicism, Queen Mary was also busying herself privately, seeking a husband who would offer hope of her producing a male heir to her throne. Potential English suitors were considered but quickly abandoned, Mary opting instead for a proposed union with King Philip II of Spain. The possibility of a foreigner becoming England's king appalled Mary's Council, the projected marriage also exciting great alarm amongst the

Protestant community more widely. The warm glow of acceptance that had accompanied Mary's initial crowning as queen was now markedly abating.

The discontent formed by Mary's proposed union with foreign shores led to more than just an impassioned outcry from Protestant quarters. In March 1554, rebellion erupted led by the staunchly anti-Spanish Thomas Wyatt. With the support of many nobles and impassioned followers, he sought to raise public sympathies across England's counties. One of the more notable members of the Wyatt rebellion was Henry Grey – Lady Jane's father. The uprising intended to remove Mary from power, replacing her instead with her Protestant sister, Elizabeth. Furthermore, the rebellion also desired the restoration of Lady Jane, the innocent puppet still imprisoned and obliviously unaware of the battles ensuing beyond her prison walls.

The insurrection would not achieve its aims. Swiftly crushed by the queen's overwhelming forces, Wyatt surrendered and was executed along with many more of the participating rebels. Mary was at this point persuaded that imprisoning Jane and Guildford was dangerous and could lead to further attempted revolts. All of Mary's political opponents now had to be eliminated. For his part in the attempted revolt, Lady Jane's father had effectively signed his – and his daughter's – death warrant.

Though Mary was resigned to the fact that the ultimate punishment was set for Jane, she was nevertheless troubled by the belief that the young girl's soul would be eternally damned within the fires of hell unless her Protestant faith was abandoned. She respited the execution for three days with a specific purpose in mind. On the morning of 8 February 1554, upon her orders, Queen Mary's personal chaplain visited Jane. Benedictine John Feckenham was tasked with dislodging Jane's Protestant faith and replacing it instead with popish mantra; success here would – to Mary's mind at least – allow the salvation of Jane's soul.

Jane, though, with commendable determination and unwavering belief, stood true to her ideals. Feckenham apparently had 'great difficulty in trying to convince her.' Despite her tender years, Jane knew her own mind and would not allow it to be swayed, even throughout the most intense and deadly scrutiny. All that now remained was for the dreadful sentence of death to be passed.

The date of 12 February 1554 was fixed for Jane's execution. As perilous a position as Jane's was, its grim reality was to be brought vividly and excruciatingly to life right before her own death. Her husband, Guildford, was to die first, the block on Tower Hill barely dry from the recent spilling of his father's blood. Guildford was led from the Tower the short distance to Tower Hill. Making no protest as he mounted the scaffold, he lay his head on the block. The axe fell and in one stroke, Guildford's head was detached from his body. As his bloodied corpse was taken back to the Tower, Jane, en-route to her own savage fate, saw her husband's carcass in the cart. 'Oh, Guildford, Guildford!' she mourned. If Jane had been in any doubt as to how her end would play out, it had surely now vanished, its reality barbarously confirmed in front of her eyes.

Whereas Guildford's end on the Hill was vastly observed, Jane was afforded a more private end to her young life. Tower Green is a small confine within the Tower, and apparently a more dignified location for nobility to meet their makers, away from the eyes of macabre spectators and their animalistic baying. As Jane reached the scaffold within the Green, it was noted that 'she turned towards those who stood by to see her die, and greeted them all asking them to take her death as witness of her innocence.' Jane appeared adamant that she would die with valour and courage, a remarkable absence of fear still defining her final moments.

Stood resolutely on the scaffold, she addressed the cruel world that had brought her to this end:

'Good people, I am come hither to die, and by a law I am condemned to the same. The fact, indeed, against the Queen's highness was unlawful, and the consenting thereunto by me: but touching the procurement and desire thereof by me or on my behalf, I do wash my hands thereof in innocency, before God, and the face of you, good Christian people, this day.

I pray you all, good Christian people, to bear me witness that I die a true Christian woman, and that I look to be saved by none other meane [sic], but only by mercy of God in the merits of the blood of his only son Jesus Christ: and I confess, when I did know the word of God I neglected the same, loved myself and the world, and therefore this plague or punishment is happily and worthily happened unto me for my sins: and yet I thank God of his goodness that he hath thus given me a time and respect to repent. And now, good people, while I am alive, I pray you to assist me with your prayers.'

These were the words for which Lady Jane Grey would be remembered, a declaration that confirmed her devout beliefs, and yet, having prepared her soul for death, doing likewise for her body would cause one final heart-rending moment.

She was handed a handkerchief to 'knit about her eyes'. The executioner then kneeled before her, and begged her forgiveness for what he was about to do. With customary compassion, she forgave him most willingly. He then asked Jane to stand upon the straw, at which point she saw the block.

'I pray you dispatch me quickly,' she pleaded to the executioner.

Blinded by the 'kerchief about her eyes', Jane moved forward, feeling for the block with her hands, but could not find it. She grasped thin air several times, the sorry episode a most pitiful and forlorn sight to the few in attendance. Her composure deserted her briefly amid the confusion, crying out desperately, 'What shall I do, where is it?'

The appalling sight of the young girl hopelessly seeking reassurance in this most frightful of moments dismayed all upon the scaffold. Eventually, she was guided to the block. She laid her head upon the beam and spoke for one final time: 'Lord, into thy hands I commend my spirit!'

The headsman raised his axe, and in one stroke, the life of Lady Jane Grey, a wretched victim of misplaced ambition, was ended. Her final words prior to execution on the block reflected both her living dignity and fortitude, as well as symbolically replicating the tragic confusion that her nine-day reign created throughout England, and indeed within herself.

An innocent victim of the sins of others, Lady Jane Grey's execution concluded another facet of incredible Tudor history. Jane's fleeting term as queen may not have elevated her to the auspicious heights of monarchs before or since, though this detracts little from her story, which retains its propensity to inspire and fascinate far more enduringly than the length of her reign.

Chapter 5

Charles Smith

If we are to be privy to an individual's last words, there is, of course, a necessity in documenting them: perhaps through written means, recording the spoken words, or simply the reliance of one's memory to call upon the utterances when desired. One of the more inventive – and certainly ghoulish – methods of preserving such words is synonymous with the case of Charles Smith, executed on Newcastle upon Tyne's Town Moor in the year 1817. A Durham newspaper dated 3 October 1818 perhaps best articulates this method, reporting that: 'An eminent collector and antiquarian of Newcastle is possessed of a piece of skin of the late Charles Smith, executed near that town last year for the murder of Charles Stewart, which he has had tanned and dressed for the purpose of binding a large paper copy of the murderer's dying speech!!!'

The animation in the reporter's writing is mirrored even to this day by those intrigued sufficiently to explore the dimly-lit recesses of Newcastle's City Library to view the macabre relic, where it resides today. This small book is specifically explicit in its detailing of Charles Smith's crime, his execution and, of course, his last dying words. Compiled through a unique collection of paraphernalia concerning the case, it is an extraordinary manuscript which offers a fascinating insight into the event. Yet towards the middle of the document, the reader is confronted with a most sinister-looking page; its thick and leathery quality offers grim confirmation that a physical piece of the murderer himself endures within its pages: pieces of skin cut from the dead man's body some two hundred years prior.

In the north-east of England on the banks of the sprawling River Tyne stands the proud city of Newcastle, iconic for its industrial heritage, distinct 'Geordie' dialect and its affable warm-hearted locals. During the Industrial Revolution of 1750-1850, heavy industry thrived in Newcastle, owing largely to its ideal location for building the ships and steam locomotives that powered the era. A city as rich in its history, however, would not be complete without a host of sinister horrors to deface its chronicles. The Castle Keep, founded in 1168, was the site for several of these grisly episodes, the 'Keep' being regularly decorated with the heads and limbs of the executed. Other landmarks would also feature stark deterrents to would-be criminals; one of the more famed saw the sizeable right arm of William Wallace displayed upon the bridge in 1305, whilst several unnamed body parts of the Scottish warrior were also strewn across the castle walls.

If Newcastle's executions were particularly bloody, those that endured plain and simple incarceration in the keep suffered too. Appalling conditions, described in *An Impartial History of Newcastle upon Tyne* as a 'den of filth', homed countless convicted prisoners whose humiliation was amplified by the morbid public who would pay a fee to satisfy their curiosities and view the prisoners' tormented anguish.

Regardless of the barbarity of punishment, throughout history it is abundantly clear that for some, no level of retribution set upon them will deter a transgression of the laws. This appeared to be the case on a wintry evening on 4 December 1816 in a dilapidated area of Newcastle.

The Ouseburn Valley is a small cradle within Newcastle which, over the centuries, suffered from severe environmental degradation through the relentless processes of industrialisation. A further decline was experienced following the disappearance of key industries from the area, though today the area's wheel has turned full circle. Gone are the slums that once lined the valley, transformed instead into a creative artists' hub brimming with innovation and quirk.

The Ouseburn Pottery Works was owned by John and Joseph Dalton. In its full working capacity it employed up to twenty-four men, but times had become difficult and in November 1816, the Daltons were served a notice of repossession whereby in such consequence, a sheriff's officer acquired possession of the premises and business was duly suspended. Under the direction of the sheriff's officer, Charles Stewart was appointed as custodian of the premises, selling any remaining articles off to interested parties. He lived and slept in an office within the building and deposited any monies generated from the sale of goods into a writing desk. As 'keeper' of the property, Stewart would have been aware of the threat to his safety and the possibilities of raiding chancers looting an apparently unoccupied building, but had presently encountered no great difficulties.

In the icy early hours of 4 December, however, Stewart was disturbed by a knocking at the warehouse door. Warily, he creaked his way towards the clamour where he was met by two intruders. The men subjected the helpless Stewart to a beating of such gratuitous ferocity that upon its cessation he was barely alive. The intruders abandoned him with the assumption that he was indeed dead.

A short time following the attack, however, Jane Buckham and Thomas Pasmore were passing the pottery at five o'clock in the morning and had their attention averted upwards as they saw 'old Charles Stewart looking out of the office window.' The distressed man summoned the energy to sound a warning to the passers-by: 'Alarm the people, for the factory had been robbed last night, they have almost murdered me, and left me for dead!'

The foreman of the works, Mr William Wilkinson, was immediately sent for, arriving at around half past five. Records of the event reveal that the foreman found little of note as he passed through the warehouse, but was left aghast upon reaching the office. There sat Charles Stewart, saturated in his own blood, his head punctuated with heavy bruising and a 'hole in his cheek large enough to admit three fingers'. Wearing only his jacket, the man was by now cold and in a state of great shock, the scene being one of much confusion. All about him were puddles of blood and sodden papers scattered about the place, acting as harrowing reminders of the brutish attack.

The injured man relayed his ordeal as comprehensively as he could under the extreme circumstances – the principal points here being that he had been attacked by two men, one of whom he was unable to identify, but the other he believed to be a man named Charles Smith, easily recognisable due to his 'broad Irish accent and his size'. The suspect was a burly Irishman, a man who had been married for seven years and had two daughters. He was of Catholic faith and was believed to have spent some time in the army prior to moving from the Potteries in Staffordshire, initially to Wearside, where he was employed for some time at 'Dawson's Pottery' at Hylton Low Ford in Sunderland, before swapping the Wear for the Tyne in around Easter 1816, and gaining a position as a pan-man at the Ouseburn Pottery Works.

Armed with Stewart's suspicions, Wilkinson alerted PC Percival Allen, who, with Joseph Dalton and John Charlton, the sheriff's officer, made the short journey to arrest the suspect. Meanwhile, the injured man was with some urgency taken to Newcastle Infirmary for immediate attention.

Charles Smith's lodgings were in Stepney Square, a matter of yards from his place of work and now crime scene. When the ensemble of men burst into his room at seven o'clock in the morning, Smith was in bed. Perplexed at their appearance, he was advised that he was being apprehended as the prime suspect in the attack upon Charles Stewart. To this accusation, he denied all part claiming he had gone to bed early the previous evening and had been there all night.

Whilst dressing himself, the accused Smith was spotted trying to conceal an item under the bed. Suspecting something amiss, Wilkinson reached beneath Smith and pulled out a shoe. He had apparently worn boots the previous evening, and upon inspection of these, they appeared to be stained with blood. Smith countered this saying that he had 'killed a hen the other day, and that sparked the boots.' He was hurried into attiring himself to be then taken before Charles Stewart in the infirmary. Visualising this scene requires some contemplation; the herding of a suspect by a rather chaotically assembled quartet, and arraigning him before the victim in his hospital bed only a few short hours after the attack, is a startlingly vivid image of contrast highlighting the shifting paradigms of justice across the years.

When the prisoner came into the presence of the wounded man at the infirmary, Smith spoke first. 'What's the matter?' he queried furtively. 'Thou rascal, thou knows well enough what's the matter!' was the unforgiving response. Stewart then went on to explain the circumstances of the incident as if to refresh the ignorance of Smith's mind. He claimed that he was seized by the hair and held down by an unknown man. He was then bludgeoned to the side of the head with either a piece of iron or wood.

Smith, implied the wounded man, then proceeded to drag him along the floor 'like a dog' to an outer ware room where he was beaten unmercifully about his head and body. Amidst his crippling agonies, Stewart attested that the attackers believed that they had 'deprived him of life', throwing an old coat over his lifeless body as he lay prone on the floor.

Next, insisted Stewart, the men ransacked the building, breaking their way into the office desks in their pursuit of any monies or valuables within the property. Adding to his unwavering belief as to the guilt of Smith, the bedridden man claimed that whilst he lay in the claret pool of his own blood, he was certain he heard Smith triumphantly pronounce: 'Charles you deserve it all – the bugger is dead!'

John Brown was the clerk to the magistrates of Newcastle. Brown was instructed to write a statement as presented in Stewart's version of events. Stewart narrated this under oath and signed the document as the whole truth. This act presents the plight Charles Stewart had been reduced to. Obtaining his written statement prior to any further physical decline demonstrates the tenuous and fragile balancing act his life had become.

Smith, though, continued to protest his innocence in the matter. With the 'trial by bedside' in progression, Mr Dalton's clerk was sent to the accused's house to look for the stick used to beat Mr Stewart with. During the house search, a large oaken stick was discovered, apparently stained with blood. It was assumed with excitement that this was the weapon with which the horrible affair had been effected. A boot besmeared with blood, one of Smith's stockings and the right knee of his breeches also appeared to be speckled with blood and as such were gathered together, though nothing else of corroborative value was found.

Charles Stewart remained consistent in respect of his testimony, declaring to all around him that Smith was his attacker. Indeed, his reiteration of such became his final act, as he sadly succumbed to his catastrophic injuries on Christmas Day 1816. The charge levelled against Charles Smith, having previously been concerned with robbery, now became one of murder.

With an indictment of murder looming over him, Smith's time spent in custody at Newgate gaol was a miserable one. Sustained with gruel and stale bread, floggings commonplace and all manner of mistreatments lurking in every sodden, verminous corner, the prospect of his trial may well have been a preferable alternative.

The trial for Smith was listed for 15 August 1817 at the Guildhall, an impressive building comprising a composite of several periods dating from 1655. Its Palladian-style entrance block provided a striking approach for those in attendance, and its handsome quayside location belied the solemnities that could be delivered within its walls. Any such delivery in this case would be made by the Lord Chief Baron Richards, a man considered a most sound and capable judge.

It was a Mr Alderson who shouldered the considerable burden of hope for Smith, acting in his defence. Fortunately for Alderson, there were several inconsistencies he wished to untangle before the jury, which offered glimpses of optimism to his client. In his cross-examining of PC Allen, for example, Alderson brought to the fore a quite inexplicable error made by the constable following his admittance of Smith into custody. When Smith's house was searched, a blood-soaked cloth was discovered. This was handed to the constable along with the other items of interest found. PC Allen saw fit to place the cloth into one of Smith's boots, thus contaminating it with blood allegedly from the victim.

'Was it not your duty, as a constable, to have kept everything from the boots when you knew the man was charged with murder?' quizzed Alderson.

'Yes, it was,' came the rather vanquished reply. This suggested undertone of incompetence and invalidity was a theme which Alderson believed ran through much of the 'evidence' against his client; his difficulty, though, would be persuading the jury to think likewise.

Next came the steady stream of witness testimonies, which once more, Alderson interrogated to the full. Miles Brown passed the pottery on the evening prior to the attack, and adamantly claimed that Smith was whispering with another man outside. Brown went on to say that his sole point of positively identifying the man as Smith was the glazed hat which he wore. Alderson immediately questioned whether there should be 'anything extraordinary in a man whispering' late in the evening – to which Brown agreed there was not.

William Richardson remembered seeing Smith at 10.30 in the evening walking towards the pottery. Under duress from Alderson he admitted that he did not know Smith, but recognised his glazed hat – a point in which Alderson affirmed that there were a great many similar hats in Newcastle, and so this man was not necessarily Smith, and as such, did not constitute as evidence against him.

James Dowling was another witness whose attestations would be disputed. At eleven o'clock, he heard two men whispering by the pottery in 'Irish dialect'. This was considered almost irrefutable proof that Smith had been involved, though Alderson quite correctly inserted the fact here that many of the pottery's employees were Irish, and furthermore, of Smith's stocky build. Dowling's evidence appeared to encapsulate the bulk of witness testimony provided – the majority of it being merely circumstantial.

The medical evidence created similar dubiousness. Mr James Church was the house surgeon of Newcastle Infirmary. He recollected Charles Stewart being brought to him on 14 December, and was evidently in a 'dangerous state'. The surgeon explained that as Stewart had suffered a fracture to his skull, an operation known as a 'trepan' was necessary – a procedure performed to relieve or remove oppression of the brain, which, importantly in the circumstances of this case, also 'causes an absence of intellect'. The insinuation here was clear: much of the prosecution case against Smith centred around the injured man's evidence, yet how much credence could be given to this in light of the severe head injuries he had received? Indeed, Stewart's 'identification' of his attacker was through voice alone, and at no point did he see his face. The surgeon reinforced the idea of contention further, adding that it would be unlikely that a man in Stewart's situation could recognise a person by his voice alone.

Charles Stewart's bedside testimony then created the greatest supposition of doubt in the entire trial. Mr Alderson submitted to the judge that the deposition should not be received as evidence, owing to the much-affected condition of its author. This aspect was, of course, of pivotal importance; here was a deceased victim's oath-sworn account that 'provided' the name of his aggressor, yet it was laden with scepticism and incredulity. The learned judge, however, overruled Alderson's assertions and admitted the deposition to be read as evidence, essentially appearing to seal Smith's fate.

The jury was finally addressed in an impressive manner, the judge summing up the evidence with neat perspicuity. The jury retired for fifteen short minutes before returning a verdict of 'guilty'. Smith, who had stood with undaunted firmness throughout the six-and-a-half-hour trial, then began to declare most strongly his innocence in the shedding of Charles Stewart's blood. When order was restored, the judge delivered a solemn address to the prisoner, culminating in passing the sentence of death to the shattered man. Charles Smith was ordered to be hanged until dead, and his body was to be then passed to the local surgeons for dissection. Smith was removed from the bar in a 'much depressed state', left to ponder his limited future shackled in squalor back in Newgate gaol. Moments of meagre cheer, though, were afforded the condemned man, enjoying several visits from his wife. She was apparently most attentive to him and supplied much-needed kindness and affection throughout, all of which softened the rigour of his confinement.

However, despite permitting the victim's testimony as admissible evidence, the case had yielded perplexity across the bar, to the point that Lord Richards decided that 'owing to a point of law, referred (the case) to twelve judges, on some informality of the deceased.' This was a process which arose when a question of law or procedure emanated during the conduct of a jury trial; the question could be reserved for collective deliberation by the twelve common law judges. So it was that in the Michaelmas term of 1817, eleven of the judges met to consider the case – C.J. Gibbs being absent.

There would be no reprieve for Smith, however. Ten of the judges considered the conviction to be correct, and that the deposition had been properly received in evidence. The sentence administered to Smith would therefore stand, and on Wednesday, 3 December 1817 on Town Moor, he would be hanged by the neck until he was dead.

The spectre of the scaffold cast a long and ominous shadow over eighteenth- and nineteenth-century England. Early on the morning of Charles Smith's execution, its morbidity was manifesting itself in Newcastle as the gallows were erected at the low end of the Town Moor, in preparation for the impending spectacle. The moor is now a vast green recreationally-popular expanse, and for a fortnight each summer, it plays venue to Europe's largest travelling fair attracting masses of revellers – the likes of which had been unwitnessed since the bloodthirsty droves shared in the merriment of capital punishment.

Whilst the grim practicalities were being implemented across on the moor, in a dank and dreary cell Charles Smith was attended by Reverend Worswick to assist him in his devotions. At some time close to ten o'clock in the morning, Smith was taken from his cell and set into a stage within the cart which would deliver the condemned man to his place of execution.

The compassionate clergyman closely followed the rattling cart and later noted that Smith appeared 'absorbed in devotional exercise from a book he held all the way'. Smith was of devout Catholic faith, yet his piety was being examined to its very highest, and under the stresses of death, Smith disclosed that his life had been a sinful one, noting particular attention to his 'neglecting divine ordinances' and 'worshipping in the alehouses instead of the house of God.' Such feelings under extreme conditions as these are not, of course, unexpected. But to his God, Smith needed to initiate the road to redemption as speedily as possible.

Having navigated through the vast concourse that had descended upon the Town Moor to witness yet another man's final moments, the cart stopped yards away from the gallows. Engaging in fervent prayers with Reverend Worswick, Smith then stood up firmly and began to address the flock about him:

'I was born in Ireland, of honest and reputable parents, who gave me a religious education. Murder, or the intention of murder, never took possession of my mind at any time. I die cheerfully, with a good conscience to all men, and I know that no one can say any thing against my character, except in foolishly spending the earnings of my industry, and a neglect of the ordinances of God, for which I am heartily sorry. I hope all good Christians will join in prayers in my behalf to Almighty God, that I may be accepted in his presence, and I do most solemnly declare, that I never knocked down Charles Stewart, – or tied him, – or shed his blood. I hope there will be none so base as to upcast my untimely end to my dear Wife and Children. I die an unworthy member of the Church of Rome, in the forty-ninth year of my age, – and may the Lord have mercy on my soul.'

His reassertions of innocence were calmly and collectedly delivered, performed in the presence of the noose's dark shadow casting out across the moor before him. He demonstrated great fortitude, but such valiance could not delay the inevitable. The cart was driven the few required yards, positioning itself under the gallows. The executioner actioned his onerous work and prepared the noose around Smith's neck. The cap was drawn over his ashen face, and before Smith could dwell even momentarily, he was quickly suspended – whereupon the commencement of a short struggle occupied all those in attendance. A short series of involuntary jolts proved to be the final actions of Charles Smith.

His body dangled for the customary hour before being cut down and hauled away to be anatomised and dissected for medical research. This prospect was one which struck untold fear into the condemned. Indeed, it is thought that Charles Smith pleaded to the sheriff that following his death, his body might be given to his dear wife, rather than 'face' the ignominy of the surgeon's slab. It was not solely the prospect of 'medical mutilation' that unsettled the condemned; what perturbed in equal measure was the significance of the body's integrity in the concern of resurrection and the prospect of life beyond the gallows. That such treatment of a body could hinder the hopeful prospect of reawakening was a tremendous apprehension. One indeed, which was often dreaded more than the hangman's work itself.

Regrettably for Smith, his body was indeed to become an object of gawped scrutiny, *The Tyne Mercury* newspaper reporting that 'numbers of persons assembled on that and every succeeding day during that last week to view it.' It seems that murderous felons have always captivated and intrigued on some level, and Charles Smith similarly so. The case retains intrigue and debate; was Smith, considered by some to be a mere statistic of a flawed and imperfect justice system of its time, or was he indeed the cruel killer of Charles Stewart? Whilst the surviving book which chronicles his last moments may not answer this question, it does offer a unique glimpse into the soul of a condemned man. It is then, perhaps fitting that a book about the human soul should contain a physical piece of the man himself…

Chapter 6

Charlotte Ellen Reeve

Suicide was traditionally viewed as a form of self-murder, an offence against God and a felony in criminal law. In the Middle Ages, suicide was met with condemnation in common law and by the church – in whose eyes it constituted a mortal sin. Within Tudor and Stuart England, the act was regarded most heinously and was subject to savage punishments. From the middle of the eighteenth century, however, a tolerance and easing of public attitudes toward suicide had emerged. An example of this shift in public opinion can be discerned through a spirited debate initiated in *The Times* in 1786, when the question was posed 'is suicide an act of courage?' This concept had never previously been entertained, attracting only negative connotations.

Juries were tending to demonstrate a leniency and refraining from imposing punitive sentences to punish 'self-murder'. Typical punishments for *'felo de se'* (felon of himself) had included the denial of a Christian burial, or stripping the deceased family of their belongings and passing them to the Crown. The suicide of an adult male had the capacity to not only devastate a family, but could reduce it to a state of pauperism.

In 1823 Parliament abolished the religious penalties for suicide, but nonetheless it continued to be regarded with great fear and abhorrence. Moreover, it was the converse of a 'good death' – a concept which preoccupied many a nineteenth-century mind, riddling it with morbid fear. Suicides were 'sudden' deaths, an issue which created much disturbance to Victorian thinking; if a death occurred without warning, there would be no time for spiritual preparation or contrition for past sins.

Many Christians of the nineteenth century, however compassionate they were becoming, still regarded suicide as a sinful act against God. Although suicide was more frequently viewed as an act caused by insanity, there remained a prevailing presumption that 'self-killing' was bad, and even if Victorian society was generally unwilling to inflict punishment upon suicides and the families, it was still an act that required concealing wherever possible. The stigma that attached itself to a grieving family following a suicide death was all-consuming and something to be avoided at all costs.

In religious circles, suicide continued amongst some to be deplored with horror. In 1900, Reverend J. Gurnhill in the *Lancet* referred to it as 'this deadly sin'. For some, however, particularly those bereft of such a platform to circulate such assumptions, or indeed lacking in any voice whatsoever, suicide was a clinical option in freeing oneself from a bitter life and putting to an end an existence of suffering.

The lives of Victorian parlourmaids have been extensively documented in terms of the degradation and servitude often endured. Whilst male servants would predominantly keep the gardens and lands of the prosperous well-tended, women were as equally likely to run the internal proceedings. Employing a male indoor servant would attract a tax, and as such, women were a more cost-effective form of labour. Of equal importance, though, women were more easily dominated and 'kept in line'. Restricted within an unbreachable hierarchy, parlourmaids generally occupied the unenviable position of society's bottom rung with little chance of advancement. In 1740 Elizabeth Branch and her daughter Mary were hanged for the murder of their maid, Jane Butterworth. On the gallows, Elizabeth's final words were an unenlightened admittance that it was her belief that servants were to be viewed as 'slaves, vagabonds and thieves', – an eighteenth-century opinion that was regularly echoed, publicly or otherwise, by much of the Victorian aristocracy.

A further distress encountered by many parlourmaids – particularly those of tender years – was their vulnerability to sexual exploitation. Allied to the physical and psychological traumas this created, the resultant possibility of being burdened with an illegitimate child compounded their miseries further. Many young women were tragically punished by the law in such situations, and in agonisingly desperate cases, newborn babies were regularly disposed of with horrifying abandonment. Even the briefest perusal of newspapers from the era confirms the frightful regularity of such episodes – ditches, wooded copses, and secluded pools of water were unwittingly transformed into burial grounds for the despairing women. Once such a desertion was discovered, the forlorn woman could be hauled before the courts and tried and convicted by the powers of a male-dominated justice system. In a sense this construct ensured that women were essentially 're-abused', many of whom ultimately paid with their lives.

In 1900, Charlotte Ellen Reeve was 23 years old. She was in the service of Mr Cooper, of Glenhurst, Clapham Park. The young parlourmaid was an unsung cog in the hierarchical ensemble employed by high society. Charlotte was mother to Clephan, her illegitimate son, and she struggled with the 'disgrace' that she believed she had brought upon her family. In an incredible series of letters written to her sister and discovered after her death, Charlotte provides a moving account of the mindful struggle endured as she concludes what her fate is to be.

Her final words are charted in the form of a diary extending over three weeks and reveal much anguish, heartache and despair. Yet through the blizzard of despondency, the young girl is fervently certain of one thing, revealing a stirring clarity of mind, as the letters tumble into an unwavering preparation for death and she definitively makes her 'forever decision'.

The opening pages of the document were dated 29 April and addressed to her sister, Clara, also a parlourmaid, across the Thames in Hyde Park Gate.

On the night I post this to you I shall have left here forever; so will you please have my boxes fetched to you, or wherever you like to have them sent? If Mrs Cooper says anything to you about our late butler spare his name, as he is nothing whatever to do with me. He is entirely innocent of the cause of my leaving here. Why I am going I need not say, and even if I did, it would do no one any good. My only wish is that I could take Clephan with me. He is my only worry now. Oh! If I could only take him with me; but that I can't do. Bad as I know I am, I must stop short at murder.

If my machine and boxes are pawned I daresay they will fetch a few shillings; enough to pay for Clephan until they take him into the union [workhouse], as that is where he must go unless I can force myself to take him with me at the last minute…Myself I hope and trust you will never hear of again. My body may be found in the river near the docks, or I may go further away than that. I cannot fix on the certain place till the time comes, but I have taken all the washing marks and names off all the clothes I wear, so that no one will know me, and I don't want any one to identify me. Better for my sake and all the others. I shall have a black silk ribbon around my neck, with a small gold heart-shaped locket and a 22-carat gold wedding ring strung on…Don't let mother know of this. Let her think I am too lazy to write to her. I have not written since January. I have left you a dreadful lot of hard work to do for me, I know, but when it is all over I am sure you must think it is the best thing I could do, and what I ought to have done three years ago, and saved my family all the disgrace of these last three years. Just fancy! My first boy in Heaven, my second on earth, and my third in hell with me. How awful to have such a record. Now, for your own sake and the sake of your family, don't scream or faint, or do anything like that when you read this, as I must warn you it is very shocking; but it can't be helped now. I am not unhappy, but I wish I could go now instead of waiting three weeks.

The prose continues under the date of 14 May 1900, Charlotte's words divulging her obvious fears of death.

My mind is slowly but surely going. I only hope it will last one more week. I wonder if anyone else ever felt this nervous about dying. I am going out tomorrow to finish up the last of my business. Then I shall have nothing else to do but wait for Monday. I am starving myself this week as much as possible so as to be too weak to struggle long in the water, as I dread a slow death more than anything else…I wish the weather was warmer, then the water would not be so cold. I tried yesterday and fairly shivered.

Finally, on 21 May, Charlotte concludes the letter, simply saying:

Goodbye, Clara. Pray for me.

The following day, the body of the young girl was recovered. On the Bermondsey side of the Thames, nestled between Tower Bridge and

London Bridge, is Stanton's Wharf. It was here that the 23-year-old was found drowned, and as to her written word, upon her lifeless body was draped the black ribbon, together with a heart locket and ring, as she had so meticulously planned. The letters Charlotte left formed the principal evidence at the inquest following her death. Samuel Langham, the district coroner presided over the hearing at Horsleydown, where the jury returned a verdict of 'suicide whilst temporarily insane', a rather customary verdict of the time, the supposition generally being that the individual was innocent of self-murder, and instead suffering from a disturbed mind.

The letters offer stark glimpses into an era defined by the constructs of domesticity and motherhood, and their centrality to the very composition of a woman in Victorian times. These 'duties' alone were considered to provide ample emotional fulfilment for the fairer sex, yet as cases such as Charlotte's show, the reality was seismically different, and such a degree of neglect was often insurmountable. Clearly the girl's thoughts are largely occupied by her children past and present; her 'first boy in heaven, second on earth', and 'third in hell with me', portraying her sense of previous loss as well as revealing her current state of pregnancy. We have no record of paternity here, but the letter may be construed as confirmation of another parlourmaid suffering the indecent vulnerabilities which often defined the employment.

Mercifully, Charlotte did not take Clephan with her, and thus succeeded in 'stopping short of murder'. Her surviving son was a mere 14 months old when his mother took her own life. Charlotte's assumption that he was destined for the workhouse happily proved an inaccurate one, for in the 1911 UK census, Clephan is recorded as living with his grandparents, John and Sarah Reeve, and indeed, Clara, at Farthingstone, Northamptonshire. In light of the tragedy that befell the young boy, we might presume that his auntie shouldered much of the care for him during his early years. If indeed this was the case, she appeared to do an admirable job; Clephan went on to live an extensive – and hopefully happy – life, dying in 1994 aged 95.

Chapter 7

Robert Catesby

On 5 November 1605, deep beneath the vaults of the Houses of Parliament, a bearded stranger was discovered. In isolation, the discovery of the man may not have caused such a stirring consternation, but the accompanying thirty-six barrels of gunpowder were proof enough that a plot of upmost treachery had been exposed. The story of Guy Fawkes has, of course, become a well-worn one; after all, had the plot succeeded, it would have been the bloodiest in English history. And whilst Fawkes' detection was paramount to the emergence of the rebellious scheme, the reality of its origins lay elsewhere.

Robert Catesby was a young, charismatic nobleman with an ebullient reputation as a man of action. A devout Catholic living in Queen Elizabeth's aggressively Protestant England, Catesby hatched an audacious revolt intended to unshackle his fellow Catholics from the subordinate regime they had long since endured. His views were total and clear; Catholics should not merely be passive and fall in line, rather they needed to seize any opportunity to improve their restricted conditions. These notions, however, if not necessarily disagreed with by his compatriots, certainly provoked an unwillingness to act upon such radical ideas.

Most Catholics had learnt to remain quietly in the shadows, begrudgingly holding their faith as an object of suppression rather than something to be publicly embraced. Seventeenth-century-England, after all, was an unforgiving landscape, a period of fierce religious conflict where competing powers of state toiled for supremacy. Catholic priests worked covertly, under the omnipresent threat of discovery which would lead to certain death.

For Catesby, his faith overrode fear and he lived with a resolute refusal to conform. Such non-conformists to the Anglican doctrine were labelled recusants by the government. This beleaguered minority was struggling to keep the 'true faith' alive, but during a period of ongoing conflict with

Catholic Spain, recusants were viewed disdainfully as a possible 'enemy within', and a problem that needed to be incessantly monitored. At constant risk of unannounced night-time searches of homes and property, and with a burgeoning fear of far more callous reprisals, the majority of English Catholics drifted into conformity.

Catesby's friend, Thomas Percy, served the Earl of Northumberland as kinsman and steward for the earl's northern estates. Percy was also the earl's intermediary in a host of confidential communications with King James VI of Scotland. In the autumn of 1602 during one such exchange, Percy sought reassurances from the would-be king that a toleration of the Catholic faith within England would be established. With Elizabeth on the throne, there was little chance that Catesby or other Catholics would be indulged, but the queen was in poor health and with James set to replace her as head of the monarchy, Catholic dreams of acceptance appeared valid and recusant prayers seemingly answered. At least this was certainly the message that Percy had taken from their rendezvous and he was eager to distribute the positive news to fellow Catholics who could embrace imminent liberation.

Six months later, on 24 March 1603, Elizabeth died and King James VI of Scotland became James I of England. His accession to the throne complete, English Catholics were hopeful of a reordering in which their suppression would be nullified. Initially, there was indeed a relaxing of persecution, however, this period of relief lasted only a year and by the summer of 1604, it was clear that no formal appeasement of Catholicism was forthcoming.

English Catholics felt betrayed, none more so than Robert Catesby and Thomas Percy, disenchanted with the new king who had, to their minds, reneged on his promises of toleration. For Catesby, a lifetime of indignation moved into sharp focus; the object of his hatred and contempt was King James, and only an extreme course of action would now suffice.

In the spring of 1604, Catesby had made his decision. He had devised a most outlandish and drastic plan riddled with untold risk, but if successful, he would not only blow King James to pieces, but the entire establishment within the House of Lords.

On Sunday, 20 May 1604, the Duck and Drake Inn off London's Strand was the venue for Catesby to meet with four friends, who, clandestinely huddled together, set in motion a most fanatical collusion – the ruthless Gunpowder Plot.

The target would be the state opening of Parliament whereupon the entire ruling class would be present and subsequently – if the plan was realised – obliterated. An act of such devastating proportions could not be achieved independently so Catesby recruited Thomas Percy, Thomas Wintour, Jack Wright and Guy Fawkes as fellow conspirators, the group brimming with impulsiveness and a resolute desire to succeed. The newest royal dynasty could never have known the grave danger that stealthily stalked it.

Percy was a vital pawn in the plot, funding the group and securing leases to properties in central London, ideal bases from which to scheme and collude. Perhaps most crucially, on 25 March 1605, Percy obtained the lease for the undercroft which lay directly beneath the House of Lords – an ideal location from which to create an explosion. Guy Fawkes, of course, was central to this part of the design, his well-established connections and knowledge in the field of explosives and mining providing access to hordes of surplus gunpowder; during the summer months of 1605, he had painstakingly stockpiled it in the undercroft where it would remain, under the very noses of the Protestant state until it was time to ignite the deadly ammunition.

Meanwhile, Catesby was embroiled in the task of seeking additional recruits for the plot. Drawing upon his vastly charismatic nature, he was able to persuade his fellow man to stand beside him, to act and finally rise up against the cruel injustices that Catholics had become accustomed to. Convinced by his flawless plot, Catesby was, however, blind to the fact that further recruitment lay the plan open to perhaps its biggest danger of detection. A careless whisper in the wrong company and the consequences would be both absolute and indescribably brutal.

Three weeks before King James would reopen Parliament, the plot appeared to be on course. Thirty-six barrels of gunpowder lay in wait, carefully watched over by an anxious Fawkes. Back above ground, however, Catesby faced a problem. With funds evaporating, he sought to address this by convincing Francis Tresham, a prominent recusant Catholic landowner, to join the conspiracy, believing that he was a man of some wealth. Tresham and his family were strict Catholics and the relentless persecution they endured led him to become hugely embittered. Nonetheless, Tresham had concerns, and was largely unconvinced by the plot. 'A great sickness requires so sharp a remedy,' claimed Catesby, his incurable mantra finally managing to secure Tresham's agreement to act as the last conspirator within the expanding plot.

The materialistic advantages of luring Tresham into the plot were obvious, but this belied an ironic paradox because Tresham also had the capacity to be its weakest link. He was a man of substantial connections with many friends within the House of Lords, including two brothers-in-law, and it would be reasonable to assume that Tresham may have wished to forewarn them of the intended scheme. Indeed, many commentators believe that is precisely what Tresham did. Only ten days prior to the planned crescendo, Catesby's plan began to crumble. Whilst at supper in his north London home, Lord Monteagle – a brother-in-law to Tresham – received an obscure letter delivered by an apparent masked stranger. The scrawled letter read:

My lord, out of the love I bear to some of your friends, I have a care of your preservation, therefore I would advise you as you tender your life to devise some excuse to shift your attendance at this parliament, for God and man have concurred to punish the wickedness of this time, and think not slightly of this advertisement, but retire yourself into your country, where you may expect the event in safety, for though there be no appearance of any stir, yet I say they shall receive a terrible blow this parliament and yet they shall not see who hurts them, this counsel is not to be condemned because it may do you good and can do you no harm, for the danger is past as soon as you have burnt the letter and I hope God will give you the grace to make good use of it, to whose holy protection I commend you.

Monteagle was a Catholic peer and at some risk of becoming collateral damage in Catesby's grand plan. He was due to attend the opening of Parliament, but the contents of the letter urged otherwise. He was confronted with a stark warning to renege on his planned attendance; 'I would advise you, as you tender your life, to devise some excuse to shift your attendance at this parliament'. The message was certainly vivid enough to evoke suspicions of a foul deed and, as such, was immediately rushed to Whitehall and into the hands of Robert Cecil, James's secretary of state – a man of notorious anti-Catholic disposition. A major function of Cecil's role was to gather intelligence of such plots and foil them in their infancy, so this letter, despite its puzzling origins of authorship, could not be ignored.

Meanwhile, Monteagle's servant, Thomas Ward, a recusant Catholic, conveyed a warning to the conspirators that a letter had been sent to the government which warned of the plot, thus confirming an almighty breach of trust and placing the entire plan in enormous jeopardy. The natural suspect was Francis Tresham, but when confronted by Catesby and Wintour, he was seemingly able to convince the seething pair of his innocence. Rumours have abounded since regarding the source of the letter, but whilst its author has never been identified, the letter did at least reveal that the act of insurgency had been unearthed – but still, even this did not deter the unwavering Catesby.

On 1 November 1605, King James returned to London from a hunting trip blissfully unaware of the plot against him and his government. Cecil was quick to correct this, however, immediately revealing the letter to his king and disclosing the horrible treason planned.

With the conspirators in the throes of their final preparations for this most drastic of rebellions, Tresham was urging Catesby a final time to abandon the plot – a plea ignored by this resolute 'moving spirit' of the gunpowder plot. Beneath the vaults of Parliament remained Fawkes; a shadowy figure shrouded in mystery lying in wait, and preparing to light a slow-burning fuse that would result in an act of anarchic annihilation of the pomp and ceremony of state.

However, just before midnight on Monday, 4 November 1605, Robert Catesby's fantastical project was quite literally unearthed. Sir Thomas Knyvett and a guard were assigned to search the bowels of Parliament, where the following day, only yards above their heads, the hall would be crammed with all manner of peerage which formed the establishment. A most theatrical image ensued with Knyvett and his guard happening upon Fawkes in the darkness as he manned the numerous barrels of gunpowder. Fawkes was swiftly pinioned by the guard, leaving Knyvett to proceed warily into the black expanse, armed with a flickering lantern to lead his eye. Unearthing a vast heap of kindling, he probed tentatively at it, before revealing the lethal barrels that lay beneath.

Without delay, Fawkes was hauled to the Tower of London for questioning. If the king and his council hoped the interrogation would extract speedy answers from their mysterious captive, they were very soon dismayed. Masquerading as 'John Johnson', Fawkes remained the epitome of self-possession and restraint, staunchly refusing to buckle under the intense examination, all the while providing his accomplices with precious time to abandon the capital.

As the news of monumental treason filtered around Westminster and beyond, the remaining insurgents bolted, riding through the wintry November night towards Holbeche House in Staffordshire, where Catesby had reckoned upon a final last stand. En route, the men plundered armoury and money from various sites, among them Warwick Castle and Hewell Grange in Worcestershire, the stately home of Lord Windsor, before continuing on their final journey through the autumnal damp towards Holbeche. The impressive mansion, owned by Stephen Lyttelton, a prominent Catholic figure in the West Midlands, offered refuge to the demoralised, weary – and now wanted – band of rebels.

As the men focused their preparations for the forthcoming fire-fight, a remarkable incident of inconceivable irony served to deplete their now-waning belief. The journey to Holbeche had dampened amounts of the gunpowder, and, in a calamitous effort to revive its use, they set about laying it to dry before a fire. The result of this was all too apparent; a stray spark ignited the powder creating an explosion that maimed the faces of four of the men, Catesby included. One of the men was so badly hurt, his 'eyes were burnt out.' A dreadful, accidental replica of what they had intended in London had served to damage their very own efforts, and also highlighted just how much they needed their expert in munitions.

Alas, he was otherwise, and somewhat agonisingly, engaged elsewhere. Acutely aware that the obscure man found beneath Parliament could not have been solely responsible for such grand-scale treason, the king was intent on syphoning any information from Fawkes that might reveal any further identities involved. Should Fawkes remain unyielding, King James advocated some means of gentle persuasion to loosen his tongue: 'If he will not other wayes confesse, the gentler tortours are to be the first used unto him…God speed youre goode worke. James.' Bizarrely, James was impressed by Fawkes' immovable manner, earning his admiration and describing him as owning a 'Roman resolution'.

Nonetheless, his admiration did not prevent James from authorising and, indeed, inflicting hell upon Fawkes. The 'gentler tortours' achieved their goal, and following a gruelling three-day stretch on the rack, he succumbed to the excruciating pain. Amid the sound of popping cartilage and bursting bones, Guy Fawkes finally revealed the identities and whereabouts of his co-conspirators.

With the list of wanted men drawn up, all eyes turned to the Midlands. The end game had begun.

The seventeenth-century mentality was decidedly providentialist, and the mood of the remaining conspirators was reflective of a group whose initial spiritual elation had long since passed. Several of them had deserted, the belief and enthusiasm drained in what had become a hopeless cause. Catesby, however, was defiant to the last and would not leave Holbeche quietly. He and the fragmented remnants of a once-buoyant group would simply wait for the arrival of the king's men. Fate would then play its hand.

On the morning of 8 November 1605, the High Sheriff of Worcester, Sir Richard Walsh, led 200 men to Holbeche and promptly surrounded the hideout. As they peered from their retreat, the thirteen remaining men were utterly besieged and resigned to the hopelessness of their situation. It seemed even Catesby accepted the morbid position in which they had tumbled. The remaining men intended to die at Holbeche; the alternative would, after all, be a far more excruciating affair that would conclude with their body parts decorating the 'four corners of the kingdom'.

Walsh and his men, aware of the quarry holed up in Holbeche, immediately started a fire in the hope of drawing the conspirators from the house. The plan worked: Thomas Wintour, John and Christopher Wright and Ambrose Rookwood, perhaps attempting to quell the fire, were soon shot in the courtyard. Wintour was wounded, but escaped back into the house with Catesby and Percy, the only other two that were not incapacitated by their injuries.

Catesby's final words reveal a gallantry befitting this free-spirited symbol of Catholic hope. They also reveal the totality of the wretched plight faced by the men, coupled with the vivid realisation that together they were stepping out to their deaths. In typically show-stopping fashion he said: 'Stand by me, Tom, and we will die together.'

The king's men, bristling with intent, awaited the merest movement from inside. Catesby and Percy, side by side until the end, stepped out into the courtyard where both were allegedly felled by a single shot. Percy was killed, but Catesby, further demonstrating his unflinching doggedness, crawled back inside the house and completed his demise most aptly – finding a picture of the Virgin Mary and clutching it in his arms until he died. The flame around which a rebellious flock had once gathered was extinguished forever.

The remaining surviving plotters were undoubtedly the unfortunate ones. On 31 January 1606, the men, including the renowned Fawkes, were dragged to the Old Palace Yard at Westminster and hanged, drawn and quartered opposite the very place they had dreamt of demolishing. Catesby, though already dead, would also suffer the fiendish dishonour of decapitation: his head taken back down to London and set upon the 'side of Parliament House', to become one of the 'sightless spectators of their own failure'.

Catesby's final moments were recorded in the confession of Thomas Wintour prior to his own annihilation. Certainly, his final declaration succinctly epitomised the defiant character which made Robert Catesby a perfect figurehead for such an audacious plot. They also resonate with the perpetual state of mind that inhabited Catesby: the overwhelming desire to restore England to its 'one true faith', regardless of how delusional and unlikely his desired outcome was. Catesby, as founder of this most notorious of terrorist plots, came agonisingly close to a complete destabilisation of the English realm, and whilst his co-conspirator lives on through burning effigies and playground song, Robert Catesby, in contrast to his crusading days, has gently faded into martyred obscurity.

Chapter 8

Helen Blackwood and
Hans Smith Macfarlane

Victorian Scotland was quite the paradox. As industry flourished, flocks of people were enticed towards urbanised districts, filling the jobs created by the increasing manufacturing of textiles, chemicals, glass, paper and soap. Glasgow's population grew vastly, as did the city's attraction to other heavier industries, diversifying into shipbuilding and heavy engineering, enthusiastically powered by the plentiful and nearby supplies of coal and iron ore.

A swelling population could satisfy the array of employment on offer, but inevitably the housing stock could not keep apace, leading to severe overcrowding and the creation of slum areas, the conditions of which were loathsome at best. Thousands of people were crammed into dilapidated 'housing' where sanitation was a literal pipe dream. The city centre was starkly described by commentators of the time as 'an accumulated mass of squalid wretchedness unequalled in any other town in the British Dominions'. Indeed, a 'warts and all' account of the Glasgow slums written in 1842 by eminent physician and inventor Dr Arnott, is particularly vivid: 'There were no drains or privies there, and the dungheaps received all the filth which the swarm of wretched inhabitants could give; and we learnt that a considerable part of the rent of the houses was paid by the produce of dung heaps.'

Croiley's Land in the New Vennel area of Glasgow was typical of the less-than-salubrious lodgings the city offered. Disparagingly referred to as 'fever-dens' or 'little hells', these crowded tenements were widespread, and whilst the threat of disease had severely inflated amongst the populace, in one of these dark and dingy addresses lurked a far more unexpected, yet equally deadly peril.

The home of Helen Blackwood was a single room on the third storey of a cramped and crowded tenement. Her homely possessions consisted of merely a bed and several cooking utensils, with seating arrangements in the form of some large stones – primitive indeed – yet with room dimensions of eight feet by six feet, little more could be accommodated.

Born in 1823, 30-year-old Helen had endured a harsh start to life; abandoned swiftly by her father, James Blackwood, she was left under the less-than-watchful eye of a drunken mother, Margaret Craig. A lack of guidance and direction ensured that Helen rapidly descended into a murky world of prostitution and criminality. Furthermore, she was fulfilling the character that her detractors had long since labelled her – Helen Blackwood apparently having 'long had the character of a desperate and wicked woman'.

Even laden with such dubious traits, however, Helen still attracted particular suitors, and Hans Smith Macfarlane, a 25-year-old collier from Partick, was the latest. Living together would, of course, be a compact affair, but remarkably the couple were not the only lodgers sharing in the ramshackle of the room. As well as two prostitutes named Mary Hamilton, 27, and Ann Marshall, 25 – both of whom would regularly use the room for 'business' – two orphaned brothers, William and James Shillinglaw, aged 11 and 9 respectively, were permitted to sleep under the bed, a gesture which perhaps partly belies the foreboding persona portrayed by Helen Blackwood.

The boys were pupils of a newly-formed educational movement known as the 'Ragged Schools'. Generally established in working-class districts of rapidly expanding industrial towns, they were essentially 'charity schools' throughout the United Kingdom, offering free education alongside food, clothing and even lodgings in some cases, for those without the means to pay for such luxuries. The founding principles were certainly just, but the realities of the Ragged Schools were dire; an early snapshot perhaps of the deprivation that many of its pupils would doubtless filter into throughout their adult lives. Indeed, it was a visit to such an establishment in 1843 that inspired Charles Dickens to write his timeless classic, *A Christmas Carol*, which provides an illuminating insight into conditions and the plight endured by children akin to the Shillinglaw brothers.

On Saturday, 11 June 1853, two ship carpenters with the merchant navy, James Law and Alexander Boyd, were merrily revelling in some long-anticipated leave. Their pockets groaning under the weight of their hard-earned coins, the two men had been drinking heavily for the bulk of the day, and 'kept up the spree all day from half-past eight in the morning'. For 39-year-old Boyd, the crawl was especially welcome. It heralded a long-awaited return to his native city, having lived in Valparaiso, Chile, for several years. A relentless succession of bars had been frequented and the two men were very visibly sodden in drink, and in a state of some vulnerability. Such targets were impossible to ignore for ladies desperate to earn money, regardless of how dubious their intents were.

Mary Hamilton and Ann Marshall were two such women, hopefully prowling the streets of Glasgow with a staunch resolve to earn some silver. Happening upon the inebriated men, they duly enticed them to Helen's room, the promises of sex frantically ringing in the men's ears. Leading the eager men up the squalid staircases to the third-floor room, a succession of the usual drunks lay about the corridors, gurgling incoherently and lying prone, unwittingly oblivious to the dangers that roamed about them.

The carpenters were in a state of utter stupor by now: Law completely unconscious on one of the stones, and whilst Boyd was little better, he was certainly the less drunk of the two. Helen, now revelling in her hostess guise and content that the men could be robbed with little resistance, lit a candle amidst the dim and drabness of the room. She craftily surmised that Boyd perhaps required some additional lubrication to have him reach the same paralytic levels of Law, and suggested he give her money for whisky. Clearly happy to keep the gathering sufficiently oiled, Boyd handed over the money and Helen obliged, soon returning with a jug awash with whisky. During her errand run, however, Boyd had fallen asleep, his hands on his knees and his head lolling down uncontrollably.

Mary Hamilton then took the whisky from Helen, adding to it a quantity of snuff. This smokeless tobacco product would deliver a swift nicotine hit to its users and was especially popular during the eighteenth century. Quite how Hamilton had concocted the snuff is open to question. However, having forced the mixture down Boyd's throat, it provoked a most curious reaction. The carpenter instantly became 'sick and stupid-like', staggering to his unsteady feet and unleashing a wild blow towards Helen, who narrowly evaded the attempt. Chaos now reigned in the tiny room as Helen retaliated by taking the chamber pot and striking the intoxicated man to the head, shattering the pot and forcing Boyd to topple backwards, slamming his head on one of the large stones. He now lay 'gasping like a dying man' on the floor, but contrary to feeling a modicum of guilt or remorse, the band of looting villains instead seized their opportunity.

'Let's strip him!' was Helen's call to Marshall, at which the pair wasted no time in tearing off his jacket, waistcoat and trousers. Helen grabbed the coins from Boyd's pocket and stashed them in the front of her dress. Macfarlane and Hamilton, who had not participated in Boyd's unceremonious exposure, were both sat by the door observing events. Having achieved the goal of ransacking Boyd, Helen required direction in terms of the next move. 'What'll we dae wi' him?' she quizzed her lover. Macfarlane's reply was less than compassionate, or indeed subtle. 'Nobody'll see. Heave him over the window!'

Short-sighted and perhaps rather remiss of Macfarlane, but somebody did see everything that happened in the grimy bed-sit on that evening; perched under Helen Blackwood's bed lay the two little Shillinglaw brothers, quite unnoticed by the anarchic mêlée, yet who through their terrified eyes witnessed everything.

Blackwood opened the window in preparation as Macfarlane grabbed Boyd's feet, with Blackwood and Marshall each taking an arm. They dismissively hurled the abject man through the window, before a tumultuous crash was heard down below. Predictably, the noise of Boyd's falling body had awakened many of those crammed into the dilapidated tenement, and had alerted a passing policeman who quickly attended the scene. Macfarlane had departed the room and was desperately seeking refuge wherever he could. Landing at the door of Charles Scott, he was fortuitously harboured; Scott sneakily sent the police away, feigning ignorance of the matter. As the police left, Macfarlane fretted relentlessly, asking Scott repeatedly; 'What am I to do? What are Helen and I to do?'

Macfarlane and the trio of culprits successfully escaped the tenement, but shortly after slipping away, the police raided Blackwood's room to discover James Law and the Shillinglaw brothers, still reeling from what they had witnessed. The three were escorted to the police station to be probed for information about the violent death of Alexander Boyd.

Early the following morning, 12 June, Macfarlane and Blackwood were spotted by night constable Duncan McInnes heading out of town together, but when apprehended, Blackwood denied knowing her accomplice at all. A thoroughly unconvincing act, the pair were swiftly transported to the police station where further elaborate fabrications were conjured up. Both provided false names, Macfarlane claiming to have been absent from the house on the evening of the murder and Blackwood rather hopelessly trying to convince the police that no such murder ever occurred, and that the man had simply 'fallen over the window'.

Mary Hamilton was seized on the same morning as Blackwood and Macfarlane, this time in College Street, close to where Boyd had been thrown to his death. Hamilton, though, contradicted Blackwood's 'accidental' version of events, instead telling Inspector Thomas Harding that 'the man was thrown over the window, and this is all I know about it'. Detective McLaughlin searched Hamilton, whereupon her person he found a small paper packet of snuff and money she had stolen from the drunken men.

The final villain of the sordid piece to be detained was Ann Marshall, picked up in King Street by Police Constable Donald Carmichael. She denied having any part in the murder, but admitted to bringing the two men to the house with the unscrupulous intention of robbing them. The foursome now successfully detained, their imminent arraignment before the court would soon determine each of their fates.

Thursday, 21 July 1853 saw Macfarlane, Blackwood, Hamilton and Marshall placed at the bar of the High Court in Edinburgh charged with murder. A prolonged indictment was declared, leaving nobody in the hushed court room in any doubt as to what grim details they would be enduring:

The said Hans Macfarlane and Helen Blackwood, Mary Hamilton and Ann Marshall did wickedly and feloniously attack and assault the said Alexander Boyd and did, with a chamber pot strike him one or more severe blows about the head...and did violently seize hold of him, and did violently grab or compress his testicles and did throw him out of a window whereby he fell from a height of twenty three feet.

An initial list of thirty-three witnesses were set to give evidence, though not all were located. There was, however, no chance the police were going to allow their two principal witnesses to evade the trial. Six weeks had passed since the murder, and in this period, the Shillinglaw brothers had spent the whole time together incarcerated in prison, largely because they had nowhere else to go. From lodging under a bed in a sordid bed-sit, they were now rubbing shoulders with scores of intimidating felons, the boys enduring a truly desolate start to their young lives. And now they were facing a highly pressurised situation whereby their evidence could help convict the very lady who provided them with 'lodgings'.

An autopsy had been sanctioned on 13 June, the day after Alexander Boyd's death. Physicians John Alexander Easton and Robert McGregor performed their solemn duties, confirming to the court that Boyd suffered heavy injuries to the head, with multiple fracturing to his skull following the 23-feet drop. He also suffered lacerations to his liver and severe bleeding in the brain. As they listened to the medical evidence from the bar, the three women appeared quite unmoved. Blackwood emanated an air of nonchalance throughout, with only Macfarlane appearing to display any anxiety. In light of the testimonies heard by the court, the laidback personas of the three women were curious to say the least.

11-year-old William Shillinglaw gave his version of events, all uniquely viewed from his dusty and cramped position beneath the bed. The boy said that he saw Blackwood enter the room with Boyd first, followed by Macfarlane and Marshall, then confirming that Blackwood robbed the deceased, and that Hamilton had added the snuff to his drink. Most damningly of all, he reiterated how he had witnessed Blackwood, Macfarlane and Marshall throw Boyd over 'head foremost'. He went on to identify the clothes of the deceased and even the stone that Boyd had fallen back onto. Tellingly, he ended by asserting that before Boyd was thrown, 'there may still have been life in him'.

The evidence of James, the younger sibling, corroborated that of his brother. Several other testimonies were heard from neighbours who all heard the raucous commotion and the sickening slamming of Boyd's body as it hit the ground. Thomas Clymont lived directly below Blackwood and Macfarlane and could always hear any occurrences from above. On the evening in question, he 'heard voices and shuffling of many feet and in a moment saw a man's body fall from the window above'.

Following the evidence and summaries, the jury returned a speedy verdict within 20 minutes. Helen Blackwood and Hans Macfarlane were found guilty of murder, so too Ann Marshall – but the case against Mary Hamilton was unproven. Despite later protestations by the press, Marshall was reprieved, the jury recommending her to mercy. Upon the judge passing down the sentences of death to Blackwood and Macfarlane, Helen responded in an apparently 'saucy' tone: 'We've got no justice. There's a higher judge for us. We are innocent.' The pair were sent back to Glasgow to await their execution and to be fed only on bread and water until their day of reckoning. As a minor concession, the water was occasionally sweetened with treacle and the bread dipped in weak tea. This infrequent gesture, though, was in sharp contrast to the dining enjoyed by other players involved in this frightful spectacle. William Calcraft had been assigned the task of hanging the doomed pair. Arriving two days prior to the execution, the *Glasgow Herald* reported that the notorious executioner 'was enjoying his beefsteaks and port wine' – here was a man unperturbed by the morbid nature of his employment; he was perfectly at peace with his work, but worryingly for his victims, not particularly good at it.

Calcraft was set to perform the execution on Thursday, 11 August. It was a hazy late summer's morning, ideally set for the multitudes to observe the ritual. Even before daylight, an excited public began to assemble, eager to claim the best vantage point 'so as to have a near view of the gallows'. The green became a literal sea of faces, a 40,000-strong congregation prickling with excitement and fervour. With an audience of this scale to aim at, entrepreneurialism could never be far away, no matter the subject. At 203 Gallowgate, an execution broadside was available for sale – a playbill for the theatre of punishment and death. Such street literature was a profitable venture, and whilst the extent of public literacy during this period is debatable, the number of pamphlets which still remain as evidence today suggests that there was appetite enough for them to make their publishing worthwhile. These rather ephemeral publications were generally intended for the middle and lower classes, and were usually sold for a penny or less. Providing lurid details of the crime committed, often in the form of poetry, they also often provided illustrations depicting the execution scene.

If the scene of Blackwood and Macfarlane's execution was relatively standard – couples being dispatched together was not unusual – what occurred upon the scaffold certainly deviated from the norm and delivered an incredible spectacle to the delight of the voyeuristic swarms.

The *Falkirk Herald* reported that the evening prior to the execution, Helen Blackwood retired to bed but scarcely closed an eye, gripped as she was in a state of 'painful mental excitement'. Tended by two female wardens she was dressed just before six o'clock, whilst her sweetheart Macfarlane rose early – three o'clock – and engaged in unremitting prayer until the chaplain, Mr Reid, arrived and conveyed Macfarlane to Blackwood's cell where a divine service was performed. With the religious elements complete, it was now time for the practicalities of the impending punishment to be enacted. Calcraft made his entry to the cell and pinioned their arms. The condemned couple bade each other a tender farewell, strikingly unfamiliar to all that had gone prior. Indeed, it was commented that they 'appeared to have cherished considerable affection for each other'.

At eight o'clock, the pair were chaperoned along the subterranean passage from the prison to the Court House. Here they were briefly seated and given a glass of wine before attempts to coax a confession were initiated; alas, it was with dogged persistence that they continued to deny the murder.

In any event, the procession was now ready to advance to the scaffold. Macfarlane was supported by the arms of the very man who would soon launch him into eternity, with Blackwood assisted by the chaplain. The pair's inevitably disturbed and troubled night had rendered them pale and exhausted, but it was with a firm footing that they strode to their deaths. As the ropes were adjusted and secured, one final event – of a highly unusual nature – unravelled on the platform, which astounded the crowds.

Speaking in a firm and assertive voice, Macfarlane had specific designs in mind for his final words. Turning to his lover amid the preparations of imminent doom, he offered an unconventional proposition: 'Helen Blackwood, before God and in the presence of these witnesses I take you to be my wife. Do you consent?'

Helen replied decisively, 'I do.'

Macfarlane continued, 'Then before these witnesses I declare you to be what you have always been to me, a true and faithful wife, and you die an honest woman.'

The chaplain replied, 'Amen.' The bolt was drawn and the couple, legally married as Scots law declared at the time, fell to their deaths. As came to regularly epitomise a 'Calcraft execution', the event was not especially successful. Whilst Macfarlane died quickly, Helen's struggles 'were very severe and protracted, indicated by the convulsive motion of the chest, the tremor of the body and the uplifting of the knees'. She endured the agonies of death for four lingering minutes. There was certainly to be no honeymoon period for this couple.

It was indeed a remarkable showing for the Glasgow crowds, and a quite unique usage of one's final words, particularly considering the ultimate hopelessness of their situation – a situation we should remember that was induced by the brave testimonies of two young brothers. The pair were later lauded for their intelligence and bravery shown 'amidst so much deplorable ignorance', and were described as 'deserving boys'.

Helen Blackwood was one of fourteen women executed in Scotland between 1800 and 1868. Together with Hans Smith Macfarlane, the couple presented perhaps the most bizarre conclusion to any of Scotland's dismal worldly departures.

Chapter 9

Jack Shuttleworth

There are a thousand doors to let out life. How we exit this world can be as hugely varied as the lives that were led before the gates of death open to receive us. Generally, life which expires following what we consider a 'good age' is something we hope for, if not only for ourselves but for those closest to us. This does, after all, follow the natural order of things, the progression of a lifetime – a span encompassing swathes of untold moments, feelings, emotions, and memories.

Of course, such is the meandering, irregular and intermittently cruel way of life that the fulfilment of an 'acceptable' duration on earth can never be certain. That we could depart life in the vein of renowned author and essayist William Hazlitt, who prior to death joyously proclaimed: 'Well, I've had a happy life,' is perhaps one of the foremost wishes an individual aspires to. Deaths that oppose this idealist notion appear to strike our hearts and minds with increased venom and grief, the sense of a pained, unfulfilled and perhaps curtailed life hammers home its fragility, serving as a tender reminder of our own mortality. Perhaps these reasons form part of our undiluted sorrow in response to suicidal death; the concept that instigating one's own demise is often barely conceivable to a mind that shudders to imagine the depths of despair to which their fellow man can descend.

In 1934, suicide in the United Kingdom was still considered an illegal act, though at this time suicide rates spiked considerably, largely owing to the Great Depression. Indeed, the highest male rates of suicide over the entire twentieth century occurred in 1934, recording 30.3 deaths per 100,000. The depression, or 'slump', along with high rates of unemployment, was categorised as a major factor in the increasing number of suicide deaths.

Jack Shuttleworth, a young man from Carnforth in north-west England, tragically became listed within these statistics when, in January 1934, he shot himself dead in the family kitchen, unable, as he stated, to 'go on any longer.' At 25 years old, the sudden death prompted an outpouring of grief from within the local community; the shocking and brutal nature of his death combined with his youth paralysing his family and friends.

Employed as a silk spinner at Nelson's Silk Works in Lancaster, Jack was adhering to a well-worn path of employment in the area. The north-west was a fulcrum of the textile industry, but as with many towns in the north of England, Lancaster was hit hard by the economic downturn of the day, which became Britain's largest and most profound period of recession of the twentieth century. The silk works, however, remained at least partially buoyant and Jack retained his employment amid the uncertainty that was blanketing much of the country.

On Monday, 22 January 1934, a little after four o'clock in the afternoon Jack Shuttleworth put a gun to his head. William Cambray, an ex-police constable, was sat in his kitchen next door to the Shuttleworth property. Without warning, John Shuttleworth – the father – ran into his neighbour's house shouting, 'Bill, come quick!' before running back to his own home. Cambray followed his panicked neighbour and on reaching the back kitchen, he saw Jack lying on his back. 'I think he is shot,' mumbled the distressed father. Cambray noticed a puncture wound in the centre of the forehead from which blood was mournfully oozing. The two men moved Jack, who was still alive though unconscious, onto the couch before Dr Moss, a Carnforth GP was sent for. Cambray also noticed a miniature .22 rifle reared up in the corner of the back kitchen, evidently the destructive implement.

Dr Moss dressed Jack's wounded head and ordered his immediate removal to Lancaster Infirmary.

Police Sergeant Frederick Sandford, stationed at Carnforth, visited the Shuttleworth home at six o'clock, shortly following Jack's transfer to hospital. Examining the scene at the rear, large amounts of blood had pooled on the doorstep and seeped into the kitchen, and a small portion of the young man's brain was found on the kitchen floor. Sandford took possession of the offending rifle, its barrel now hauntingly empty.

Jack Shuttleworth succumbed to his head injuries a few hours after his admission to hospital. Medical efforts proved in vain and life was pronounced extinct at twenty past eight, his body conveyed to the infirmary mortuary. The horrible news of their son's death could barely have registered before the crestfallen parents were required to provide statements to the police. At this time, suicide was technically an illegal act, but considered, as it is today, as an unnatural death and as such the authorities were required to investigate. The immediacy of investigative procedure in such instances can compound the early stages of grief, the process appearing insensitive and unnecessary, yet practically the actions are essential in ascertaining, beyond doubt, the manner of death. In essence, with cases like Jack Shuttleworth's death, although seemingly a glaring case of suicide, a certainty to that end had to be established, therefore eliminating the possibility of something more sinister.

On 23 January, statements were taken from Isabella (Jack's mother) and John Shuttleworth, the latter's statement detailing the moments directly prior to his son's death. Father and son were sat together in the kitchen when Jack suddenly reached past him for the rifle which stood by the fireplace. The weapon was specifically used in the extermination of rats around the property. He picked up the rifle and, walking to the scullery, called out to his father, 'I will go and see if I can get anything,' before closing the door behind him. John, assuming his son was referring to the vermin, remained seated and was oblivious to any sense of the forthcoming dread. He then heard the discharge of the rifle, a sharp cracking sound intimating that the elusive rat that had perpetually plagued the back yard for days was no more.

At this point, Isabella Shuttleworth came downstairs, entered the kitchen and queried where Jack was. Her husband informed her that he had gone out into the yard to shoot the rat. John's statement then described the moment he discovered his son.

I got up and opened the kitchen door and found him lying down on his back, and slightly to the left with his head on the back kitchen step. I ran for the next door neighbour's and returned and helped to pick him up and put him on the couch. There was blood on his face and head. I went with Jack to the infirmary and stayed with him until he died.

Both Mr and Mrs Shuttleworth declared in their statements that Jack was 'always cheerful', and had 'never threatened to do any harm to himself,' reinforcing the shock and unexpected nature of his death.

An inquest into the death was held at Lancaster Town Hall on 24 January, where the cause – suicide – was formally confirmed, recorded explicitly as via 'a bullet in the brain'. However, the receipt of a letter on the morning of 23 January had already helped to dismiss the possibility that any person other than Jack was responsible for his death. Alice Dixon, a 20-year-old nurse at the County Mental Hospital, received a letter addressed to her ward:

Dear Alice,
This is the end. I can't go on any longer. Please thank your mother and [sic] for being so nice to me.

I thank you for the nice times we have had, and I forgive you for the others. Don't think I'm a coward for doing this, you don't understand; I am sending your letters back, as I don't want anybody else to read them.

Well, goodbye Alice, I'm sorry we couldn't have parted friends, but never mind.

All my love
Yours for ever.
Jack x x x x x x

The letter did not initially alarm its recipient. As she read the letter, Alice 'did not attach much importance to it,' having received similar letters from him previously. According to Alice's statement, the pair had kept company together the previous two years, admitting they had, like most couples, shared a 'few quarrels'. Alice last saw Jack on 21 January, the day prior to the suicide, where he had remained at her home until nine o'clock at night; there had been nothing untoward, no disagreements, and no apparent identifiers that may have alerted Alice to Jack's disposition. Previous probing into why he had formerly sent similar letters were flippantly dismissed by Jack, claiming that he 'didn't mean anything by them,' but was just 'fed up with work'.

He had promised to meet Alice at the hospital after her shift on 23 January so they could spend time together before his nightshift at the silk works began at ten o'clock. This, as we now know, never happened.

The County Mental Hospital where Alice worked was originally the Lancaster Moor Hospital. Opened in 1816, it was the first asylum of its kind in the county. Attractively located with Morecambe Bay and the Lakeland hills in the distance, the hospital could at one stage house over 3,000 patients. It is likely that a proportion of these would have incorporated those that attempted suicide whilst of an 'unsound mind', therefore it would not be unreasonable to suggest that Alice would perhaps have had at least some layer of experience in working with suicidal patients in her time there. In many respects, herein lies the great difficulty in such deaths. There are often no signs or indications, to even the professional mind, of the extent of despair that can be endured by our fellow kind. Where written last words are expressed, they do not always offer clarity or a reason behind an action which can appear so desperate. In Jack's tragic case, the note left behind appears to fit this mould, with no apparent motive for his suicide and leaving behind a grieving family in a state of abiding wonder. Indeed, whether connected or not, nobody could know, but shortly following his son's death, John Shuttleworth passed away at the family home in Carnforth. Had a broken heart prompted the beleaguered man's passing? In any occurrence, the Shuttleworth men were reunited in death, and hopefully, finally unburdened from the rigours of life.

Chapter 10

Frederick George Richardson

In 1914, Britain was no longer merely teetering on the brink of world war, but was by now destined to face the grim realities that would shortly ensue. Such realisations were etched on faces throughout the land, though the unanimous agreement that the cause was a just one ensured that Britain's streets still bristled with ample patriotic jingoism to encourage its departing men.

In the historic city of Canterbury, practical preparations and reminders of the commencement of war gazed apologetically at its residents. If it wasn't Lord Kitchener pointedly recruiting Canterbury's young men, it was the town's shops apologising for the necessity of hiking up their inflated prices. 'Owing to the very grave position into which our country has suddenly been plunged, the butchers are to face an appalling rise in the price of all live stock!' was the message adorning the windows of one local butchery.

This was certainly not an easy period of time to be born into, but for Frederick George Richardson, this was his reality. Nobody could have foreseen then, through the gloom of war, that forty years later he would be at the epicentre of a quite extraordinary and harrowing Canterbury tale.

In 1954, Richardson lived with his wife Violet and three young children, David, Anne and Joan at 19 Cambridge Road, Canterbury. He was a miner at Kent's largest colliery, Betteshanger, and though working in desolate, back-breaking conditions, he enjoyed sharing in the unique camaraderie with his fellow workers. Mining – though important work – was not extravagantly paid employment and the family became saddled with financial difficulties. It is not clear how they plunged into substantial levels of debt, though the upkeep of three young children would certainly not be easy, intensified in a time of economic troubles that were smothering Britain following the Second World War. Certainly, the latter part of the 1940s was a period of austerity and economic restraint, and whilst a modicum of prosperity returned in the 1950s, it nevertheless remained a difficult time for many.

Richardson had approached various associations to obtain money to pay off several debts and loans he had incurred. The Alford Aid Society had refused him, as had the Soldiers, Sailors, Airmen and Families Association (SSAFA). Now known as the Armed Forces charity, the organisation was originally created in 1885 by James Gildea, a British Army militiaman, who served as chairman and treasurer until his death in 1920. The action of seeking aid from the organisation suggests that Richardson served a period in the armed forces prior to his work in the coal mines.

Henry Charles Miller of Canterbury's sheriff's office visited the Richardson family on the morning of Friday, 18 June 1954. Miller advised that he had a writ of execution for £34 6s. 10d. The stresses of such a dialogue at his family home must have been considerable, elevated further still once Richardson was advised that he had until Tuesday, a mere four days, to find the money. Nonetheless, and fully aware of how unlikely it would be to produce the required sum in such a short time, Richardson signed the form of possession to the creditor, an Edmund William Baldwin.

Miller's unrelenting pursuit of the money was continued on Monday afternoon, the day before the agreed deadline. It was half past five and Mr Richardson was not home, making attempts, no doubt, to seek the money he desperately needed. Miller spoke instead with Mrs Richardson, though the course of the conversation is not clear, neither indeed is the knowledge she had in regards to the extent of the debt owed. It may well be that Mr Richardson was shouldering the crushing financial pressures independently, concealing the woes from his wife. Although women had secured the vote by this time, this was pretty much the extent of the equality they 'enjoyed.' In many such cases of fraught worry, the truth would be obscured from wives for fear that their perceived limited emotional capacities would not cope. Mrs Richardson was apparently not alone in being unaware of the plight of the family. Mr Benjamin Baker, father of Mrs Richardson, would later state that he had no knowledge whatsoever of the family's burdening financial troubles.

The creditor did not attend the Richardson house on the agreed Tuesday, having been made aware that Richardson had again applied to the Alford

Aid Society and presumably expected things to be in order the next time he called at Cambridge Road. Miller visited once more on the Thursday but received no reply. The blinds were drawn at the windows, and nothing could be heard from within the house. Abandonment upon a doorstep would surely not have been a new experience for the debt collector, and he was clearly insufficiently concerned to adopt more forceful means of entry. Instead, he returned the following day, Friday, but again received no reply. His presence at the property had alerted the Richardsons' neighbours, some of whom stepped out to express their concerns that none of the family had been seen for several days. To have not seen or heard even one of the family's three young children was an uncommon occurrence upon the street, their boundless energy conspicuous in its eerie absence.

Genuine concern now reverberated around Cambridge Road. The police were called, PC Pearce swiftly arriving at the scene. Informed that the family had not been seen for three or four days, he made an initial external check of the house. The blinds were all drawn, all doors and windows were secured with no sound audible from within. The constable had no option but to force an entry inside. Having breached the premises, the sense of foreboding and sombre expectation weighed down his every move. A sudden movement then caught his jittery eye: a dog was tied to a drawer handle. Whimpering, it appeared withdrawn and perplexed, but alive. A cat, evidently permitted a fraction more freedom, was roaming freely around, appearing befuddled with more curiosity than even its standard disposition.

Continuing through the house, PC Pearce reached the kitchen. It was here that he became greatly disturbed. From behind the gas stove led an attached rubber pipe trailing through the hall and over the bannister, to where it had been secured by an old bootlace. The pipe then led over the landing rail and into the double bedroom to the front elevation of the house.

The pipe finished beneath the right hand of a motionless Frederick Richardson. He was kneeling beside the bed, with only his right arm upon it. His wife Violet was lying on her back in the bed, inanimate and unresponsive. Aware that three children also lived at the address, the constable continued his search, more in a vain hope than expectation of finding them alive and well. Creaking open the door to the small front

Hyde Road, scene of the murder of Katie Reeves. (*Courtesy of P.A. Williams*)

St Margaret's Church, location of the grave of Katie Reeves. (*Courtesy of P.A. Williams*)

The chair on which Sir Henry Irving died. (*Courtesy of the Garrick Club, London*)

The execution of Miss Mary Blandy, for the murder of her father, near Oxford on 6 April 1752, with the Rev. Swinton in attendance. (*Wellcome Collection. Attribution 4.0 International (CC BY 4.0)*)

Statue of Sir Henry Irving on Charing Cross Road, London. Irving is the only actor in the capital to be honoured in this way. (*Author's collection*)

Execution scene of Lady Jane Grey. Here she is being guided to the block where her executioner awaits, axe in hand. (*Wellcome Collection. Attribution 4.0 International (CC BY 4.0)*)

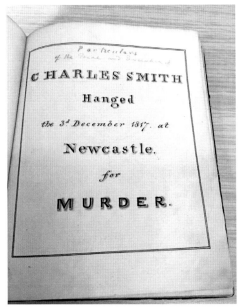

Opening page of Charles Smith's 'Skin Book'. (*Author's collection*)

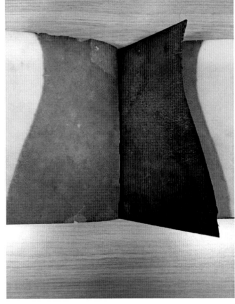

Tanned sections of Charles Smith's skin, taken from his body following his execution for murder. (*Author's collection*)

The death of Robert Catesby: with his final words, Catesby implored his friend and fellow plotter, Thomas Percy, to stand by him and 'die together'. This image shows Catesby in the final death throes, clutching the Virgin Mary. By George Cruikshank. (*Public Domain*)

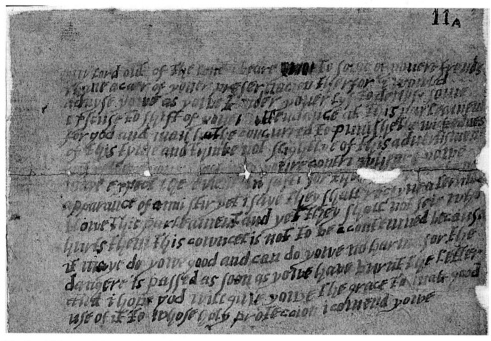

The Lord Monteagle Letter. On 26 October 1605, while sitting at supper in his house in Hoxton, London, Lord Monteagle received a letter warning of the Gunpowder Plot. It is believed by some historians that he authored the letter himself to win acclaim and favour with the King. (*Public Domain*)

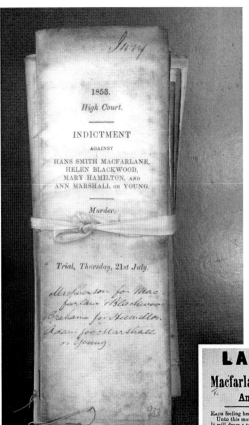

Indictment against Helen Blackwood and Hans Smith Macfarlane. The pair were found guilty and sentenced to death. Just before they were hanged, Macfarlane proposed marriage to Blackwood. She agreed, but they were then both immediately dropped to their deaths. (*Crown Copyright. National Records of Scotland, JC26/1853/525*)

Broadside sold on the day of Helen Blackwood and Hans Smith Macfarlane's execution. Such street literature was a common feature on execution days. (*Reproduced with permission from materials on loan to the National Library of Scotland by the Balcarres Trust*)

LAMENT ON Macfarlane, Blackwood And YOUNG.

Each feeling heart pray lend an ear
Unto this mournful tale,
It will draw a tear of sympathy,
I'm sure it cannot fail ;
It's of three wretched criminals,
In prison now we lie,
For the murder of Alexander Boyd
We are condemned to die.

On the eleventh day of the next month,
What an awful sight to see,
Macfarlane, Blackwood, and Young
Are to die on the gallows tree,
A public show to high and low,
O, Lord, to thee we pray,
Our wretched souls for to receive
Upon the judgment day.

In our gloomy cells, when 'tis midnight,
His dying groans we hear,
And no rest here can we find,
For his murdered form appears,
Pointing unto us with scorn,
Which makes us quake and pale,
As he with solemn words does cry
For vengeance on us all.

Oh, much better we had ne'er been born
To feel the grief this day,
But fate ordained it otherwise,
And we must not say nay ;
When unto us the judge did say—
No mercy you did give
To your victim, Alexander Boyd,
And none you will receive.

For the awful crime that we had done
He bade us watch and pray,
And to prepare ourselves to die
Upon that fatal day ;
An awful sight unto the friends
Whom we shall leave behind,
Hoping with the Lord to dwell,
Where we will comfort find.

What must our friends and parents feel,
When they our sentence read,
And see that we're condemned to die,
'Twill make their hearts to bleed ;
But life for life it is the word,
By the laws of God and man,
And may our fate a warning be
When we on the scaffold stand.

Now all young men and maidens fair,
To you we write one word,
From virtue's paths, Oh, never stray,
But love and fear the Lord ;
Earn your bread in honesty,
And shun bad company,
If by our parents we'd been ruled,
We now might happy be.

Unto our friends and comrades dear,
We write our last farewell,
Hoping such a horrid deed
You never more may tell ;
It will cause many of you to shed a tear,
And tremble, when you see
Us launched into eternity,
Upon the fatal gallows tree.

LAMENT OF MACFARLANE, Blackwood and Young,

At present under Sentence of Death in Glasgow Jail.

Good people attend to our sad dismal tale,
And let our latter end be a warning to thee,
For base cruel murder we're doomed to suffer,
On the eleventh of August we must die on a tree.

Whilst others are sleeping we're constantly weeping,
No rest to our bosom now e'er can we find ;
In sorrow we're bounded and with grief surrounded—
From the thoughts of our fate no peace can we find

Alas, that Macfarlane should e'er have been tempted,
With Blackwood and Young, poor Boyd to destroy,
Had we but remained in the bright paths of virtue,
Our lives might have ended in comfort and joy.

Oh, little we thought on the twelfth day of June,
When our poor deluded victim from the window we threw
That in two months thereafter our doom should be sealed,
That our lives should be taken for the one that we slew.

We murdered poor Boyd, and now we must suffer,
O, heaven ! have pity, and do not judge we,
But grant us relief, for our poor mind's distracted,
In the height of our prime we must die on a tree.

On the twenty-first of July, in the year fifty-three,
Before the bar of justice our trial came on,
For the horrid crime of murder we were indicted,
To answer for the cruel deed we had done.

Our trial being over, our doom was soon sealed,
And now the hand of justice doth us pursue,
But the hour's fast approaching will end all our sorrow—
Dear friends and relations a long long adieu.

O, may our sad fate unto all be a warning,
To both young and old that our sad tale does hear,
Our life in this world it soon will be over,
There's no one to pity us—Lord our prayer hear.

GLASGOW :—Sold Wholesale at 203 Gallowgate.

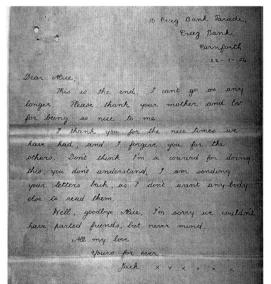

Copy of the suicide letter Jack Shuttleworth sent to his girlfriend. She did not believe his threats in the letter, but Shuttleworth took his own life in the kitchen at his family home in Carnforth. (*With permission of the Lancashire Record Office (DDHD/39/3)*)

Poor people having dinner in a workhouse, 1840. The rules were often strict in the workhouse, and one day in 1934, it all became too much for resident William Watts, whose dying wish came true at the dinner table. (*Wellcome Collection. Attribution 4.0 International (CC BY 4.0)*)

A Representation of the Manner in which the infatuated Mob cruelly Murder'd Ruth Osborne on Marlston Green in the Parish of Tring in Hertfordshire.

The Mob tying Osborne and his Wife's Great Toes and Thumbs together, their Legs and Arms being first cross'd.

Colley in ỹ Marlston Mere turning & Pulling ỹ poor Woman about, and Humbles and Red Beard holding ỹ Ropes that they draw'd her in by.

The remarkable confession of Thomas Colley: the drowning of an alleged witch (Ruth Osborne), with Thomas Colley as the incitor. Colley would be made an example of following the murder, and was himself hung for his crimes. (*Wellcome Collection. Attribution 4.0 International (CC BY 4.0)*)

Good People I beseech you all to take Warning by
an unhappy Man's Suffering, that you be not
deluded into so absurd & wicked a Conceit, as to
believe that there are any such Beings upon
Earth as Witches.

It was that foolish & vain Imagination
heighten'd & inflamed by the Strength of Liquor
which prompted me to be instrumental
(with Others as mad-brain'd as myself) in
the horrid & barbarous Murther of Ruth
Osborn, the supposed Witch; for which I am
now so deservedly to suffer Death.

I am fully convinced of my former Error,
And with the Sincerity of a dying Man declare
that I do not believe there is such a
Thing in Being as a Witch: And I pray
God that none of you thro' a contrary
Persuasion, may hereafter be induced to think
that you have a Right in any shape to
persecute, much less endanger the Life of a
Fellow-Creature.

I beg of you all to pray to God to forgive me
& to wash clean my polluted Soul in the blood
of Jesus Christ my Saviour, & Redeemer.

So Exhorteth you all the Dying

Signd at Hertford aug.st the 23 1751. Thomas Colley
just after Receiving the Sacrament
In Presence of Edw: Bourchier minister
Rob.t Keep Parish Clerk

The confession letter as written by Thomas Colley.
These would prove to be his final words and were used
as a warning from the authorities to deter anyone that
may have had plans to carry out similar brutalities.
(*With permission of the Hertfordshire Archives and Local
Studies (DE/LW/Z22/13)*)

A group of Greenwich Pensioners
smoking and drinking. These were
common pastimes for them, and it was
such debauchery that led John Smith to
kill Catherine Smith. His final words
included what he described as 'a history
of his life' in doggerel verse. Etching by
G. Cruikshank, 1834. (*Wellcome Collection.
Attribution 4.0 International (CC BY 4.0)*)

The Execution of Sir Walter Raleigh. Apparently
unperturbed by his impending doom, Raleigh found the
words to goad the axeman into taking off his head, the
executioner having shown reluctance to perform his duties.
(*Public Domain*)

The wreckage of the doomed flight that killed eight of the Manchester United football team in 1958. (*Wikimedia Commons*)

The tombstone of Liam 'Billy' Whelan. Whelan was killed in the disaster at Munich, but his final words aboard the plane before it crashed have become symbolic of the bravery demonstrated by many on that fateful night. (*Public Domain*)

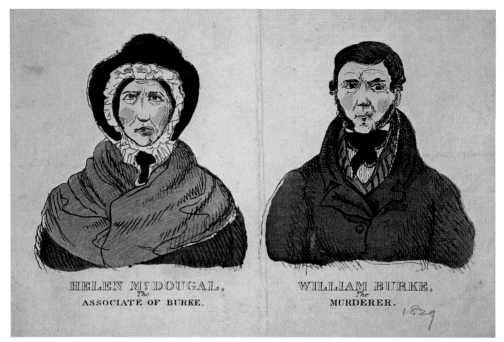

Artists' impressions taken within court on the day of William Burke and Helen MacDougal's trial at Edinburgh; the portraits bear the pencilled date '1829'. MacDougal's case was 'not proven' but William Burke suffered the ultimate fate. (*Wellcome Collection. Attribution 4.0 International (CC BY 4.0)*)

The interior of a dissecting room in Edinburgh, with half-covered cadavers on benches, 1889. Bodies for dissection were a much sought-after commodity in William Burke's day. The price that a fresh body could command saw him sink to deplorable depths, keeping Dr Knox happy with a steady supply for dissection. (*Wellcome Collection. Attribution 4.0 International (CC BY 4.0)*)

EXECUTION of the notorious WILLIAM BURKE the murderer, who supplied DR KNOX with subjects.

Execution of Burke.
From a Contemporary Print.

Execution of William Burke. Burke's final words were allegedly to offer the hangman some advice. His execution caused much excitement in Edinburgh's Lawnmarket. The mob, however, remained irate that Burke's accomplice, William Hare, did not suffer the same fate. (*Wellcome Collection. Attribution 4.0 International* (*CC BY 4.0*))

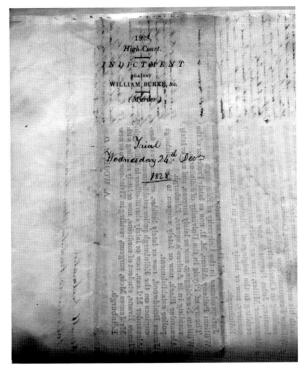

Indictment against William Burke. (*Crown Copyright, National Records of Scotland,* (*AD2/1*))

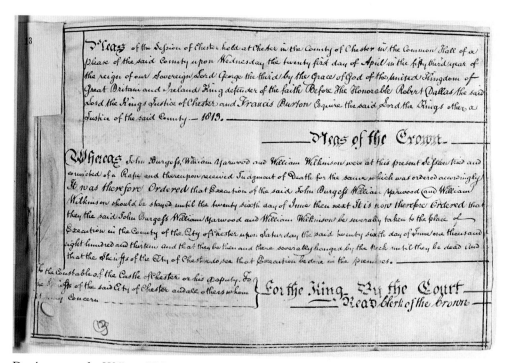

Death warrant for William Wilkinson, James Yarwood and William Burgess. The trio were executed together for the savage attack on a young lady. Each of the men approached their doom in varying ways. (*With kind permission of Cheshire Record Office (QAB 5/8/13)*)

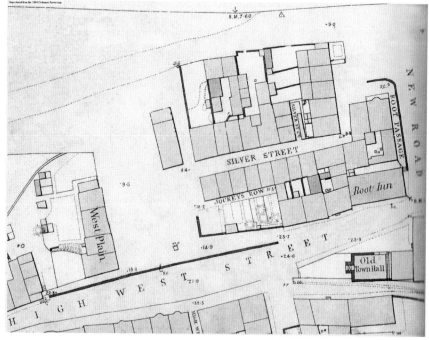

OS Map showing the murder site (near the Boot Inn) of Tillroyd Morgan in 1792. The murder would go unsolved for some sixty-five years until the deathbed confession of an old woman. (*With kind permission of Richard Samways*)

Application for the Admission of a Child.

NOTE.—This Form when filled up and certified by a Clergyman of the Church of England, should be returned to
E. DE M. RUDOLF Esq., Secretary, CHURCH OF ENGLAND CENTRAL SOCIETY FOR PROVIDING HOMES FOR WAIFS AND STRAYS,
Church House, Dean's Yard, Westminster, S.W.

QUESTIONS TO BE REPLIED TO.

1	Give the child's christian name and surname	Frederick Fleet
2	State the exact age, and give the date and place of birth	Born Liverpool, 15 October 1887
3	Legitimate ?	Illegitimate
4	If baptized, state place and date of baptism	Yes — Walton Parish Church — date unknown
5	Parents living ?	Mother living — nothing known of the father.
6	If, however, either or both are dead, state of what disease they died, and give the date of their death.	Mother — Father —
7	If living, give their exact places of abode, and state how long they have resided there.	Mother Went to U.S.A. October 1890 — 15 care of a Sister living there present address ... Longs St. Springfield . Mass. U.S.A. Father unknown whereabouts unknown
8	Give the christian names and surnames of parents (in full) and state their ages	Mother Alice Fleet . 22 — Father Frederick Lawrence — age unknown —
9	What was or is the nature of the father's occupation and the amount of his weekly earnings? Give the name and address of his present or last employer	Was a private in the 4th Dragoons — has not been heard of since 1889 —
10	What was or is the nature of the mother's occupation and the amount of her weekly earnings? Give the name and address of her present or last employer	The Mother works in a mill of some kind in Springfield Mass. U.S.A. exact nature unknown also amount of earnings —
11	Have the parents or guardians ever received parish relief? If so, to what extent?	So far as is known, nothing —

12 Give the names, addresses, ages, occupations and earnings (if any) of all the brothers and sisters of the child				
NAME	ADDRESS	AGE	OCCUPATION	WEEKLY EARNINGS
This child was the mother's firstborn — since then, she is believed to have been living a respectable life, & is unmarried				

. Replies to this question must be very full and exact.

No application can be received without full enquiry as to earnings having been made, and result stated.

The lifeboat in which Frederick Fleet escaped the freezing Atlantic waters. Fleet was in the *Titanic*'s crow's nest when he saw 'a dark object up ahead'. Although he survived the disaster, his subsequent life was fraught with difficulties, many of which stemmed from his experiences of that night. (*Public Domain*)

Frederick Fleet at the time he served on the *Titanic*. (*Public Domain*)

The Life and Trial of William Shaw

Who was
EXECUTED INNOCENT

For the MURDER OF HIS OWN DAUGHTER. Catherine SHAW
With the Confession of her Sweet-heart 2 Hours after the Execution

WILLIAM SHAW, a respectable Upholsterer residing in a Village near Edin, had a Daughter Catherine, who lived with him, and who encouraged the addresses of John Lawson a Jeweller, contrary to the wishes of her father. who had inseperable objection against him, and urged his Daughter o receive the addresses of a son of Alexander Robertson, a friend and neighbour the girl refused most peremptorily

The Father grew enraged; passionate expressions arose on both sides and the words Barbarity, cruelty and Death, frequently pronounced by the Daughter. at length her father left her, locked the Door after him. The appartment of SHAW was only divided by slight partition from that of one Morrison. a Watch-case Maker, who had indistinctly heard the diabolical conversation & quarrel between Catherine Shaw, and her Father: and was particular struck with the words she had pronounced.

For some time after the Father had gone out, all was silent, presently Morrison heard several groans, from the Daughter, He called some of the neighbours ; and these listening attentively, not only heard the groans. but her Faintly exclaim. 'CRUEL FATHER, thou art the cause of my Death ;' Struck with the expression, they got a ┈┈┈┈┈ and Broke the Door open.

of SHAWS Apartments; where they found the Daughter Catherine weltering *IN HER BLOOD*, and a Knife found covered with blood. near were she was laying, a Surgeon was immediately sent for, and on Examining the Wound there was no hopes of ever her recovering, has the Wound was mortal, she was a live and Speechless. but on Questioning her as to owing her Death She pointing to her Father who was present in the Room, in custody of an Officer, She was just able to make a motion with her Head and shortly after she expired amidts several Neighbours who witnessed this awful Catastrophe,

"At this moment Shaw enters the room, all eyes are upon him ! & seems much disorded in his mind with Horror but at the sight of his Daughter he turns pale and ready to sink, the first suprise and the Succeeding Terific countenance, little doubt of his Guilt in the breast of the beholders, and even that little is done away.

He was instantly hurried before a magistrate, and upon the deposition of the Parties committed for trial, in vain did he protest his innocence, & declare that the blood on his shirt was occasioned by his having blooded himself some days before, and the bandage having become untied, The circumstances appeared so strong against him. that he

was found guilty, was Executed. and his last words were 'I am innocent of my daughters murder ,'

There was scarcely a person who thought the father innocent, but a short time after, a man, who had become the occupant of Shaw's apartment, accidently discovered a paper which had fallen into a cavity on one side of the chimney

It was folded as a letter, and on being opened, it was found to contain as follows :—*Reading*

COPY
OF A LETTER,

Barbarous Father ! your cruelty, in having put it out of my power, ever to join my fate to that of the only man, I could love. and tyrannically insisting upon my Marrying one whom I always hated, that has made me form a Resolution to put an end to an existence which is become a burthen to me.

This Letter was Signed Catherine Shaw, and on being shown to her relations and Friends, it was recognised as her writing, The Magistracy of that Town examined it, and on being satisfied of its Authenticity, they ordered the body of Wm. Shaw to be cut down, from the gibbet, and Given up to his Friends with honour. as the Innocent Blood Cries for forgiveness to those that swore false againts him,

---

Broadside of the harrowing case of William Shaw, who was wrongly executed for the murder of his daughter, Catherine. Catherine had killed herself, which she stated in a suicide note. The note, however, was not discovered until William Shaw was already swaying in the gibbet. (*Harvard Library*, © *[2020] President and Fellows of Harvard College, licensed under a Creative Commons Attribution 4.0 International License*)

The execution of Ernest Brown at Armley Gaol, Leeds. Was his final word on the gallows an admission of guilt to a previous unsolved murder? (*With thanks to the British Newspaper Archive*)

The village of Otterburn in Northumberland. (*With kind permission of the Otterburn History Society*)

bedroom, he found David, the oldest of the children at 10 years old, lying on his back, dead. Any lingering hopes of discovering the two girls alive were now effectively vanquished in the heart and, indeed, head of the constable as he despondently walked towards the final bedroom.

The back bedroom, a room that would only a few days previously have been filled with the shrieking and rapturous laughter mustered by the care-free frolics of youth, now lay in ominous silence. The awful truth was then confirmed as Anne, 7, and the youngest child, 6-year-old Joan, were discovered dead in their beds. All except Frederick Richardson were in their night attire, suggesting that they were all in bed during their passing. Richardson himself was dressed in day clothes.

PC Pearce, much shaken by what he had witnessed, then made his way downstairs. Suspecting gas poisoning as the cause of death, he was surprised that he could not smell the pungent odour anywhere in the house. Stepping through the tide of unopened mail littering the hallway, he next entered the lounge, and curiously noticed that the three-piece suite and carpets were all deeply slashed, with a sheath knife menacingly embedded in the carpet. There were also a host of unopened letters addressed to several people.

One of these letters was addressed to the Canterbury Coroner, Mr C. A. Gardner.

On Monday, 28 June 1954, the inquest was held into the five deaths that had stunned the local community. The coroner then read the letter which had been addressed to him from the deceased father.

I regret to state that the action I have taken, although judged by earthly laws as criminal, is, to my mind, necessary.

I have tried for help. I have been allowed until to-morrow to raise £36.

I have destroyed the furniture because the Service and Government have taught us the scorched earth policy – let nothing of value fall into the enemy's hands.

To all people I swear that my wife is innocent. I am afraid my last debt now is to the Gas Company. I have stored a large quantity with a single shilling and a key.

I enclose a pay packet for a penny. Can any company other than the National Coal Board beat that for audacity?

This letter, although short, reveals much of importance. The admission of murder clearly reveals the complexity of the man's state of mind, particularly in that he felt it a necessary action. The desperate tone of the letter is tangible; his pleading for help went unheard, the result being one of awful tragedy. The language used in this letter is significant – addressed to a government official, Richardson is clearly intimating his distaste towards the very heart of the establishment, and almost proclaiming a posthumous victory over the 'enemy' in destroying the furniture, such is his wish that the state emerge with nothing following his death.

Dr G. J. E. Wood attended the address in the aftermath of the police discovery. At the inquest, he asserted that the family had all died through coal gas poisoning. He explained that the pipe which was connected to the gas stove from the kitchen was responsible, as 'enough gas could be carried through this pipe to cause death.' It was his estimate that the family had been dead for several days, and that the children could very well have succumbed without a struggle as it would have been a gradual process; 'a fully conscious person,' he added, 'would not even be aware of it happening.'

As the inquest progressed, PC Pearce was then called to read Richardson's final words, expressed in the letter which he had himself found in the house. The crestfallen man was evidently moments from ending his own life. His writing by this point had become shaky and erratic, a tragically symbolic document of how life itself had become for him:

Please put the cat and dog to sleep too. I find them awkward. I haven't much strength left. I have got to the stage of dragging myself across the floor. I will drag off to my death upstairs with my darling wife and children. The time is now 5:55 a.m. I feel so sick and my head is swinging around.

It is believed that at the time of writing these final words, Frederick Richardson's family were already dead upstairs. His remaining strength, it seems, he used to end his own torment.

The coroner, in summarising the events, commented that Frederick Richardson had tried relentlessly to secure assistance, 'having gone round the various associations for more money'.

'No doubt he was extremely fond of his family,' exclaimed the coroner. 'He says in the letter to me that he would rather take them with him than let them suffer with the stigma of being a suicide's children. I don't think we can say other than that he deliberately murdered these three children. He waited until the early hours of the morning when they were asleep, gassed the children, wrote those letters, and then went and finished himself.'

The jury of the inquest returned a verdict that Frederick Richardson had murdered his wife and three children before taking his own life, whilst the balance of his mind was disturbed.

Although attitudes to suicide had progressively shifted from its sinful label to one of medicalisation which recognised connections with mental health issues, in 1954, its stigma still clearly troubled. Richardson's foremost concern was, after all, protecting his children from becoming 'a suicide's children'. This is perhaps not surprising; it was not until the Suicide Act of 1961 that the action was no longer deemed criminal. Several writers have specified that much of the stigmatisation of suicide stemmed from the use of unhelpful language around it. The term 'commit suicide' – still used even today – can evoke a feeling of criminal wrongdoing; the connotation of 'committing' an act is often considered in a law-breaking sense, to commit robbery or murder, for example.

In the case of the desperate Frederick Richardson and his family, however, his final written words reveal that the five deaths appear to be linked almost entirely to the economic plight in which they became engulfed; they became further statistics within a tragic correlation between financial burden and suicidal ideation, one that has endured throughout history and continues to do so.

Chapter 11

William Watts

The concept of the 'dying wish' is synonymous with highly-charged and emotionally-packed desires expressed by an individual as they drift towards their ultimate end. A poor thing, it is said, to fear that which is inevitable, yet death has timelessly instigated a trepidation perhaps based around its undeterminable and mysterious nature. Death's resultant ambiguity, then, accounts for a general aversion towards it, something to be staunchly fended off at all costs – yet in some instances, a final wish for some people involves a beckoning of their own demise, actively imploring the solemn shackles of doom to pluck them from life and accelerate their final parting. Whilst such statements may often merely be the substance of jest and triviality, one such declaration made in a fit of rage by an inmate of a London workhouse, whether intended or not, resulted in the most ironic of consequences.

William Watts was born in the unforgiving terrain of Stepney in London's East End, in 1856. The Industrial Revolution's relentless sprawl had advanced its way through the capital, its population growing in tune with the unwavering urbanisation of the area. As the population exploded, districts in the East End became overcrowded slums, an epicentre for crime and deviance amid the filth-ridden tenements. Even before the most-famed slasher of them all stalked Whitechapel in 1888, the East End was well accustomed to unscrupulous and unforgiving conduct. The dense fog-filled air and dimly-lit streets aided both the petty criminal and the more foreboding villain in the perpetuation of felonious actions. This veiled cover of darkness may have perhaps even abetted the youthful Watts himself as he navigated his way through life in a brutish and pitiless London, such was the rifeness for infractions of the law.

If Watts' dalliance with delinquency did indeed begin as an impish youngster, it would not end within the confines of juvenility. At the turn of the twentieth century and in his forty-fifth year, Watts was hauled in front of the Westminster magistrates on charges of 'stealing 51 battens' from his employers, Joshua Knight & Sons. Watts had worked as a carman – essentially a horse and cart man delivering goods around the city. A carman was a common occupation of the time, a fact highlighted within the court records which displays the occupations of all those reprimanded before the magistracy. Watts was received into custody on 10 October 1901 alongside his co-accused, Joseph Ambrose Williams, and the supposed 'handler' of the stolen battens, William Frederick Benn. A little over a week later, however, and Watts was released, the record stating 'bill ignored' – thus confirming that the indictment was dismissed as unfounded. In early November, Williams was found guilty of the charge and sentenced to '8 months hard labour at Wormwood Scrubs Prison', whilst Benn's role landed him a full year of the same gruelling sentence.

If criminality in the dark rookeries and alleyways of London's East End was indicative of the Victorian era, so too was another equally painful blight on the social conscience of a generation – the Victorian workhouse. Intended as an institution to provide work and shelter for the poorest in society, it instead came to embody a prison-like system that simply detained the most vulnerable whilst failing most emphatically in its proposed visions of tackling pauperism. State-provided relief for the poor has its dubious origins in 1601 following the passing of the 'Act for the Relief of the Poor'; an ordinance that bestowed a responsibility upon parishes for their own impoverished transients. Parish officials were legally able to collect money from local property owners to fund 'poor relief' for the sick, elderly and infirm. Parish poor relief was initially dispensed through monetary grants, clothing, food or fuel to those living in their own homes. The workhouse concept began to evolve with prominence in the seventeenth century, fuelled by the belief that providing care under one roof was the most prudent and cost-effective way forward; this type of 'mass-produced' beneficence led to a flurry of workhouses opening in the early 1700s. After 1723 the workhouse began to form a part of Britain's social fabric, when Sir Edward Knatchbull's Workhouse Test Act gained parliamentary approval. According to the act, the workhouse should act as a deterrent, and relief was only provided to the desperate unfortunates who had no other option but to accept its rather tyrannical regime.

A traditional workhouse welcome was not a thing infused with amenable warmth or hospitality. New residents were issued with a uniform to be worn throughout the duration of a stay and subjected to a medical examination. Then a selection process would begin; the men, women and children were separated, before the able-bodied and infirm were then, too, grouped accordingly. Despite the haunting similarities here to the infamous Nazi 'work' camps discovered many years later across Europe, these classifications were mercifully not a morbid measure of who would live or otherwise, rather an indicator of the residents' physical capacities to fulfil various tasks within the workhouse.

Conditions inside the workhouse were intentionally repugnant. Although each workhouse was managed by a board of different guardians, their intentions were always consistent – to be as unpalatable and unappealing as possible. Meals were a lesson in the rankest of fare, eaten in a large communal dining hall, with endless rows of forlorn faces grimacing through their gruel. Families were callously splintered, with parents permitted a meagre hour with their children on a weekend. The message was very clear: entry to a workhouse was no premium for idle habits, rather, it swiftly became the ultimate degradation within Victorian society.

Falling on lean times, William Watts admitted himself into the Whitechapel workhouse. Regrettably no records exist of the date of his entry to the 'South Grove Institution', though the area was clearly regarded as a 'hub' for those maimed by misfortune. It was Whitechapel's second such establishment, erected in 1871 at the south side of Mile End Road between South (now Southern) Grove and Lincoln Street, opposite the City of London workhouse.

One morning in February 1934, the bell had summoned the inmates to the communal hall to take breakfast. As Watts made his way with the assembled flock, the prospect of the offerings that would soon be laid before him would hardly have filled him with delight. Perhaps this revolting anticipation and the relentless rules and regulations had finally breached his tolerance levels. Now at 78 years of age, he was still occasionally prepared to flout the commands of the workhouse orderlies. Mealtimes insisted that 'silence order and decorum shall be maintained' throughout – although the word 'silence' was belatedly dropped in 1842, this was a rare easement of in-house law. Watts had decided to wear his hat to breakfast, an act that was strictly prohibited. A bowler-style hat was a part of the male uniform within the workhouse, but was never to be worn during dining. An attendant immediately requested that Watts remove it. The demand enraged Watts, tipping him into an infuriated state, prompting him to holler a decidedly drastic request: 'I wish I was dead, and out of this!'

Regardless of how genuine Watts' outburst was, nobody could have foreseen that it would materialise with such unearthly immediacy. For no sooner had the words passed his world-weary lips, than Watts slumped forward in his chair, dead. Pandemonium erupted through the clanking of crockery as the attendants rushed to his aid, efforts that were ultimately to no avail. The ensuing inquest recorded a verdict of 'death from natural causes', though for the onlooking inmates on that late winter's day, the death of William Watts bore little resemblance to anything of a 'natural' composition. Watts' apparent conjunction with a higher being ensured his final wishes on earth were mystically granted. Famous last words indeed.

Chapter 12

Thomas Colley

The origins of this bizarre and tragic tale begin with the animated clamouring of a trio of town criers from the towns of Winslow, Leighton Buzzard and Hemel Hempstead in 1751. The three had been paid to announce the 'ducking' of two persons suspected of being immersed in the practice of witchcraft in the market town of Tring, Hertfordshire.

Sixteen years prior to the events in Tring, Parliament had deemed, in the name of justice and reason, that witchcraft would no longer be considered a criminal act. The notion that witchcraft was ever considered within the statute of criminal law is, of course, baulked at by modern eyes, yet for centuries, it claimed a plethora of unfortunate victims as those suggested to have partaken in its 'sorcerous' ways were subjected to an execution that dripped with excruciating barbarity.

By the time the Witchcraft Act was passed through Parliament in 1736, it was generally thought that witchcraft was a vulgarised notion bred through ignorance. This was certainly the feeling rife among the ruling classes as they looked to assert their educated superiority over the masses. This, however, was not exclusive; long after the amended legislation was introduced, there were still significant numbers of intellectual people that continued to express ambivalence towards the conclusive rejection that a supernatural evil existed. The English politician and writer Joseph Addison, for example, a man of considerable standing in his new and 'enlightened' time, believed that 'there is, and has been such a thing as witchcraft'.

The idea, then, that the elite had moved beyond such preposterousness and the oft-cited belief that witchcraft was consigned only to the heathen minds of the ignorant, is perhaps a misleading generalisation; portions of the country's educated men and women continued to believe in its existence and the principle that it certainly *could* exist, but that it had not existed in their own times. After all, ideas of fantastical devilment were perhaps not something one wished to attribute to their own more 'progressive and informed times'.

The doctrine of witchcraft had foundations grounded in Europe in the mid-1400s. The *Malleus Maleficarum* – translated as *The Hammer of Witches* – was a leading medieval work written by Heinrich Kramer, first published in Germany in 1487. The work elevates sorcery to a criminal status and is wholly defiant and unapologetic in its response to those who may dabble in the dark arts. *Malleus* lays out the procedures that ought to be followed in the trial of a suspected witch, before ultimately advocating the death penalty against them as the only certain remedy against their evils – burning them alive at the stake being the typical 'solution'.

One of England's more infamous proponents of such a bible was the self-styled 'Witchfinder General', a ghastly man named Matthew Hopkins who roamed East Anglia searching for witches and, together with his equally vile sidekick, John Stearne, was responsible for the condemnation and execution of approximately 200 alleged witches. His reign of terror from 1644 lasted only a few years until his death in 1647, and was substantiated by nothing more than gregarious claims of owning 'special commission' from Parliament to erase witches from the country. He is thought to have earned close to £1,000 for his atrocious 'employment'.

Almost 100 years later in 1751, however, this 'hammering of witches' was allegedly an outdated concept, the 'crime' of witchcraft freshly erased from the statute books and consigned to its own bloody and repulsive history. It would appear, however, that it was somewhat more difficult to eradicate witchery and its mischiefs from the minds of some of the more cynical country folk.

Folk whose ears were pricked when, on Monday, 14 April 1751 – Hemel Hempstead's market day – they heard the enthusiastically delivered announcement from William Dell, the town crier of Hemel Hempstead, holler the following: 'This is to give notice that on Munday [sic] next there is to be at Long Marston in the Parish of Tring two hill [sic] desposed [sic] persons to be ducked by the neighbours consent!' The same notice was also cried at both Winslow and Leighton Buzzard on their respective market days, ensuring the fullest public congregations.

Upon the news, a maniacal buzz of anticipation swept across the lands of the parish. The prospect of a public spectacle would certainly gather the crowds; the fact that the anonymous pair were to be 'ducked' confirmed to the excited village dwellers that they were facing accusations of witchcraft, whipping them into a further state of frenzy. Following the decriminalisation of witchcraft, lynchings became the sole means by which villagers who believed that witches had wronged them could bring the alleged malefactors to justice. So long as there was a belief in these arts, such illegal attacks could continue and create gushing excitement.

Ruth Osborne was a rather peripheral figure in Hertfordshire. At 56 years old, she and husband John Osborne had fallen on lean times, their days filled with battling the constant peril of poverty which would often lead to begging from local farmers for food and water. The Osbornes were marginalised from the collective and had become shunned as whispers across the air suggested the pair may have had 'abilities' of sorcery. One particular incident with a local farmer incited this speculation.

In the hamlet of Gubblecote, near Tring, the elderly Osbornes visited local farmer John Butterfield on an errand of desperation, imploring the man for some milk. Butterfield, though, was not in a charitable mood. Angrily dismissing the wretched pair, they trudged away disconsolately, muttering their dissatisfaction with the farmer as they left.

Following Butterfield's encounter with the impoverished couple, many of his cattle soon began to die inexplicably. The extent of these mysterious deaths bewildered Butterfield but before long, he was attributing the carnage to a curse the Osbornes had bestowed on him during their fiery encounter on his doorstep. Certainly, witchcraft was regularly adopted as an explanation for misfortunes endured in village life, and this appears to be the case for the befuddled farmer; unexplained losses of livestock at this time often gave rise to suspicions of sorcery. Butterfield may well have considered the woman's very appearance as further testament to his beliefs, as some years earlier it was thought that 'every woman with a wrinkled face, a furred brow, a hairy lip, a gobber tooth, a squint eye is not only suspected but pronounced a witch!' This mantra had not yet completely filtered away into ignorance, and may well have contributed to Butterfield's suspicions.

As the carcasses piled up, so it would also seem did financial troubles, which ultimately led to the decision that Butterfield could no longer sustain the farm. This, to Butterfield, was plain evidence that a dark and unnatural power had been at work, and was most likely the ill-effects of 'the witch Osborne' seeking retribution against him for the altercation at his farm. The man took little time to be convinced of his newly 'bewitched' status, even claiming that the witchcraft had not only plagued his livestock but had likewise seized upon his person, which operated upon him in such a manner, that 'sometimes he barked like a dog, at other times mew'd like a cat, and then again made a noise like a fox.' If these ailments were formulated by Butterfield with a deceitful intention of 'proving' the old woman's witching ways, he certainly succeeded.

Butterfield's claims of such animal imitation may well have been quite purposeful, for a common motif in witch legend was the ability to turn people into animals. Hares and cats were popular transformations but any animal shape could allegedly be assumed to meet a particular purpose. An antiquated tradition records that those 'in the form of a hare would suck the udders of a cow at night leaving them dry for milking the next morning.' This notion certainly has extensive origins; *Giraldus Cambrensis* – Gerald of Wales – wrote as far back as the twelfth century that sucking teats under this counterfeit form allows one to 'stealthily rob other people's milk'. This was something that the 'witch' Ruth Osborne was surely capable of without the pleadings on random doorsteps – the irony seemingly lost on everyone, not least Butterfield.

Butterfield's friends and neighbours had been thoroughly convinced that the man was bewitched and desired to gain absolute proof of the fact. Thomas Colley, a friend of Butterfield, had, along with a host of others, heard of a most 'cunning woman that liv'd further in the country', who once consulted, would determine whether or not Butterfield had indeed been riddled with mystical roguishness.

The mysterious woman – ironically not considered of possessing any arts of witchery herself – confirmed that Butterfield had indeed been afflicted by the dark arts and that the Osbornes were the pair responsible. With this confirmation, several other farming men agreed to draw up the paper which was subsequently cried in the market towns.

As the day of the ducking drew closer, the rumour mill gathered a fervent pace throughout the area. Across bars in the alehouses and over hedgerows of the fields and meadows, talk of the impending delivery of justice occupied all minds. Hostility towards the Osbornes was ratcheting up to fever pitch, to such an extent that Matthew Barton, the overseer of Tring's impoverished, wisely sensed that the increasing mob mentality was plotting much mischief. Seeking to avert wholesale anarchy, he moved the Osbornes to the workhouse for their own safety.

However, during the evening of Sunday, 21 April, it was apparent that this course of action, however prudent, would be insufficient. Large crowds were beginning to gather, swelling in both their numbers and states of antagonism. In the early hours of Monday, 22 April, the terrified pair were clandestinely moved from the workhouse to the vestry of Tring Church as a further safety precaution. The master of the workhouse, a John Tomkins, portrayed a vivid account of the happenings around the workhouse shortly prior to the Osbornes' merciful relocation: 'A great mob came to the workhouse and demanded the old witch and wizard that came from Long Marston, meaning the said John Osborne and his wife, upon which he told them that they were not there, but the mob insisted that they were and if he did not let them in they would force in by violence.'

Faced with a relentlessly increasing mob, Tomkins was forced to open the yard gate and allow them to search the house and its grounds. Unable to discover their desired quarry, however, served only to incite the rabble to new lengths; stones were flung at windows until all were entirely demolished, one brick end of the house was pulled down and very real threats were made to burn the remainder of the building which would then, it was promised, be followed by the destruction of the town itself. Under such duress and fearful of the ill-consequences if the pair were not delivered unto the mob, they were immediately taken to the vestry in the church where the bloodthirsty hunt continued. The vestry door was hoisted open and a great number of people rushed in, seizing the cowering couple, whereupon Ruth was grabbed by one of the mob and lain across his shoulders 'like a calf', and carried upwards of two miles to the designated site of doom.

It would be feasible at this juncture to query the lack of authority; the whole affair was advertised and hardly a closely-guarded secret, yet nothing was done to halt the destruction in progress. Eventually, though, the local blacksmith and Tring constable, Sebastien Grace, was summoned, though his appearance did little to quell the attitude of the marauding masses: 'He is only the Constable, don't mind him!' they were heard to yell, whilst others even threatened his life. His presence there was essentially anonymous; by this time, the mob had inflated to an estimated 4000 – it would take a substantially greater authoritarian presence to have any effect on this multitude.

They had come to Tring to share in the spectacle, and now, with their victims forced through the crowds and beaten with sticks, as some kind of pitiless curtain-raiser to the centrepiece of the day, they made their way to the watery place of justice at Wilston Wear in Tring, the assumed witch helplessly pleading along the way: 'For God's sake, don't murder me!' The couple were acutely aware of what was about to befall them as the horrors that lurked in the murky waters of Wilston were not shrouded in any mystery. Trial by immersion in water has an extensive history – in England, it was used to try witches from the early-seventeenth century onwards. A so-called 'ducking' saw suspected witches have their right thumbs tied to their left toes, and their left thumbs to their right toes. To complete the degrading spectacle, a rope was then tied around the waist of the wretched soul before being unceremoniously thrown into a river or pond. Two men would hold either end of the rope, and the unfortunate victim would be 'ducked' repeatedly; if a suspected witch floated, then justice had delivered a guilty verdict, the premise being that the 'sacred water of baptism' had rejected them owing to their crimes. Conversely, if they sank, then God's water had clearly embraced them, therefore signifying their innocence.

Accounts offered by several onlookers describe the furore that surrounded the pond as the Osbornes were brought to the water. Local farmer Mr Nott Gregory stated that on Monday, 22 April between the hours of two and three o' clock, his children came into the house saying, 'They have got them.' Understanding this to mean the elderly couple, he went into one of his fields and witnessed 'a great number of people going towards some water in a meadow'. This excerpt certainly reveals the sense of local notoriety of the case at the time, even Gregory's children being aware of the plight of the pursued fugitives.

Harry Archer witnessed a man he knew as Charles Young and several others fetch the dazed woman to be ducked. Young proceeded to wrap her in a sheet and tie the rope around her. She was then carried into the middle of the pond and laid down in the water which was approximately 5 feet deep, 'till it was thought she might be drowned', before being carried out again and placed on the bank for half an hour.

Ruth Osborne's dogged tormentors were not finished yet though, and once more she was carried into the water and repeatedly 'turned' by a local man Archer knew as Thomas Colley, who, with a large stick, relentlessly turned and prodded her frail and expiring body. On any occasion she was able to summon the energy to lift her head from the depths, she cried and attempted to grab the stick for support, but, seemingly enjoying his role, Colley cruelly wrenched it from her, leaving her lying prone in the water and extinguishing any minuscule hope that may have remained for her. Following the struggle, her lifeless body was then carried from the water and dumped by the water's edge.

Edward Chapman also witnessed the events. He saw two men take Ruth in their arms and drag her to the middle of the pond. Once finished with her, her husband John was also dragged across, though his treatment was not as brutalised. Whilst dragging the suspected witch to and fro, the sheet came off her, leaving her 'quite naked', Chapman believing at this point that she was already dead, 'drowned in the manner aforesaid'. As a scarcely believable aside, Thomas Colley, one of those responsible for the ducking of Ruth, stepped over her prone and muddied body, mingled into the crowd and brazenly requested monies for 'the sport he had shown them in ducking the old witch'.

Ruth's limp and wrinkled body was then conveyed to the Half Moon public house on Wilstone Green. The landlord stated that Ruth Osborne was brought to his house by a 'very great mob of people, in a riotous manner and carried upstairs'. At odds with the unnatural and wild events of the day, she was then placed in a bed and left to rest in some semblance of 'peace'. A local surgeon, John Foster, viewed the body as it lay at Wilstone Green. His lamentable conclusion was that 'she came to her death by being suffocated with water and mud and suffering to be on cold ground for a considerable time.'

Meanwhile, the mob, content with their day's revelry, began to drift back to their homes. The landlord claimed that he did not know any of the persons concerned in the said mob, but as a local victualler, one may question the validity of this statement. However, his reluctance to name any of those involved was certainly not exclusive – the majority of people were hugely disinclined to name those involved, quite probably for fear of reprisals if particular names were revealed. They had, after all, revealed their destructive form with their demolition of the workhouse.

One man, however, was not as lucky to escape identification. Perhaps his shameless appeals for silver at the pond following the murder had served to lodge himself firmly in the psyche of those that witnessed the events. Or, as the 'Tring Chimney Sweep', Thomas Colley would surely have been a fairly notable, if not grimy, face in the area.

Despite the obvious delight that Ruth Osborne's demise had caused, the actions of the guilty parties were, nevertheless, altogether illegal. Attempts to amass those involved were difficult and often fruitless. Colley was relatively straightforward in bringing to custody; his mind and body largely impaired with drink, he was rapidly apprehended to the County Gaol at Hertford, charged with the murder of Ruth Osborne. Destruction and attacks on property were regarded with as much – and often greater – severity as those on a person. To this end, those responsible for the riotous behaviour in the search for the Osbornes were also sought out, though not with much haste. A month elapsed before an enquiry was held before the justices in Tring, giving those concerned ample time to flee the decimated scene they had created.

On 25 April, the Half Moon alehouse opened its heavy creaking doors to a far more solemn crowd than usual, as coroner Samuel Atkinson presided over the inquest held there, with twenty-five 'honest and lawful men from several parishes' together returning a verdict of wilful murder against Colley and a further twenty-one known and some unknown persons. The trial against Colley was set for 30 July 1751, but ambiguity remained over who might stand indicted with the chimney sweep. The Reverend Johnson, one of Tring's justices, stated that: 'A man named Charles Young and another named William Humbles, both of Leighton Buzzard, were as much concerned as Colley in exercising cruelty on the body of Ruth Osborne at the ducking place'. He went further, claiming that there were many others notoriously guilty of the riot who had already absconded and thus beaten the warrants out for their arrests.

The escapees' fates lay in stark contrast to the situation Colley found himself in. He was incarcerated at Hertford awaiting trial for murder, with only his contemplations and fears for company. He could, however, clutch on to a modicum of heart in that the record of prosecutions which resulted from the ducking of suspected witches was negligible at best. As Hertford's Summer Assizes loomed ever larger, Colley would soon learn of his fate.

Tuesday, 30 July 1751 was a day which had been much publicised, not only locally but nationwide. The case had become something of a national sensation, which politically speaking was a favourable outcome; with the ongoing drive to eradicate the 'yokel beliefs' of witchcraft and to encourage its extinction from England, such cases needed to generate a commotion of the masses, which could hammer home the understanding that the vilification of suspected witches would be severely punished.

The meting out of such punishment rested on the broad shoulders of Lord Chief Justice, William Lee. A trailblazer in his stance upon women, Lee was renowned for standing up to their rights more strenuously than any English judge before or since his time; perhaps then, he was the ideal appointment in this instance.

Lord Chief Justice Lee controlled events on that day in late July. As the indictment against Colley, Humbles and Young was announced, Colley was seen frequently weeping as he reflected upon the deplorable circumstances he had got himself into. Despite his lamentations, however, he did in the main appear composed. Despite returning home from the trial late into the evening, the Reverend Johnson provided a brief written commentary of the events, which he would later submit to Lord Cowper. We learn that Mr Fagin Slale was the foreman of the grand jury, the man that pronounced a verdict of 'guilty' against Colley, and his two compatriots in the accusation of murder. Lord Chief Justice Lee then passed his sentence of condemnation. Thomas Colley's body was to be hung in chains on Wilstone Green, but with a caveat inserted that this was to be kept a closely-guarded secret so that the 'Sheriff may not be interrupted with too great a mob at the erecting of the gibbet, or suspending of the body thereon'; this was another example of just how prominent the case had become. Humbles and Young were also deemed guilty of murder, but with a lesser involvement, and fortuitously escaped with their lives.

The indictment for tearing down the workhouse was found against Richard Symonds, John Eastoffe, John Waters, John Mayos, Benjamin Price and Henry Worster, though only the latter was apprehended; discovered in the county of Buckinghamshire, he was imprisoned at Hertford until more of his comrades were also taken, upon which time they would all be tried together at the next assizes.

As well as a concern for preserving peace within the county, Lord Chief Justice Lee stressed his desire that such 'dangerous riotous assemblies' were suitably punished, this being absolutely necessary for the 'common people who were more instigated to commit disorders of this kind.' Moreover, he asserted that unless restrained by examples of punishment inflicted upon like-minded offenders, such occurrences would continue to blight the county. Thus, his desire was to sentence accordingly in such a fashion that would 'deter them from spitting on the same rocks.'

Having had his fate laid bare before him, all Thomas Colley could do was live in the fear of death. This fear pains many more than the very pangs of death itself, and on Friday, 16 August, the day prior to his expected execution, he was informed by the Reverend Mr Bourchier that he would endure these fears for a week longer – a reprieve had been handed down, thus prolonging his torment. In this exchange of limited sugar-coating, the reverend also informed the condemned man that he was to be carried alive to the murder location, and there meet his doom, before afterwards being hung in chains. On hearing these harshest of realities, Colley was very much shocked – perhaps he had become dumbstruck with deafness when the Lord Chief Justice had earlier announced his fate – and hoped that his constant and fervent prayers to almighty God would give him the strength to bear the huge weight of his afflictions.

That evening, consumed by the dread of his finality, he wrote a letter to his wife committing his continuance of love to her, and that he 'has a very great desire' to see her before his execution. Colley insists that if she could endure such a visit, that she go to him immediately whilst he remains 'sensible', as he feared his senses would begin to waver as his final day approached. He begs that his children grieve his troubled heart before signing: 'From your dying husband, Thomas Colley.'

He further echoes such sentiments in additional letters sent to friends. Of particular interest are his writings to Samuel Holmes, in which he acknowledges the 'poor unfortunate act' he committed and has undeservedly brought such affliction upon 'the best of wives', and 'the honestest poor loving creature that ever a poor unhappy man had'. The letters behold an undertone of abject fear should his sins not be forgiven by God. Very much indicative of its time, Colley pleads for prayers directed towards both him and his family, whilst desperately hoping to make true repentance with God; the suffering of physical death was one matter, but the agony of uncertainty of God's judgement was hugely significant – no man was assured a state of grace.

Shortly after Colley had written these letters, he was visited in the gaol by a gentleman who had been sent to reason with the doomed felon and convince him of his 'erroneous opinion in believing that there was any such thing as witchcraft.' Colley firstly relayed his account as to the circumstances of his entering into the unhappy affair. Having parted with his farm following the death of many of his livestock, Colley claimed that the allegedly wronged farmer, John Butterfield, took over a local alehouse. As the mob descended into town on the day of the murder, Colley left his work and went to Butterfield's inn where he and others were subsequently plied with 'gin and other liquors'. The landlord spirited Colley and the other inebriated men on to proceed in the design of this rash and wicked action. Colley did own the fact that he was at the workhouse during its demolition, and apparently could not remember actively searching for the Osbornes.

Colley also relayed an odd and rather fanciful tale of his reasoning in believing that Ruth Osborne was a witch, she apparently having bewitched her own brother some years previously. Having listened to these stories, the gentleman then endeavoured to convince Colley that there was no foundation or reason to ground his notion of witchcraft upon, for if she had indeed been adept in such ways, surely she would have foreseen and so prevented the cruel ordeal she was subjected to. After further discourse between the pair, Colley was supposedly brought to a thorough conviction that witches had no 'manner of existence but in the minds of poor infatuated people'. Satisfied in this point, an epiphany of realisation as to the heinous nature of his crime had finally dawned upon Colley.

As his understanding became more enlightened, however, so too did the horror of his approaching death. He became affected to the degree that he was now convinced he would lose the use of his senses once at the place of execution. This would amount to an inability to produce his final words which he wished to offer to the onlookers present. Colley suggested that he would therefore write these words down so they may be carried to the execution site as information for the 'ignorant and misled country people'. By doing this, Colley was ensuring that should his mind be suppressed under such extreme terrors that he was rendered incapable of delivering his words orally, his message and final pleadings of forgiveness could still be expressed.

The day before his execution, Colley was taken from his gaol at ten o'clock in the morning and conveyed to a room in the keeper's house, where Reverend Bourchier administered the sacrament. This was followed by a 'suitable and excellent' sermon whereupon Colley displayed great emotion. At its conclusion he was then put into a one-horse chaise, driven by the very man who would, in only a few short hours, be responsible for ending Colley's purgatory by hanging him until he was dead. Arriving at St Albans at three o'clock, he was then deposited into the gaol where he would spend his last earthly evening. His final visitors were his wife and daughter, who valiantly tried to raise his morose spirits. We know not of his feelings during his last evening, though it could be safely assumed that Colley would have endured a particularly restless night. At five o'clock the following morning, he was put into the same chaise, with his executioner once more in control of this, Colley's final journey. Ingesting the sights, the smells, the minuscule things once regarded with everyday tedium, they now reeked of significance as his concluding minutes whittled away.

When the chaise reached the location of Butterfield's alehouse, Colley made the staggering declaration that had he known the consequences of destroying the innocent woman, he would not have engaged in such exploits. Glaring accusingly at the tavern, he further reiterated that its landlord had been the fuelling force behind the diabolical act. This may be seen as displacing his own portion of culpability, though perhaps his claims of ignorance to the consequences of 'ducking' deserve some credence; had he understood the severity of the repercussions, for example, surely the foul display would not have been advertised throughout the county so blatantly.

Arriving at the place of execution at eleven o'clock, he was escorted by an incredible 108 men and seven officers of the Horse Guards. A force of these proportions to guard one felon was unusual, but symbolically amounted to a display of defiance and force in the hope of deterring future offending and, of course, eradicating the belief in witchcraft itself, its prevalence in this part of the country seemingly still so embraced.

Lord Chief Justice Lee's proviso that Colley's hanging be publicly concealed was at best a fanciful idea. Even in the relatively primitive times of 1751, an affair of this nature being kept undisclosed was distinctly improbable. Indeed, if this command from the justices was intended rigidly, the flocks did not heed the directive. The *Everyday Book of 1751* reports that 'Thousands stood at a distance, muttering that it was a hard case to hang a man for destroying a wicked old woman that had done so much mischief by her witchcraft.' Even in Colley's death, public opinion was very much on the side of the guilty man.

At the tree, Colley was reported to have behaved with great decency and resignation. Attended by the Reverend Mr Randal, Minister of Tring, the pair prayed together as Colley was prepared for the practicalities of death. As per his aforementioned worries of becoming senseless at the event, Colley was explicit in his desire for the minister to impart his final words, which he had written the previous evening. Mr Randal took hold of the script and with a firm voice verbalised Colley's departing speech on behalf of the condemned man:

'Good people!
I beseech you all to take warning by an unhappy man's suffering; that you be not deluded into so absurd and wicked a conceit, as to believe that there are any such beings upon earth as witches.

It was that foolish and vain imagination, heighten'd and inflamed by the strength of liquor, which prompted me to be instrumental (with others as mad-brain'd as myself) in the horrid and barbarous murder of Ruth Osborne, the supposed witch, for which I am now so deservedly to suffer death.

I am fully convinced of my former error, and with the sincerity of a dying man, declare, that I do not believe there is such a thing in being as a witch; and pray God that none of you, thro' a contrary persuasion, may hereafter be induced to think, that you have a right in any shape to persecute, much less endanger the life of a fellow-creature.

I beg of you all to pray to God to forgive me, and to wash clean my polluted soul in the blood of Jesus Christ, my saviour and Redeemer,
So exhorteth you all, the dying
Thomas Colley'

The words complete, the cart was drawn from under Colley and in resounding contrast to Ruth Osborne, he dropped silently to his death, signalling the end of this unhappy man. Having hung for the allotted time, Colley's perished shell was then prepared for the chains. Whilst his life was now extinct, his penned terminal words would form part of an ongoing quest to rid minds of the implausible 'logic' of witchcraft. His letter bore out an unequivocal communication almost certainly intended to permeate the public consciousness and evoke a shift in the gullible beliefs which were still so deeply ingrained by some.

Colley's words may well have been a reflection of a man learned of the undoubted error of his ways. Or, perhaps more likely, the words were enforced upon Colley by law enforcement and government officials of the day who could cunningly seek to capitalise on the tragedy at Tring to aid efforts to disseminate the word that witches were beyond existence. Armed with such a 'confession', the signed document and its warnings within could be circulated to the wider community to reinforce the much-aspired towards and desirable concept that witchcraft was purely a fallacy. The corridors of power could use such an incident to trumpet this message to some of the more unreachable pockets of the 'unenlightened' and similarly bring to a close the barbaric witch hunts that had been a filthy stain upon England. Ironically, in his death, Colley's closing remarks on Earth may well have provided an unlikely platform in eradicating the oppressive behaviour he himself had partaken in and thereafter led to him suffering the ultimate penalty.

Chapter 13

Thomas David Cunnington

The penned final musings to a life are not ordinarily linked to humour. Yet, if we are afforded the control of our own final destiny, partings can, intriguingly, be scripted to reflect the personal character of its author. A message of this ilk may then be seen to serve as an eternal memorial to the departed, an encapsulation of sorts within their final words.

The words written by Thomas Cunnington, a London valet, prior to him taking his own life in 1930 were doused in humour combined with a distinct lack of trepidation or fear towards his looming death. Indeed, in a letter he sent to his brother, he opted for a most unusual approach, providing a form of 'commentary' of his actions as he edged closer to his final release.

Thomas David Cunnington was born in Westminster, London, in 1883. Little is known of his early life, but he appears in the census of 1901, 18 years old and lodging with Aron and Anne Gay. Service records relating to the First World War do not exist for Cunnington, though this does not amount to confirmation that he did not endure warfare in the trenches; only approximately 40 per cent of these service records now exist, more than half being destroyed by bomb damage in the Second World War.

Frederick Charles Cunnington, Thomas's younger brother, was born in 1885. Military discharge and pension records are in existence for him, which confirm his discharge from the army in 1918, and that he was living in Mayfair's prestigious Mount Street with his wife and housemaid.

What appears certain is that the brothers both suffered considerable grief when, in 1929, they were bereaved by the loss of their mother. Thomas was much affected by her death, the pair relying on each other for company. They had both lived in Winchester Street in the Pimlico area of London, and Thomas was described as having 'brooded over his mother' following her passing. One Saturday morning, a letter arrived at Frederick's Mayfair address. The contents ordered him to collect a key from the lamp stand in the hallway of his flat which had been left hanging there. It was the next part of the letter, though, that made Frederick's blood run cold.

> Don't make a noise when you come in. You might wake me up, and if I ain't dead, there is a chopper in a box, or I will leave the damn chopper out. Hit me hard for I can't be seen alive again. Don't expect me to answer the door. Just get the key off the lamp stand. I have two, but my own will be locked from inside and of course, I must take it out for the key I am leaving outside. Don't call Tom, for my spirit is with mum. Don't look any bluer than I hope to be. Am putting on the silk sleeping suit. Haven't bothered to wear the thing for a long time, but I must 'dye' a good colour.

As Frederick accessed the property, he found his brother lying dead on the floor, wearing a pair of silk pyjamas. His head was positioned near a gas oven, and the gas source had been completely exhausted. Lying next to the lifeless body was another letter, addressed again to Frederick, but this time detailing Thomas's final living actions, his articulation apparently maintaining a jocular tone.

> 1:30. – Just returned from posting a bundle of letters. Dare not be found alive after this lot, so here goes! Wish I knew a bit more about poisoning, but have no nerves. Only hope it isn't a failure.
>
> Half an hour with my head in the oven. Never dreamt I could swallow so much gas.
>   I'm getting to think gas will run out and what a fool I'll look in the morning. Fancy waking up and finding I am not dead. Terrible. My luck is out. Can't get enough gas! Can't even smell it. I must be gas-proof! Am trying.
>   Hope I'll wake in heaven. It would be funny if I opened the door to you in the morning. God forbid. I won't want to die only once.

As the gas began to take its mortal effects, Thomas Cunnington, in his forty-seventh year, signed off his life issuing his final words directly to his brother.

Am going to sleep. Good-night Fred.

The words of Cunnington's final letter offer a remarkable insight into the mind of the man. It appears clear that in light of his mother's death only a year previously, he yearned to reconvene with her 'hopefully', as he states, 'in heaven'. Purveyed throughout the text is a definite clarity of mind in a man intent and seemingly untroubled by his actions. This may appear a juxtaposition in regard to a man resolved to ending his life, yet it is a course of action he holds no obvious fear toward. Indeed, any fear indicated by Cunnington's words appear to be focused around a failure to perform the deed 'successfully'. Certainly, the thought of being found alive and having to face the recipients of the 'bundle of letters' he posted prior to his death did not enamour him greatly – an interesting bundle of documents they would surely prove to be!

The Westminster inquest into Cunnington's death recorded the familiar line of 'suicide whilst of unsound mind'. The cause of death required little unearthing. The incidence of suicide by gas poisoning rose rapidly in the early part of the twentieth century. It was readily available and considered a painless method of suicide. At the time of Thomas Cunnington's death, gas poisoning was the most common method used by women, and it remained so for over a decade.

The highly-revered London coroner, Mr Samuel Ingleby Oddie, oversaw the inquest and followed up his standard conclusion with the surely narrow-minded assessment that 'a man whose attitude to death is of that kind, clearly has an unbalanced mind.' That Cunnington had 'cracked jokes about his death' created much perplexity to the coroner, thus reinforcing his conclusion of insanity. There was clearly great flippancy to which cases of suicide were simply castigated as owners of 'unsound minds'. The coroner's comments indicate a misguided sense that an outlook towards death could only be considered rational if it followed a particular narrative – anything in direct contravention to this, it was assumed, must indicate an insane mind.

In the case of Thomas Cunnington, his final words to his brother perhaps disclose less of an unbalanced mind, offering instead a vivid portrayal of a man who simply felt beyond hope following the death of his mother.

Chapter 14

John Smith

An individual's final words can vary hugely depending on a variety of different elements. Possessing an awareness of imminent expiration does, of course, provide a degree of pre-selection and free will. There may not be quite the ingredient of spontaneity, but rather a more controlled and deliberate array of expressions which the grieving recipient may well treasure and behold thereafter as a source of unique comfort.

It would appear that far from expressing sentiments of love and adoration, for example, dying declarations can sometimes be infused instead with hatred, jealousy or guilt, cemented by the embittered lamenting of a stricken situation and ultimately blaming all others for their arrival at such a desperate predicament. For Greenwich pensioner John Smith – under the sentence of death for murder – the latter was certainly evident in his final words. Yet he also exhibited one of the most remarkable instances of mental abstraction possible, particularly when considering that Smith was an illiterate man of almost 80 years old.

In 1822, John Smith was in his seventy-eighth year, an impressive figure to reach in a time when he would not be expected to surpass 40 years old. Described as a 'fine and robust old man', quite what the secret of his longevity was is unclear, though according to the man himself, Smith adored the fairer sex and 'had a hundred in his time' – perhaps his alleged dalliances did indeed maintain his years, though it is with great irony that he also attributed his ultimate downfall to womankind.

Smith was a pensioner of Greenwich Hospital which had become a home for pensioned seamen, admitting its first pensioners in 1705. By 1815, the hospital housed almost 3,000 sailors and played a crucial role in supporting those who were unable to return to sea, whether through injury or increasing age. The youngest 'pensioner' on record was a John McKerty, just 12 years old, who was admitted in 1750 suffering from 'dropsy'. All of the men admitted to the hospital had befallen difficult times, the majority emanating from poorer backgrounds without the means to save for their advancing years. Life at sea was, of course, a perilous prospect in those times, with accidents and illness rife among the sailors. Living as a Greenwich Pensioner meant following a strict routine. On first entering the hospital, the men were issued with a uniform, initially grey, then brown, before the more iconic blue frock coats were introduced. Each man would be woken daily at seven o'clock when they would be expected to attend chapel and prayer services. As an institution, Greenwich bore a greater resemblance to a retirement home than a hospital, so medical provision here was limited – for the unfortunate pensioners suffering serious ailments, they were transferred to other London hospitals to secure the care they required. The standard diet 'endured' by a Greenwich Pensioner would include a staple of bread, accompanied by beef for three days a week. Mutton, pease soup and cheese would fulfil the rest of the week's offerings. Pensioners were entitled to leave the hospital during leisure hours, where they would most commonly frequent the numerous alehouses dotted in the area.

Painting a vivid portrayal of its clientele, one former hospital governor, Sir Thomas Hardy, described it as homing men of 'all sizes and outlies, including some who almost assume the appearance of four-footed animals, from their bending so low'. The hospital was forced to finally close its doors in 1869.

Prior to becoming a Greenwich Pensioner, John Smith had spent some time cohabiting with a Catherine Smith, living together for fifteen months. Upon his arrival at Greenwich, John had managed to procure her a position as a ward assistant in the hospital, but Catherine's behaviour towards him had begun to alter, appearing cold and aloof, though on John's part at least, she remained his sweetheart.

On 4 October 1822, John visited The Cricketers public-house and sat at the bar. Having ordered his 'pot of porter', Smith summoned the landlord enquiring if he had 'seen my woman this morning?' Replying that he had not seen Catherine, the landlord agreed that he would call her in should he see her pass the window. Moments later Catherine did enter the pub, but in the company of another man, a fellow Greenwich Pensioner named Levett. Feelings of jealous rage were engulfing John as he quietly concluded the reasoning behind her change in attitude towards him. Catherine was heard to order two glasses of gin. Upon receiving the first glass, she exclaimed: 'You know I take it with peppermint!' As the landlord turned for the peppermint bottle, John had risen from his seat and stood over his woman before thrusting a knife into her right breast. Not a word had passed between the pair to this point, but with a clear comprehension of her plight, Catherine uttered: 'You have killed me! You have killed me!'

She managed to stagger from the bar but fell forty paces beyond before collapsing to the ground, dead. The landlord had in the meantime seized the aged transgressor who demonstrated little remorse, asserting that he had committed the act in vengeance of Catherine having 'been with that fellow all night'. Smith's warped justification of the wicked deed appeared to leave him unmoved. When searched, the murder weapon was quickly discovered on his person, a common pocket knife having recently been purposefully sharpened, suggesting that the act perhaps was not quite as spontaneous as Smith would later suggest.

In December 1822, John Smith faced a most bleak mid-winter. As he entered the Kent Assizes indicted for the wilful murder of Catherine Smith, this old and robust man standing almost 6 feet tall amazed those in attendance – not merely for the shock that a man of such impressive seniority could plummet to such depths, but that he should tread with such a firm and steady step.

The pensioner's defence was based upon the premise that Smith was overcome by that wretched and baneful passion of jealousy; witnessing Catherine with another man prompted his hands to commit the cowardly deed. He confessed that he had been fuelled heavily from drink the previous evening and thus his mind was befuddled and unknowing of his actions, pleading that there was no intention to kill the defenceless woman. Under these circumstances and his advanced years, he clung to the hope that a merciful view would therefore be taken. But this was early-nineteenth-century justice where only a month prior, William Reading had been executed at Newgate for shoplifting, hardly the gravest of crimes, but perhaps epitomising the despondency of the old man's position in an age where examples of mercy were limited at best. The jury returned an immediate verdict of guilty, and Smith's name was penned to an unenviable list of doom, enrolled to die the following Monday.

The condemned man did not wallow. His days may have been reducing but his penitence inflated and he displayed contrition throughout. A remarkable clarity of mind instigated Smith to send for a gentleman of Maidstone, whom Smith vehemently beseeched to ensure that he make public a document he had prepared following his execution. The document, Smith's final prose and written in doggerel verse, proved to be a concise narrative informing of his place of birth, ranging through to his motives for committing murder. *Literatim et verbatim*, it read:

> In the County of Wicklow I was born'd
> but now in Maidstone die in scorn
> I once was counted a roving blade
> but to my misfortune had no trade
> women was always my downfall
> but still I liked and loved them all
> a hundred I have had in my time
> when I was young and in my prime
> women was always my delight
> but when I got old they did me slight
> a woman from London to me came
> she said with You I would fain remain
> if you will be constant I'll be true
> I never want no Man but you –
> and on her own bible a Oath did take
> that she never would Me forsake
> and during the time that I had Life
> she would always prove a loving Wife
> and by that Means we did agree
> to live together she and Me –
> but soon her vows and Oath did break
> and another Man did take
> Which she fetch'd home with her to lay
> and that proved her own destiny
> So as Jack Smith lay on his bed
> this notion strongly run in his Head
> then he got up with that intent

to find her out was fully bent
swearing if he found out her Oath she'd broke
he stick a knife into her throat
then to the Cricketers he did go
to see if he could find it out or no
not long been there before she Come in
with this same fellow to fetch some gin
immediately stab'd her under the Chin
and in five minutes she was no more
but there laid in her purple gore
Now to conclude and end my song
they are both dead dead and gone
they are both gone I do declare
gone they are but God knows where –

The gentleman, on examining the paper, was greatly surprised – this was, after all, the production of an illiterate man of venerable age and under the most stressful and exhausting of circumstances.

At twelve o'clock on Monday, 23 December, the lurid sentence of law was effected on Penenden Heath. It appeared the public were unperturbed by the age of the hapless man, his demise attracting the usual assembly of prodigious numbers. John Smith's final words, smattered in irony, left no doubt as to whom he believed was culpable for his sombre situation: 'Women are the cause of my downfall. They have all through my life been my ruin, and they have at last brought me to this untimely end.'

With these words upon his lips, and the clamour his declaration did incite, he was dropped to his death, leaving in his wake his aged body for dissection and a confessional ode to murder.

Chapter 15

Sir Walter Raleigh

Walter Raleigh was born in 1552, a time when England's youthful King, Edward VI, presided over his kingdom, unaware of the incumbent illness that would soon besiege and ravage his body ahead of a period of political and royal uncertainty. Amid the fertility and richness of the Devonshire lands, however, Walter Raleigh could not have been further removed from the disorientated capital. Hayes Barton, a pretty farmstead in the parish of East Budleigh, was Raleigh's childhood home, its affinity evidently never deserting him, for when the property passed out of the family in 1584, the smitten Raleigh attempted to buy it back. 'For the natural disposition I have to the place, being born in that house, I had rather seat myself there than anywhere else,' he wrote to its new owner. In the event, Raleigh's proposition was refused, evidencing a rare occasion that his flamboyant and alluring writing style did not secure his wants. This poised finesse, however, would eventually bear its fruits, and of the very ripest kind.

The young Raleigh weaved an inordinate plethora of 'careers' into his wholesome and crammed lifetime: courtier, navigator, poet, writer, adventurer, sailor and soldier among his endeavours. To express all aspects of such a bounteous life within the confines of these pages, it is necessary to pass swiftly over particular features of which he played a secondary part, albeit these were rare occasions in which he faded from prominence.

His multi-faceted approach to life ensures his position as one of English history's most compelling characters, a man brimming with intellect and a sparkling imagination, flanked by a rascally and roguish inclination. Raleigh's richly multifarious character appealed greatly to the 'Virgin Queen' – Elizabeth I – who elevated him to such dizzying heights before a resounding fall from grace and an ultimate engagement with the headsman whereupon, as we shall see, despite the quite horrible circumstances, Raleigh still managed to entertain the masses with his usual ebullience.

Born into a well-connected gentry family, Raleigh's beginnings were relatively humble, particularly in consideration of his eventual meteoric rise to prominence under Elizabeth I. He was the result of his father's third marriage, when in 1548 he wed Katherine Champernowne. Raleigh was a boy infused with masses of energy – something that never subsided – boundlessly assisting in farm work and excelling scholastically. His learning prowess was underpinned by a natural scepticism and questioning approach; to Raleigh, ancient philosophers were not the fount of all knowledge they were so often assumed to be, but instead merely a point of critical consideration.

One aspect Raleigh was certainly convinced of was his commitment to the Protestant faith. Sunday school attendance was compulsory in his early years and laid the foundations of his staunch beliefs. In addition, Raleigh developed a bitter distaste towards Catholicism, brought about largely through the persecution of his father, Walter Raleigh senior, endured at the hands of the previous monarch, the Catholic queen, Mary I. The most notable of such instances saw his father desperately take refuge from popish henchmen in a church tower to avoid execution. The threat at this time was very real; Mary's final four years of reign saw no fewer than 288 executions, all owing to an adherence to the Protestant faith. However, her passing in 1558 brought much joy – Elizabeth I now reigned at last and with her came an abiding assurance to re-establish the English Protestant Church, a champion of the reformed faith who now offered limitless hope to the Raleigh ménage.

By the time of his latter teenage years, Raleigh was already strongly advanced by academical learning at Oxford, becoming a revered ornament of the juniors, most proficient in oratory and philosophy. It was here that an everlasting passion for poetry was ignited, but scarcely could he have known then that one day he would pen verses for his revered queen. The education of his youth was a training in the arts of a gentleman and a soldier, but it extended further even than this, also embracing an impeccable knowledge of the oceans and naval warfare that would prove invaluable. Indeed, practical experience in this vein had already been gained; his hands were bloodied in merciless battle abroad with his fighting in support of the Huguenots, a band of French Protestants embroiled in civil warfare, with Raleigh fighting their Calvinistic cause over in France. This first taste of travelling adventure thrilled the man, leaving an indelible appetite that would require frequent fulfilment throughout his lifetime.

In 1578 Raleigh's exploratory curiosity was pricked when, together with his half-brother Sir Humphrey Gilbert, he sailed in search of new lands and territories as yet unpossessed. The venture's principal aim was to mobilise landed-class Catholics to 'establish estates in the new world,' probably in the Caribbean. Raleigh experienced his first enthralling bow as captain, guiding the *Falcon* with its seventy-five strong complement aboard. The vessel was tiny, and conditions were cramped and harsh. The crew slept on folded sails between the guns close to the waterline, constant deluges ensuring the men remained in eternal discomfort, their skin rotting damp. Those were the fortunate ones. Others less so griped agonisingly with dysentery, others with typhus. Edible offerings were insalubrious at best, but attempted theft of the dismal stuff resulted in the nailing of an offender's hand to the mast for a time, before the removal of the limb. The stump would then be dipped in oil as a permanent reminder, and as a vivid deterrent to others.

The treacherous conditions Raleigh and his crew encountered ensured that for many, it was the last voyage they would sail. Large numbers of the crew died and the expedition, such as it was, was obliged to return to Plymouth in May 1579. Raleigh and his band never reached their destination, the mission free-falling into a privateering foray against Spanish shipping. The ill-fated voyage secured a cynical mention from the monarch's advisers in her Privy Council, such was the infamy of his rather brash actions. Both Gilbert and Raleigh were forbidden from sailing future voyages – if Raleigh was to gain advancement, he would be forced to seek alternative methods of achieving it.

By 1580, Raleigh had returned to London, a young man on the mere fringes of court. Inebriated by its pomp and ceremony, he yearned for an involvement within. The tempestuous aspect of his character, though, appeared to hinder this desire further when he and another young courtier were hauled before the Privy Council following a quarrel that resulted in six days in Fleet Prison in the hope it would 'cool his heels'. He was released on a promise of good behaviour, yet before his heels had even slightly chilled, he was again before the Council for an affray at a tennis court in Whitehall and ordered to serve time within Marshalsea Prison. Neither stint was particularly harsh; indeed, the young upstart would have endured far more severe conditions at sea, but both incidents highlight the vigorous enthusiasm of a young man determined to assert his force of personality.

This unflinching character then saw Raleigh sent to Ireland, in the command of a band of men to fight in the Second Desmond Rebellion. The first such rebellion was an armed protest in response to English intrusion into the 'Desmond' territories of South-West Ireland, which in contemporary terms incorporate the counties of Cork and Kerry. A four-year battle ended in 1573 following the crushing of the rebellion by Elizabeth's forces. Although Ireland was one of her two kingdoms, Elizabeth's Irish subjects viewed her with great disdain in a province infused with an overwhelming Catholic inclination. Her courtiers were granted Irish lands in order to prevent uprising rebels from providing Spain with a base from which to attack England – Ireland and Spain were united in the Catholic cause.

The Second Desmond Rebellion began in 1579 and left a far bloodier imprint on the record, in which Raleigh himself was mercilessly engaged. Raleigh and his troops are thought to have systematically slaughtered 300 Italian and Spanish troops, who had been sent to Ireland by the Pope and King of Spain. The landing of the doomed papal forces was in response to the widespread dissatisfaction of English rule of the country, derived largely from religious conflict, the rebels forlornly attempting to uphold Catholicism against the Protestant Queen Elizabeth. Furthermore, concerns that English policy was deposing Gaelic traditions, coupled with the infringement of central government upon the lands of the feudal lords, all conspired to trigger the insurrection across the south of Ireland. The rebellion, though, was once again thwarted by the crown's forces after four brutal years of bloody warfare, whereupon our man distinguished himself with his ruthlessness, earning status as a military hero in many quarters.

The result of the failed rebellions prompted the colonisation of Munster with an array of English settlers. Indeed, Raleigh himself was awarded some 40,000 acres upon the seizure and subsequent distribution of land which arose from the rebellion, elevating him to one of the foremost landowners of Munster. His Irish exploits had also enamoured him to the queen of the realm herself – moreover, his extensive writings to the Privy Council had acted as a seductive reminder to its grandees of his existence. Walter Raleigh now finally appeared firmly set on a course of royal reverence, a course he had so desperately craved.

His name was sweeping the nation, on the lips of the great and good. He became a mystical and somewhat alluring character, the figurehead of inspiring escapades which were recited throughout the lands, emphatically capturing the legend that he was living. Perhaps the most famed of these narrations was recorded by the antiquarian Thomas Fuller in his *History of the Worthies of England*: 'This Captain Raleigh, coming out of Ireland to the English court in good habit found the queen walking, till, meeting with a splashy place, she seemed to scruple going thereon. Presently Raleigh cast and spread his new plush cloak on the ground; whereon the queen trod gently.' The validity of the account is questionable as Fuller was renowned for a penchant for embellishment; nonetheless the gallant anecdote serves to encapsulate a legend that was fast embracing the ambitious Raleigh, as well as highlighting the relationship he would seek to cultivate with his queen.

Raleigh's physical prowess added to his commanding and confident demeanour. To this end, he was perfectly sculpted for the role of courtier; 6 feet tall, with plentiful dark, curling hair and a natural swagger, he exuded an authority that even the queen herself could not overlook. This new face at court, whilst reflecting rivalry and jeopardy to his peers, was the manifestation of renewed vigour and energy to Elizabeth. Delighting the queen with his every move, so it seemed, Raleigh, in the prime of his strength and beauty, was reshaping himself into the perfect Elizabethan courtier, whom she was determined to have at her side.

As far as can be perceived, Raleigh's success as a courtier was unblemished from 1582 to 1586. He took a confidential place by the queen's side, though in spite of his influence with her, his standing never exceeded to the echelons of the Privy Council, for if Raleigh, so accomplished a figure in such an array of fields did have a void amongst his compendium of abilities, it was a vulnerability in statecraft. That said, Elizabeth lauded vast affection toward her handsome courtier; indeed, the recordings of a

Pomeranian diarist documenting a dinner at Greenwich in 1584 noted that Queen Elizabeth, though surrounded by 'great noblemen', was said to 'love Walter Raleigh above all others.'

To be held in such esteem led to an accumulation of vast wealth. He began to reap untold rewards as the fortunate beneficiary of gifts and titles from his queen. In 1583 he was given possession of two estates, Stolney and Newland. In the same year he became enriched further, becoming the recipient of a license duty on the sale of wines; each vintner in the United Kingdom was ordered to pay Raleigh a fee of 20 shillings per year. An estate at Sherborne, Dorset, and Durham House in the Strand were gifted to Raleigh and titles were vehemently thrust upon the young man, culminating in a knighthood in 1585. Two years beyond this, Raleigh then became captain of the queen's guard. He was granted a royal charter which authorised his exploration and colonisation of 'any remote, heathen and barbarous lands' within North America. He was trusted with extensive rights and freedoms for the seven years that his patent existed and although Raleigh himself never visited these lands, his skills of delegation were suitably enhanced.

His influence at court was now prominent, his queen joyous as Raleigh adopted his intelligent charm to woo her further. Though forced to remain at court with Elizabeth, he sponsored an expedition landing near North Carolina, claiming the territory for himself before naming it 'Virginia' in honour of his virgin queen. This servant of the crown was many things, with a competency in gracious flattery surely heading the list. Further explorations saw Raleigh return with a multitude of treasures from exotic plants and foods, and even some of the natives who would serve Elizabeth's court. Raleigh's overtures and grand gestures, however, did not enamour him to all in the court of Elizabeth. He had few allies or, indeed, friends there and although he had caught the eye of she that mattered most, he was by contrast a loner – a prisoner of his own vanity and confidence.

Despite this, his unpopularity in court was not universal. It is perhaps with some inevitability that a man of his daring panache with such alluringly handsome features would prove irresistible to some within Elizabeth's court. This certainly proved true of Elizabeth 'Bess' Throckmorton, one of her majesty's ladies-in-waiting. A youthful and fresh-faced 19-year-old when she first appeared among the throng of vestals that surrounded the queen, she shared similar attributes to Raleigh himself; she was intelligent, courageous and voracious, though Raleigh, now in his early forties, was considerably advanced in years by comparison. Nevertheless, the discrepancy did little to quell the passion that developed between the pair, who fell hopelessly in love with one another, embarking on a dangerous liaison which would herald dreadful consequences. In the summer of 1591 Bess fell pregnant, prompting a secret marriage between the pair. The requirement of secrecy may not be obvious at this point, but this urgent need stemmed from Queen Elizabeth's demand for absolute loyalty from those around her. The fact that a secret tryst was blossoming within arm's length would prove wholly unsatisfactory should the affair be uncovered.

As Bess's maternal bloom ripened, the 'secret' of her pregnancy was inevitably short-lived. Bess gave birth to a baby boy – Damerei – who was immediately 'put out to a wet nurse' so Bess could retain her position in court, Raleigh arranging for his baby and nurse to go to Durham House. Efforts to maintain the charade ultimately proved in vain as, on 31 May 1592, the marriage was discovered. Royal permission had not been granted for the union, enraging Elizabeth by the perceived stealth shown by two of her more favoured confederates. Bess was swiftly dismissed from duties and, together with her husband, imprisoned in the Tower of London. Once her favourite, Raleigh had fallen into a pit of barely retrievable disgrace with his queen. Furthermore, her own eyes had wandered, shifting towards a new beau: the Earl of Essex, a 20-year-old 'petulant beauty', who was now enjoying the admiring glances from his queen, a perfect Raleigh replacement.

Much has been made of the apparent excessive punishment inflicted upon Raleigh and his lady. That Elizabeth viewed the breach of trust with such abhorrence has been linked by some commentators to a romantic jealousy on Elizabeth's part, though there is no evidence for this. There was adoration lavished over Raleigh certainly, so an assumption of this nature is not preposterous, nor indeed unexpected; amorous rumour is often a popular one and even if unfounded in this case, it adds a further layer of intrigue to the relationship between Elizabeth and her most renowned courtier.

Raleigh's time within the Tower was short and, within a matter of months, he had been released, Elizabeth requiring his naval expertise to supervise an unruly crew which had docked in England brimming with captured Spanish goods. Perhaps this action reveals what Raleigh was to Elizabeth: a pawn to use to her advantage rather than a central character in some dizzy love affair. The release and request no doubt fuelled Raleigh's ascended ego further as a somewhat irreplaceable and necessary aide to the queen.

Lady Raleigh was forced to endure incarceration for several months beyond her husband's release, though tragedy was central to this. Damerei died in infancy – another victim of the horrible plague – and Elizabeth bowed sympathetically to the stricken mother. The pair may have regained their freedom, but the queen's trust and adoration had left them forever. The couple were, in effect, exiled from court and indeed life, beginning a new rural existence in Sherborne, Raleigh's country residence.

In the early months of 1593, Bess was again pregnant – this time without concealment – and Walter, 'Wat', was born. Raleigh had devoted much of his time to studying and writing, and for a while domestic bliss was attained, though Raleigh, ever the thrill-seeker, continued to travel extensively. In 1595 he voyaged to Guyana, upon his return writing a particularly fantastical account of it as an incredible gold-rich land where gold could be plucked readily from the ground. *The Discovery of Guiana* was an example of Raleigh at his embellishing best, his claims tempting a host of subsequent gold-diggers greedily swept up in his propaganda-fuelled texts.

A man with such a preoccupation with his queen could not, of course, simply fade from obscurity indefinitely, particularly one in the mould of Raleigh. He went about regaining royal favour, and though Elizabeth's fervent objections to the marriage continued, Raleigh did remain devoted to his young wife. The latter part of the sixteenth century saw Raleigh restore a modicum of royal favour, however. His zenith had long since been reached; his fame and fortune surpassing anything he could dare to have dreamt, but as such, there was only one direction for Raleigh to tumble – and this he certainly did, almightily. Yet, true to the man, his resilience ensured a recovery of sorts. In 1596 the queen sent Raleigh and his rival – the Earl of Essex – on a daring naval raid against the Spanish port of Cadiz. The attack was essentially of a pre-emptive nature, rendering the port useless if Spain was to attempt to launch a new armada, of which the first and most famed of all had already been sunk in 1588. Cadiz was stormed and ultimately decimated, with Raleigh receiving gunshot wounds to his leg as a serving reminder of his heroism.

Perhaps this physical emblem of bravery impressed Elizabeth too, for on his return, Raleigh's stock had risen again. In 1597 he was elected as Member of Parliament for Dorset, and a few years later, for Cornwall also. It appeared that Raleigh had been re-elevated to lofty heights in his queen's eyes, but his good fortune would endure no further. On 24 March 1603, Queen Elizabeth's death signalled the end of the Elizabethan era and decades of female rule. It also spelled mournful disaster for Walter Raleigh. James VI of Scotland succeeded Elizabeth and immediately Raleigh's landscape dramatically shifted. In contrast to Elizabeth, the new king was unmoved by Raleigh's charms. Moreover, James, although Protestant, was eager to improve relations with Spain, which directly opposed Raleigh's bitter hatred of Catholicism and of Spain herself, having essentially been Raleigh's eternal foe.

His plentiful enemies at court were happy to poison the king's mind against him, his political opponents delighted to seize upon their opportunity. The secretary of state Robert Cecil had greatly resented Raleigh's previous influence over the queen. Unhappily masked in Raleigh's shadow for so long, he persuaded King James to remove Raleigh's titles and privileges. Dismissed as captain of the guard and governor of Jersey, Raleigh's exclusive trading rights were also removed before also being ordered to leave Durham House.

Raleigh's next 'abode' was a familiar one, though hardly one that resonated with happy memories. His clutch of enemies conspired against him in the gravest of fashions. King James's new subjects had initially rejoiced that a 'natural order' had been restored upon his succession to the throne, but these celebrations were short-lived. England's Catholics had hoped and expected increased toleration under their new king, a desire that never came to fruition, instead prompting an outbreak of rebellion. Raleigh was falsely implicated in the 'Main Plot', an attempted plan to overhaul the new king from power and be replaced with his cousin, Lady Arbella Stuart. The evidence against Raleigh was dubious at best, but he was charged with treason and once more imprisoned in the Tower.

In late July 1603 and awaiting trial, Raleigh's feelings of wretched despair overwhelmed him. The verdict of a seventeenth-century trial for treason was a foregone conclusion, and now those who had once swooned over his stylistic and ceremonial relationship with his queen relished the idea of his guilt. Raleigh did not. He attempted 'to murder himself' in the Tower, stabbing himself with a table knife. Far from being provoked into a sympathetic state, Cecil simply dismissed the actions as rather playful: Raleigh had wounded himself under the right pap, but in no way mortally, being in truth rather a cut than a stab.

Whether the attempt on his own life was a serious one or not, there is little doubt that Raleigh understood the desperation of his situation. On 17 November 1603, his trial at Winchester merely confirmed this, being found guilty and sentenced to death, the might of royal authority pronouncing a sentence of hanging prior to mutilation. None of the counts against Raleigh were proven and as one of the judges would later declare, 'that trial injured and degraded the justice of England.' His condemnation appeared to come from, quite simply, being Sir Walter Raleigh.

King James, however, unexpectedly issued clemency to the prisoner, postponing the sentence of death, instead ensuring that Raleigh began a period of thirteen years in which the Tower would home its most-famed prisoner. The Tower's foreboding reputation is something of a mythical one, and Raleigh's incarceration there certainly did not equate to a period of torturous barbarity. Dating from 1066, the Tower was indeed perceived as a symbol of state authority and fear, an imposing showpiece of power and domination. It was, however, not built as a prison and as such had no specific 'accommodation' designed for incarceration. In reality, it acted as a desolate departure point for those to be executed, and any affiliated exaggerations to its brutality would only help in its ability to extract confessions from tight-lipped prisoners.

Raleigh's quarters were befitting a man of such status. Two rooms were afforded him, both relatively spacious and well-furnished. Having been stripped of his array of titles and considered 'civilly dead', Raleigh, in typically buoyant fashion, continued to add to his labyrinth of abilities and expand upon existing ones. Self-taught in apothecary knowledge, he grew exotic plants from seeds he had collected from his travels around the world, brewing herbal medicines and remedies. As his captivity became increasingly hopeless, more of the stateliness and energy of the man emerged. Many an impressive work has been penned in a dungeon, often destined for immortality, and in 1614 Raleigh began work on his own: *The Historie of the World*, an astonishing ode to his intellectual capacities and, although ultimately uncompleted, most revered.

Despite his love of writing, Raleigh's undoubted highlights were his visits from Bess, proving that her love and loyalty had not dissipated toward her stricken husband. Indeed, in 1605, the couple added to their family, Bess birthing a further son – Carew – in the Tower itself. Bess was not his only visitor, Raleigh becoming quite the attraction. Upon his daily sojourns within the gardens, common folk would congregate to see the man, leering into his confines to glimpse the hitherto fabled character. The king's son, Henry, Prince of Wales no less, paid visits to Raleigh, chastising his father for his actions, claiming that 'only my father would cage such a bird.'

Perhaps his son's words pricked the conscience of the king, for in 1617, he released Raleigh, albeit momentarily, granting him permission to conduct a second expedition in search of the fabled El Dorado and its rumoured gold mine. The fateful voyage would be Raleigh's last. Despite promises to the contrary, a section of Raleigh's men attacked a Spanish outpost on the Orinoco River. These foolhardy actions were in direct contravention to the peace treaties with Spain, and almost certainly against Raleigh's own orders. Raleigh was by this time a frail imitation of the spirited man who had first quested for the bounteous bullion. Worse still, Raleigh's son, Wat, was killed amid the Spanish skirmishing, ensuring that Raleigh's return voyage was a horribly grief-stricken one.

Raleigh returned to England with no gold, and having failed emphatically to avoid conflict with Spain; it was a truly disastrous expedition. The actions were tantamount to an incitement of further warfare with Spain, which enraged King James. Count Gondomar, the Spanish Ambassador, demanded that Raleigh suffer the ultimate punishment, and James had little choice but to initiate Raleigh's fate and invoke the original sentence made back in 1603.

The star at which the world had gazed so inquisitively was mercilessly cast back into the Tower to await his inevitable execution. This time, the imprisonment was short, however. His impending destruction appeared not to concern Raleigh, an unwavering ambition to face death with dignity and without fear empowered him. 'When I come to the sad part, thou shalt see, I will look on it like a man,' he told friend Charles Thynne. He even insisted that the brutalised mode of his approaching death was preferable to 'dying by some fever.' We ought not to forget that Raleigh had witnessed first-hand the final moments of many a subject, his idealised preference coming indeed from a place of macabre knowledge and experience gained throughout his years.

On 29 October 1618, Sir Walter Raleigh was taken to the Old Palace Yard at the Palace of Westminster to face the axeman. With an almost gleeful flippancy, Raleigh had by this time heartily eaten a breakfast and taken some tobacco. Safe in the knowledge that his final public appearance would be a much-anticipated affair, he typically dressed magnificently for it; he wore a satin doublet with embroidered waistcoat and nightcap, and silk stockings, all wrapped gracefully within a black velvet cloak. Even in his final hour, Raleigh's image mattered to him.

As Raleigh expected, the grim pageant had attracted huge crowds. For their part, they would witness the stately murder of an innocent man and with it, the death of the last Elizabethan. Led through the crowds to the scaffold, Raleigh was shaken slightly as he reached the platform. His platform. This was a final opportunity to embrace the masses, flaunt his bravery and valour, and appease and entertain his audience. Once upon it, his usual composure was quickly regained.

He flung aside his hat and nightcap and handed money to the attendants present. In dramatic fashion, he next removed his gown and doublet before asking the headsman to show him the axe which would soon be rained down upon him. Bewildered, the man hesitated.

'I prithee, let me see it. Dost thou think I am afraid of it?' Raleigh ran his finger over the edge of the blade. 'This is a sharp medicine, but it is a physician that will cure all my diseases.'

The executioner pleaded for Raleigh's forgiveness, to which he willingly obliged. He laid his head down on the block. He had refused a blindfold, arranging prior that his readiness for the axe would be indicated when he stretched out his hands.

Raleigh was now ready. He stretched forward once. Then again. Still the headsman hesitated. Whether his apprehension emanated from awestruck affection towards his distinguished victim, or if he believed the execution to be an unjust one, we will never know. It is clear, however, that Raleigh wished to offer some final and encouraging words to his hesitant headsman, encapsulating his brazen bravery: 'What dost thou fear? Strike man, strike!'

And, strike he did. Then again.

Raleigh's severed head was displayed to each side of the scaffold. Those who witnessed Raleigh's execution documented that he behaved with 'outstanding dignity and bravery'. This only enhanced the palpable sense of grief amongst those in attendance; indeed, even the executioner, when holding up Raleigh's cleaved head, could not bring himself to muster the usual words, 'behold the head of a traitor.'

That evening the newly-widowed Bess took her husband's head home in a red leather bag. It was later embalmed and kept in a cupboard to show her husband's many admirers. It is easy to imagine that such a display of eternal love is something that Raleigh would be distinctly happy about.

The Elizabethan epic had ended, finally lifeless – though never forgotten – and this too, is a legacy that would surely thrill the most-famed courtier of his time.

Chapter 16

Liam Whelan

In the south-east corner of the Old Trafford football stadium in Manchester, a clock remains permanently frozen, the date and time etched motionless at 3:04 pm on 6 February 1958. Below this is the solitary word 'Munich'. The time records the moment which left an indelible mark on the history of Manchester United Football Club and indeed the wider sporting world, which would be tragically robbed of one of its most prodigious teams.

The side's unique potential was already in the glittering throes of recognition with two consecutive domestic league titles, which offered a route to participation in the European Cup, a competition open to the winners of Europe's domestic leagues. Competing with the elite from across the continent was, and still remains, the holy grail for professional clubs – a unique barometer demonstrating their abilities on a global scale.

Matt Busby was at the helm, his team a creation crammed with the ebullience of youth, captivating a nation with his bold investment in developing young players, helping to create one of the most exciting teams in English football history.

The 'Busby Babes' as they became affectionately known – though Busby himself never liked this term, preferring 'Golden Apples' instead – were not merely the product of chance and good fortune, however. Matt Busby had laid the foundations years earlier, developing a 'nursery' system to help his young players develop. Nothing was left to chance in the development of his 'apples', to the extent that landladies were interviewed and appointed to ensure that boys who joined the club would have as comfortable a lifestyle as possible whilst in their unfamiliar lodgings.

Busby's nurturing and, indeed, resolute faith in his youngsters was soon spectacularly rewarded. In the 1955-1956 season, his team, featuring players whose average age was just 22, stormed to championship glory. They repeated the feat the following season, and having already had their appetite whetted by a semi-final appearance in the previous season's European Cup, the club and indeed, the country, were excited to see if they could venture one better and reach the final.

Having safely negotiated the early rounds of Europe's foremost competition, Manchester United found themselves in the quarter-finals to face a stern two-legged test against Yugoslavian champions, Red Star Belgrade. The first leg saw United secure a narrow 2-1 victory, before the return fixture in Yugoslavia on 5 February 1958.

A greater acid test of youthful character could not be envisaged for the group of fledglings. Representing their club and country in the raucous Belgrade arena, they played on a pitch littered with clumps of icy snow, a physical testament to the freezing and inhospitable conditions; amidst the passionate bellowing of the partisan crowd ringing in their ears, a pressurised cauldron of intimidation was created.

These youngsters, though, had been moulded not solely into capable technicians of their art, but accompanying this craftsmanship was an undaunted lion-hearted approach that just would not waver.

A hugely entertaining tie warmed the chilled bones of all in attendance. A 3-3 draw ultimately resulted in a 5-4 aggregate victory for the Manchester club, and ensured progression to another European Cup semi-final. The reverence of Busby's 'Golden Apples' was no longer confined to the British Isles. The rest of Europe was now in full recognition – and indeed fear – of the exhilarating capabilities of Busby's budding side.

Following the match, celebrations were relaxed but relatively limited; much work was still to be done if the previous season's exploits would be surpassed. Rounds of poker accompanied by a few drinks was the extent of the post-match frivolity.

The following morning, spirits were high as the players assembled for their return to Manchester. The flight from Belgrade, though, had a scheduled refuelling stop in Munich to contend with before they could return home.

Upon arrival at Belgrade airport, the flight was initially delayed owing to a player, Johnny Berry, misplacing his passport. An immigration officer finally decided to scour the luggage in the plane's hold, discovering the passport in Berry's suitcase. Flight 609 was finally ready for boarding by mid-morning. Outside, the weather was particularly dreary, the murk and gloom obstructing visibility.

The plane was an Elizabethan Class G-ALZU AS 57 Lord Burghley, and at its numerous controls were Captain James Thain and co-pilot Captain Kenneth Rayment. Thain was a man with considerable experience in the air, and from 1941-1946, he had served in the Royal Air Force. In March 1955, he took a conversion course on Elizabethan aircraft, upon which he had completed close to 2,000 flying hours. Rayment, too, had served with the Royal Air Force and had similar levels of experience to Thain, though he could boast more flying hours in an Elizabethan than his captain, with over 3,000. Captain Thain had flown from England to Belgrade, though for the return journey, a decision was made between the pair to allow co-pilot Rayment to act as pilot in charge.

Despite the unfavourable flying conditions, early progress was good, and following a short fuel stop in Munich, expectations were that the plane would arrive back in Manchester by teatime. As the Elizabethan landed in Munich, however, snow was falling at a steady rate. The refuelling process was short, taking less than 20 minutes to transfer in excess of 3,000 litres of aviation fuel, and by two o'clock (pm), the pilots were once more ready for take-off and to complete the journey to Manchester. At 14:31, clearance was given for take-off, only for the attempt to be abandoned following the engines sounding an unbalanced note. This, though, was not a cause for widespread panic or concern. Such sounds were not unusual for Elizabethan aircraft, and Rayment even attempted take-off again at 14:34, but was once more forced to abandon the attempt having encountered the same issue.

The pilots agreed that the best course of action was to taxi the plane back to the airport terminus where further investigations could be carried out. This left some 'down-time' for the players who disembarked and occupied themselves buying presents for their waiting families back in England. The two pilots remained on the flight deck whilst Mr Black, the BEA station engineer, climbed aboard to uncover why the aircraft had returned. Black advised the pilots that the variations in the 'boost pressure' which they were experiencing was connected with the elevation of Munich Airport itself. A short discussion ensued, the men concluding that another attempt at take-off should be made, and as such, the passengers were once again asked to re-board the plane.

The previous failed attempts at take-off had created some restlessness amongst the passengers, but generally they remained in good spirits.

At least one passenger though, Duncan Edwards, had assumed that no further attempts to take-off would be ventured, the young player diligently sending a telegram to his landlady back in Manchester reading: ALL FLIGHTS CANCELLED – STOP – FLYING TOMORROW – STOP – DUNCAN.

Prior to the latest attempt at departure, a further engine run-up was carried out to verify its working order. The maintenance check raised no issues, so without delay the passengers were asked to re-board the plane. Clearly, the previous failed attempts had created some trepidation as a number of passengers opted to move to the rear of the aircraft where they considered it was safer.

The plane was once again soon rumbling down the runway. What transpired to be the plane's final run was witnessed by several people. Those with the best view of this were, of course, the air traffic controllers based in the control tower. It is insightful here to refer to the officer in charge, Kurt Gentzsch, and the statement he offered following the crash:

> It [the aircraft] began rolling normally and built up speed until it was about half-way along the runway; the nose wheel left the ground, but touched down again after about 60-100 metres. The aircraft continued to roll as far as the very end of the runway, then unstuck but gained only a little height. Approximately above the west boundary of the airport it seems as if the aircraft was going into a turn and was not gaining any appreciable height.'

The Lord Burghley careered off the runway, screeching and skidding erratically out of control before crashing through an airport fence and across a road towards a residential area. Its left wing crashed against a house, the impact wrenching off the wing and part of the tail. The cockpit crashed into a tree, with the fuselage smashing into a wooden hut containing a truck filled with fuel, which exploded into a huge fireball.

The statements procured by those fortunate enough to not be aboard the plane offer valuable external testimony, though they cannot transmit the mood and feelings of those on the doomed flight. To understand this, the accounts of the surviving passengers are revealing, yet they indicate a lack of panic contrary to what one may expect in such dire circumstances.

The mood was one perhaps more indicative of apprehension, rather than wholesale panic and terror. The prospect facing the passengers, however, soon moved into abject focus – perhaps best described by survivor Johnny Berry. 'We're all going to get killed here,' he yelled. Yet one man remained the epitome of calm, displaying sangfroid bravery and remarkable restraint as the plane hurtled along the runway towards its destruction. Liam 'Billy' Whelan, just 22 years old, was a devout Catholic hailing from Dublin. In response to Berry's forewarning of doom, Whelan simply replied: 'Well, if this is death – I am ready for it.'

In the face of death, the young man was almost belittling its significance. Unafraid and undaunted, underpinned by his resolute and staunch faith, he was ready. These words would indeed be his last, Whelan being one of eight Manchester United players who were killed. Of the forty-four passengers aboard, twenty died at the scene with a further three eventually succumbing to their injuries in hospital.

The scale of the disaster was huge, amplified in part by the esteemed cargo aboard the plane. The Manchester United team was at this time front-running and was laced with household names. The young men, many at the peak of their powers, often represented the common man's sole entertainment, offering an escape from the monotony of everyday working life. Inquests into the tragedy would inevitably follow for a protracted time – the final report from the Board of Trade would not be published until 1969, eleven years after the crash. The essence of the investigation was to ascertain 'Whether blame for the accident is to be imputed to Captain Thain'. The extensive report rebuked initial findings from a West German airport authority investigation which originally blamed Thain, suggesting that he failed to de-ice the wings of the aircraft. This final report, however, established that the crash was, in fact, caused by the slush on the runway, which essentially slowed the plane to an extent that take-off was not possible. Captain Thain was deemed 'at fault in permitting Captain Rayment to occupy the captain's seat, but this played no part in causing the accident.'

The ultimate conclusion exonerated Captain Thain from any blame attached to the accident, reporting that 'in our opinion blame for the accident is not to be imputed to Captain Thain.'

The events of Munich fostered a warmth and affection for the club, and there was a solidarity through the sadness as football's tribalistic allegiances were cast aside, if only fleetingly. Underlying each tragic death, there was a multitude of separate pain and heartbreak, each one layered with remorse and regret.

Liam Whelan's prodigious talent may have been extinguished in a cruel and premature fashion, but his legacy has continued to evolve in the years since his death. Bobby Charlton, the sole surviving player of the disaster still alive in the twenty-first century, claimed that he knew he could never be the best player at Manchester United – 'not while Liam Whelan was there.' A greater testament to his profession and talent could not be envisaged.

Chapter 17

William Burke

A brief dictionary consultation will uncover one of its pages' darkest and most salacious terms, the one of 'burking': 'To murder as by suffocation, so as to leave no or few marks of violence.' The act derived from the surname of one half of Britain's most infamous, murderous pairings: William Burke and William Hare. The idea that the very *modus operandi* adopted by the duo became named after one of its confederates says much about the ongoing notoriety of one of Scotland's grisliest chapters.

It is, though, with curious irony that William Burke and William Hare have, over time, become a vivid embodiment of the 'body snatcher', yet it is likely that neither man ever actually muddied themselves in the loathsome act of grave robbing; instead they grotesquely opted to create their own corpses through cold-blooded murder. And yet, this macabre pilfering epidemic, which ravaged places of rest for years, lies central to the story which culminated in legend casting two Irishmen as the archetypal body snatchers.

The nineteenth century was a period of pioneering advances in surgery and anatomy. Doctors' understanding as to the causes of disease and deformity were improving, whilst medical techniques were increasing in their sophistication. To aid the continual advancements, the medical profession had always depended upon the dissection of human corpses, so a frequent stream of bodies was required for the surgeons' slabs. Strong religious and social objections throughout eighteenth-century Britain ensured that only the bodies of hanged murderers, suicides or orphans were legitimately delivered for dissection. The Murder Act of 1752 directed that the body of an executed felon be delivered to the 'company of surgeons', where they 'shall be dissected and anatomised by the said surgeons.' This mandate, then, could supply a proportion of bodies to the anatomists, but the demand for the deceased far outstripped the numbers of hangings that were taking place. Furthermore, a hostile by-product of the Murder Act was the fact that there were often fights and brawling by family and friends of the dead, seeking to prevent the delivery of their adored corpse from the scaffold to the surgeons. The Tyburn riot of 1749 was am eminent example of this retaliatory backlash.

Specimens for the anatomists did, with a moribund literality, grow on gallow trees, but this was a limited source which failed to keep apace with the volume of fresh material required, creating an intolerable shortfall for the medical profession in their efforts to uncover further developments in anatomical science. So, a supply to fill this gaping void became a lucrative dealing, giving rise to the creation of the repugnant 'resurrectionists' – essentially body snatchers who operated, quite bizarrely, within the confines of the law as the bodies of the dead were not legally 'owned' by anyone. This deathly grey area of law enabled the trade to flourish across the eighteenth and nineteenth centuries. It needed to as medicine was becoming a fast-developing business; by the 1820s, Edinburgh University alone was educating some 1,000 medical students.

These burgeoning students worked under the tutelage of Dr Alexander Monro, the anatomist and medical educator of Edinburgh's medical school. Charles Darwin, no less, had been a student of Monro, though he was less than complimentary towards his former mentor, claiming that 'Monro made his lectures on human anatomy as dull as he was himself'.

In 1826, the wretched and tiresome professor – his laurels now greatly rested – faced a fresh challenge, greater than any dissection that had gone before him. It came in the guise of a youthful upstart, whose name would forever evoke a quizzical glance as to his complicity in Burke and Hare's crimes: Dr Robert Knox. Within the academia of Edinburgh's Surgeons' Square, he commenced a course of lectures from the Museum of Comparative Anatomy, a position which he had succeeded following the death of Dr Barclay. Knox's anatomy hall became something of a Mecca for medical students throughout Britain, as they swarmed to observe his practical dissection lectures. His charismatic and flamboyant style placed him in direct contrast to the stale schooling offered by Dr Monro, to the extent that Knox's morning classes required an evening duplication to allow for the considerable overspill of interest they generated. Whilst Knox was certainly revered for his eloquence and undoubted skill, his popular prominence was perhaps clinched by the seemingly endless supply of fresh dissection material he had at his disposal – his suppliers were clearly very competent.

And so we arrive at the principal protagonists of the piece. William Burke was born in 1792 in County Tyrone, Ireland. It is an ill-judged yet oft-cited belief that casts the man as a perpetual monster, and whilst this depiction amidst hindsight certainly fits his crimes, Burke is known to have been a man of affable nature, agreeable and an example in amenity. Neither was he work-shy, attempting a succession of trades, none of which suitably captivated him until he enlisted in the Donegal militia in 1809. Of Catholic parentage, he was a man of a naturally religious turn of mind, though not bound up in any particular form of faith. He married a young woman from Ballina and when his regiment was disbanded, he took up residence with his wife and family. It would appear that at this point things unravelled irretrievably; a quarrel between him and his father-in-law concluded in Burke emigrating to Scotland, abandoning his wife and family in the process. He would never again return to his native land.

William Burke arrived in Scotland in 1818. The Union Canal between Edinburgh and the Forth and Clyde Canal was in the course of its construction, whereupon Burke secured employment as a labourer. The completion of the canal was in large part owed to the sweat and toil expended by many an Irish navvy. Indeed, one of Burke's colleagues, though never known to each other during the work, was one William Hare, also of Irish origin and a man of similar age to Burke, though with a vastly different constitution. He was widely considered an illiterate and amoral man, having a rather debauched and quarrelsome nature.

Around this time, Burke, perhaps hankering after female allurement, became involved with a disreputable sort by the name of Helen MacDougal, an alleged 'loose and dissolute woman with a dull and morose temperament'. The unlikely pair soon combined their paltry lots, lodging at various addresses together across Edinburgh, living a fairly unhappy life punctuated by the regular taking of excessive drink, fuelling many a rowdy quarrel.

With the canal completed, Burke reverted to a former trade he had once entertained, that of a cobbler. He would buy old boots and shoes and repair them before MacDougal hawked them among the city's more destitute subjects. It wasn't profitable work, but a lot more wholesome than Burke's final vocation would prove to be.

Of course, if fate had cast a different hand, there may have been a happier outcome, but this is merely conjecture. In the autumn of 1827, whilst working the harvest near Penicuik, William Burke and William Hare were finally acquainted for the first time. From this point onwards, their names would forever be indissolubly entangled in the concern of a wicked depravity that would haunt the annals of Scotland's history for ever more.

William Hare lived in a lodging house in Edinburgh's Tanner's Close with his wife Margaret. Mrs Hare maintained the house while her husband was a hawker on Edinburgh's streets. Hare was a hard-drinking Irishman with an equally hard temper which, when steeped in drink, became perfectly unbearable. In early November 1827, Burke and MacDougal first encountered Margaret Hare and, upon sharing a dram with her, the couple were urged to take an abode in the Hares' rooming-house. Here, Burke would have every facility for continuing his cobbling trade, so he and MacDougal consented, subsequently setting up his business in a cellar attached to the house. The arrangement, though, was hardly one bestowed with creature comforts and agreeable company; both Hare and his wife were as prepared as the other to engage in heavy drinking, followed up by illustrations of raucous and savage brutality.

Despite the rather stormy predilections of the hosts, Tanner's Close did attract tenants. Residing for some time here was an elderly pensioner named 'Donald'. On 29 November, the old man died in the house, probably the last to die naturally within its walls, though he did so in debt to his landlords, owing a sum of £4. The substantial sum was proof enough that the man had lived on credit, surely a kindly arrangement forged through Margaret rather than the unforgiving Hare. Moreover, as if in confirmation of this aspect of character, Hare quickly informed the authorities of the death, thus removing the possibility of him landing an unwanted funeral expense.

Donald, then, was set for a 'parish burial'. The parish representatives delivered the coffin to the lodging house and laid within their departed subject before nailing down the coffin lid. As preparations unfolded for the consignment of the old man's remains to their kindred dust, William

Hare had an epiphany of the sort that should surely never be disclosed for fear of blackening one's character, though this was of little concern to Hare. Furthermore, old Donald's inconvenient death had lumbered Hare with debts he would struggle to contend with, so it was at this point, according to the later confession of Burke, that Hare proposed that rather than bury the veteran, they might instead sell the body to the city surgeons, promising Burke a share of the proceeds as an enticement. After some initial hesitation, Burke agreed to the scheme and the pair were soon chiselling open the coffin lid and removing the lifeless old body, concealing it in his bed. The pair then ran from the house, gathering heaps of bark to act as a crafty substitution for Donald's body. The coffin was then taken and interred in the West Church Yard with all the solemnity afforded by the parish in such affairs.

With the spurious entombment safely completed, the two men set off for Surgeons' Square. Upon reaching Old College, the mysterious-looking pair were spotted by a medical student who, upon quizzing them, was told that they 'had a subject to dispose of.' The young student referred the vendors to No. 10 Surgeons' Square, the premises of Dr Knox. This was further evidence that Knox was the foremost name on the lips of the medical fraternity, and with it, confirmation that the ponderous Dr Monro was a spent force. Burke and Hare soon reached Knox's address where they were confronted by the doctor's three assistants. With a growing sense of ease, Burke once again explained that he had a subject for sale. The assistants did not seek answers as to 'how they obtained it,' but asked Burke and Hare to return with their asset under the cover of darkness, and warned them 'to be upon your guard so that no one sees you.'

And with urgency, this they did. Laden with their cadaverous cargo, they set off in the darkness towards Surgeons' Square. The putrid scene, reminiscent of some outlandish Hammer Horror, takes some comprehending as the pair clumsily heaved a sack containing Donald's body through the streets. It is unlikely at this point that Burke and Hare were particularly perturbed at their actions. The old man had died naturally, but moreover, he had owed Hare money so Hare was entitled to the proceeds of the Donald estate – which now only comprised the dead man himself. So to this end, the natural order was being reinstated and to their minds, this fully legitimised the transaction.

Upon their arrival, Burke and Hare were unsure of delivery arrangements so they merely laid the sack at the door of a cellar, before returning inside to their new acquaintances. They were asked to then place Donald's corpse onto the dissection table. As the men stared at the old man – he being thankfully oblivious to the indignity of them leering over him – Dr Knox entered the room. He examined the body and proposed a price of £7 10 shillings before asking his assistant to 'settle with them.' Burke's account claimed that Hare received the greater sum – £4 5 shillings – and Burke £3 5 shillings. Whatever the truth here, the entrepreneurial duo had both earned profits with comparative ease, and if any doubts lingered as to further such negotiations in future, these were wholly eradicated as, when leaving the building, the words 'we would be glad to see you again when you have any other body to dispose of,' followed them out into the night. Burke and Hare's horrible course of crime had begun in earnest.

The success of this first transaction with the doctors initiated quite a dilemma for the pair. As the old pensioner had shown, 'obtaining the remains of their fellow creatures' was a far easier method of obtaining a comfortable livelihood than their usual mundane lines of work. Though, of course, access to a naturally expiring body is an infrequent thing, but with their minds now firmly engaged in a rotten degrading process, even the realisation that committing the highest felonious act in the land could bring them the valuable commodity did not deter them.

The men were contented with the venue they had to commit such atrocities, and the scene of the enactment for most of the crimes was, of course, Hare's lodging house. A 'Beds to let' ticket invited prospective victims inside, many a squalid wanderer seeking refuge there and suffering the ultimate fate. The house was the arena where these filthy tragedies were committed, and also where the plan was concocted; the two women, MacDougal and Mrs Hare, we can assume, were aware of the acts during the actual happenings, but it is doubtful they contributed to the formation of the plan itself.

The strategy involved unleashing Hare upon the streets, prowling the wynds of the old town for a vulnerable soul to fall in with. Burke's confession of 3 January 1829 reveals that Hare met a much-inebriated woman one afternoon in the Grassmarket. Abigail Simpson was considered a fitting subject, elderly and frail with little remaining strength of mind or body, weakened further by her sodden state. If Hare could get her to the boarding house, surely further profit would soon ensue. In her doted state, she readily entered into conversation with her conniving suitor and was soon accompanying him to the house. Once there, she was introduced to Burke and treated like a long-lost friend. Liquor was relentlessly taken and soon the woman was crooning the musical memories of her youth, with everybody now awash with drink. It was proposed that Mrs Simpson remain the night at the house, to which she happily assented in her obliterated capacity. The opportunity, it seemed, had presented itself, though perhaps through their own intoxication, Burke and Hare's evil intentions were not fulfilled. It is tempting to consider an impassioned doctrinal 'U-turn' as the motive for the mercy shown upon Mrs Simpson that night but, of course, this was fanciful thinking. The following morning, her entertainers became her makers; Hare placed his hand over her mouth and nose to prevent her breathing whilst Burke laid himself across her ailing body to stifle any resistance. In minutes, she was dead and being bundled up into a chest ready for the medical men, and the terminal action of 'burking' had been invented. In his own confession, Burke described the method vividly:

> When they kept the mouth and nose shut a very few minutes, they [the victims] could make no resistance, but would convulse and make a rumbling noise in their bellies for some time; after they ceased crying and making resistance, they [the murderers] left them to die by themselves; but their bodies would often move afterwards, and for some time they would have long breathings before life went away.

The body was conveyed to Surgeons' Square where Knox approved of its freshness but did not ask any questions, instead paying the murderers £10 for the corpse. The work of wholesale murder was now well-established and the conspirators were gaining confidence as well as wealth. Any qualms of conscience were speedily drowned in drink, and even the fear of discovery evaporated when they realised how easily and quietly they could 'work.'

Over the next eleven months, at least sixteen people were murdered at the hands of Burke and Hare, though in these pages we shall deal only with the murders which engaged the judicial process. The crimes are impossible from this point to categorise chronologically, certainly with any accuracy, but needless to say the ugly slaughter of the weak continued. Never was a strong or able man selected on which to practise their fatal skill, only ever the old and the 'silly in body and mind'. On one occasion, the duo stooped further still and committed perhaps their most heinous murder, one which according to Burke haunted him thereafter and thus requires recounting, if only to evidence the diabolical extents to which they were now prepared to explore for monetary gain.

In the midsummer of 1828, Burke befriended an elderly Irishwoman and her grandson. The boy was 'about twelve years of age', and deaf and dumb, a more vulnerable pair Burke could not wish to find. Burke happily led them to the lair, his mind curious no doubt as to the value that two corpses may fetch. As usual, a bottle was produced and the woman was invited to indulge. The drink operated rapidly on her sapped senses, forcing her to lay down on the bed. In her prone state, at some point through the night, she was in the usual fashion brought to a premature and cruel end. Unconscious to the dreadful work occurring in the next room, the poor boy was becoming anxious as to his grandmother's absence and gave such expression 'as his dumbness would permit'. The accomplices now faced the residual quandary of what to do with the boy; imprudent they thought, to take two slain bodies to Surgeons' Square together, yet they concluded, what else could be done with the boy? They toyed with releasing him into the streets of Edinburgh, but as discussions abounded, a more fiendish outcome was decided upon and here the tragedy becomes more horrible.

The following morning, Burke took the boy into the back room where his grandmother lay, and as Burke himself expressed it, 'took him upon his knee, and broke his back.' From the ever-increasing catalogue of barbarous instances in which Burke was becoming embroiled, it is of little wonder that he described this scene as the 'one that lay most heavily upon his heart,' claiming that he was haunted by the 'recollection of the piteous expression of the wistful eyes, as the victim looked in his face.' The final degradation was for the couple to be tossed into an old herring-barrel to await delivery unto Surgeons' Square and fall under the well-worn scalpel of Dr Knox.

Whilst the procession of devilment was progressing with such apparent ease, things were not always running so fluently between Burke and Hare themselves, or indeed their loathsome ladies. The four persons, bound together by this joint commission of horror, were beginning to fall out amongst themselves. It is important to indicate the part played by the two ladies at this point, for though they did not actively kill, they certainly assisted the victims into a state of which they could be easily nullified and dispatched. One of the more vociferous skirmishes between the men – fuelled by Burke's belief that his accomplice was short-changing him – was probably responsible for Burke and MacDougal leaving Hare's lodging house in Tanner's Close and moving to a house owned by John Broggan, whose wife was a cousin of Burke. The house was not far from the previous lodgings, but Burke's room here was the epitome of modesty; a very small place and 'more like a cellar than the dwelling of a human being, the two beds filled with old straw and rugs'. This room would later, in all its bareness, host its very own part in this macabre journey, but first to one of the most infamous of the Burke and Hare victims.

Perhaps none of the murders caused so much communal regret as that of James Wilson, known emphatically throughout the murderous narrative as 'Daft Jamie'. He was one of those 'wandering naturals known to everybody', deficient in intellect but huge at heart and described as a universal favourite. This murder, above all the others, excited the most cutting horror to the public mind. Daft Jamie's name was even among 'the yells into the ears of Burke on the scaffold during his last minutes on earth' – let there be no doubt, Edinburgh was grief-ridden by Jamie's killing. But Burke and Hare's snuffing out of the simpleton is an important facet in the dismal journey of the Irishmen. Whilst it was true that they had developed a most clinical and efficient method of dispatch, they were not above making errors. Daft Jamie held a cult-like status within Edinburgh, so when his lifeless body appeared on Dr Knox's dissection table, many in attendance recognised the poor boy. It is certain that at least one of these men of science identified Jamie, for following news of his disappearance, it was quickly affirmed in the town that one of Knox's students had seen him on the dissection table. The affair was now a matter of great public wonder, a concern that Edinburgh would not allow to merely dissipate into idle rumour, and one that perhaps caused Burke and Hare to begin to fear the dire consequences of their reign of villainy.

If suspicion had been ignited in the aftermath of Daft Jamie's slaying, then the murder of Mary Docherty – the final victim – generated an explosion of such cynicism that would ultimately seal the very different fates which lay in store for the two men.

On the morning of 31 October, an appropriate and devilish date for the intended deeds of this pair, Burke spotted Mrs Docherty in a grocery store and, she being in every way suitable for his wicked purpose, entered into conversation with the old dear. His technique, now refined with such potent panache, soon saw him setting off to his depraved den, his new acquaintance in tow utterly oblivious she was meandering to her imminent death. Mrs Docherty's arrival at the house received a pleasant welcome from mistress MacDougal and an invitation of breakfast prepared by the obliging Burke. With pleasantries exchanged and Mrs Docherty comfortable, Burke then left to find his accessory in crime, whom he located in a local alehouse. Over a gill of whisky, Burke excitedly told his colleague that he had at home 'a good shot to take to the doctors.' The dutiful Hare, never work-shy in this grisly trade, was, of course, happy to participate, the pair quickly ushering off to the freshly-acquired bounty. When they arrived at the house, MacDougal and the intended quarry had busied themselves in tidying the dilapidated room of Burke's in preparation for an evening of revelry, to be then followed by the usual tragedy.

Alas, there was a stumbling block of some severity which needed eradicating before any burking could happen. Lodging in the house with Burke was an old soldier named James Gray and his wife Ann. The Grays had been there merely a week but clearly, they needed removing from the house without creating suspicion. Burke, then, cunningly explained that the old woman was a relation of his mother, and Docherty also being of Irish descent, no doubt confirmed the fable to the minds of the unsuspecting Grays. This being the case, it was considered most uncharitable for Mrs Docherty to be the one to seek accommodation elsewhere. The Grays readily agreed to the suggestion, and Burke, of course, could offer alternative lodgings for the couple, in the guise of Hare's lodging house. As evening approached, the unwelcome couple left for their new abode, inadvertently freeing up the henchmen to perform their monstrous work at their own pleasure.

The night was one of great junketing, with drink being taken rapidly, Burke indulging his musical tastes with renditions of his favourite songs, and dancing was happily engaged in, quite the paradox of a precursor to the forthcoming main event.

Between ten and eleven o'clock, the neighbours heard a great disturbance from Burke's riotous dwelling and, to satisfy their curiosity, some were tempted to peer through the keyhole. Helen MacDougal was seen pouring whisky down the throat of the old woman, forcefully lubricating the victim into utter incomprehension. With the ultimate aim in mind, this certainly worked; Mrs Docherty was now beyond tipsy, her senses greatly weakened. Hare took swift advantage of this, striking the woman to the floor. Falling heavily and under the burden of drink, she was unable to rise to her feet. MacDougal and Mrs Hare, who had been sharing in the merriment only minutes earlier, made their convenient exit, allowing their brutal beaus to begin their crude work on the helpless woman.

The usual method was adopted, this time at Burke's hands, and very soon another body was ready for Knox. Burke undressed the corpse and laid it among some straw beside the bed. MacDougal and Mrs Hare had both returned to the house, aware that the act would have already been performed and another subject primed for the surgeons. The four connivers resumed their debauchery, spending a riotous night together for the last time. As the clock passed into the next morning, the group finally lay down to rest, the body of the murdered woman beside them, a grim reminder of the work that had afforded such carousing evenings during their profitable 'employment'.

As dawn broke on Saturday, 1 November, the assemblage awoke, pained from the excesses enjoyed only hours earlier. Very soon though, they would have a far more pressing matter to contend with. At around nine o'clock, Burke visited Hare's house, hospitably checking in on his lodgers, who had been unceremoniously omitted from his residence the previous evening. He invited the Grays back to his own home for breakfast and, with no prospect of such a thing in their temporary lodgings, they happily agreed. This invitation belies an absolute impulse of self-destruction on Burke's part. In full knowledge that the body of Mrs Docherty lay in that small lodging where he resided, there was an almighty risk of discovery. Perhaps he longed to be uncovered, the burden of his actions overcoming him, or his decisions may have been simply induced by the amount of alcohol he had drunk, providing him with a more *laissez-faire* outlook than he may otherwise have entertained. Whatever the reasoning, when Mr and Mrs Gray entered Burke's house, they could not see the old woman for whom they had been shifted, prompting Mrs Gray to curiously ask where the 'little old woman' had gone.

MacDougal's reply intimated that through drunken impropriety, she had been 'put out' of the soiree. Having seen the woman evidently worse for wear themselves, the Grays presumably believed the story, initially at least.

Burke now began to behave with some agitation; perhaps the gentle sobering of his mind was beginning to bring to light the perilous position he and his comrades found themselves in. The latest offering for the surgeons did, after all, lie boldly in the corner of the room, only scantily hidden by a few lengths of straw. Burke aroused further suspicion when Mrs Gray found reason to search the room when looking for a sack of potatoes. Burke became disproportionately concerned at her scouring of the room and demanded that she stay clear of it. These circumstances created a suspicion in Mrs Gray's mind, and she waited patiently for an opportunity to clarify them.

When the moment came, she did not delay. Both Burke and Hare had since left the house, so Mrs Gray saw good her opportunity. The straw in the corner had appeared a great object of attention so she went directly to it. Carefully lifting the straw, the first thing she caught hold of was of infinitely different texture to dried straw – she was clasping the cold arm of a dead woman. Mr Gray rushed across, immediately recognising the body as the woman Burke had led there the day prior. The horrified couple hastily threw the straw back over the corpse and sought a hurried exit from the place. Upon leaving, Mr Gray met MacDougal on the stairs. Quizzing her as to what they had just found in the room, MacDougal dropped to her knees pleading that he remain quiet to what he had seen, even offering him money for his silence. She managed to persuade the Grays to share a drink with her at a local public house, whereupon she hoped she might convince them that Docherty's death had no sinister attachment. She plied the couple with a concoction of arguments that sought to relieve any wrongdoing, even apportioning blame to Mrs Docherty herself, claiming that an alcohol overdose had been responsible for her death.

Try as her deceitful tongue might, MacDougal's protestations did not impress her audience, Mr Gray asserting that his conscience would not allow him to remain silent. MacDougal, now bristling with anxiety and panic, hurriedly left the bar. The Grays were obdurate and firmly intent on informing the authorities of what they had found. In the meantime, Burke and Hare were busily making arrangements for the removal of the body to Dr Knox. It is unlikely that either man was at this point aware of the earlier discovery by the Grays and their subsequent disclosure threat; certainly, the pair performed their usual routines in preparing the body for the dissection table, and did not appear fearful of impending discovery.

Burke had enlisted a street porter, John McCulloch, to call at the house for a box and have it taken to Surgeons' Square. The box's contents we know, with the now-dreadful familiarity, contained the wrapped body of old Mrs Docherty. Bundled and trussed into an innocuous box, her final journey was not one towards a gentle laying to eternal rest, rather a discourteous dumping in a dank cellar at Surgeons' Square.

Mr Gray was as good as his threat and did indeed visit the police office to relay what he had seen at Burke's address. Sergeant-Major John Fisher and a Constable Finlay accompanied Mr Gray to Burke's house. He pressed both Burke and MacDougal as to what had become of their lodger. The pair offered conflicting accounts, so the sergeant thought it prudent to apprehend both and remove them with immediacy to the police office. Later in the evening, the officer and his superintendent were accompanied by Dr Black, the police surgeon, to visit Burke's den, intent on searching it thoroughly. They found the straw under the bed soaked with blood and a striped bed-gown apparently belonging to the slain woman. A case was forming around the possibility of some grotesque undertaking, and following interviews with the accused, Dr Knox's implication became apparent. On the morning of 2 November, Fisher visited Surgeons' Square and Knox's premises in the hope of finding further evidence. He would not be disappointed. Stumbling through the dampened and dimly-lit cellar, he found the box containing the body of a woman. Mr Gray was sent for to oblige in a rather haphazard identification of the body, yet this he did, immediately recognising the corpse as old Mrs Docherty whom he had seen in Burke's house.

Hare and his wife were still in bed when the authorities arrived to detain them. Mrs Hare displayed tentative amusement at the arrest, doubtless aiming to exude an air contrary to their predicament, though this did not save them from apprehension. The pair were taken to the police office and lodged in separate cells. The four were now all committed to custody, the end now near and hurtling towards a dreadful crescendo.

The news of the tragedy prevailed quickly; the *Edinburgh Evening Courant* of Monday, 3 November headlined with an 'Extraordinary Occurrence', which, whilst in essence, reported accuracies in the Docherty case, it merely whetted a public craving for more, culminating in a flurry of incredible rumours and speculation regarding further grim discoveries made by the police. Meanwhile, the authorities busied themselves with their inquiries. In the first instance, a cause of death was required – particularly in light of the ludicrous suggestions MacDougal had offered for Mrs Docherty's demise – so they had Docherty's body examined by several doctors, thankfully prior to any dabbling from our foremost Dr Knox. The results proved beyond any doubt that she had suffered a violent death by suffocation, the revelation important in both discrediting MacDougal and strengthening the Crown's case.

On 3 November, Burke and MacDougal both gave declarations before Sheriff George Tait. Burke's first account – he ultimately provided two contrasting versions – was riddled with improbability and inconsistencies. It is certainly the work of an able storyteller, claiming that an unknown man dressed in a greatcoat 'the cape of which was turned up about his face,' visited him at his dwelling asking him to repair some shoes. As he reverted back to his once principal trade, the man apparently wandered the room remarking on its quiet position which would make it perfect to store a box for a short time. Burke consented to accommodating the box which the man then left to retrieve later and placed it on the floor near the foot of the bed. Burke received a sixpence for his cobbling and the stranger left. Burke immediately went to investigate the contents of the mysterious box, but finding it empty, he looked among the straw beneath the bed where he saw a corpse, though he was unsure of its gender. The man then called again at the house later on, where Burke remonstrated with him for 'bringing such an article into his house.' The stranger promised to remove the body in a short while, but did not do so until the following evening. The document in its entirety does include some plausible points and, bizarrely, even his version of the body's arrival was not completely incompatible with an age where a man could earn money by taking in a resurrectionist delivery.

Regardless of offering Burke's story any benefit of doubt, his telling of it was somewhat blundering and, ultimately, condemning. As his statement progresses, Burke is enlightened by the sudden acquisition of identity regarding the strange man who delivered the body, claiming him to be none other than William Hare. Burke proposes that Hare returned with a street porter to transport the body to 'any person in Surgeons' Square who would take it.'

Burke was re-examined privately before Sheriff Tait once again on 10 November, a week following his initial declaration. He declared his first statement to be incorrect in several aspects. His amended version stated that he had not caused Mrs Docherty's death and offered his opinion that she had been suffocated by laying herself down in the straw in a state of intoxication. He alleged that he and Hare had found her among the straw, her face turned up with 'something of the nature of vomit' oozing from her mouth. He went on: 'No violence was done to the woman when she was in life, but a good deal of force was necessary to get the body into the chest, as it was stiff; and in particular they had to bend the head forward, and to one side, which may have hurt the neck a little.'

The declarations made by Burke and MacDougal were contradictory in themselves, and directly opposed to the inventions made a week previously. Despite the seemingly hopeless position in which William Burke now found himself, Sir William Rae, the Lord Advocate, still faced a difficulty. The evidence of the Grays was, of course, useful but was entirely circumstantial and might fail to convict. Murder had been committed and so far as the police were concerned, at least one of the four were guilty of such. The wily and ever-cunning Hare, though, understanding how the land lay, responded in a manner which would have resounding implications in the distribution of justice.

The Lord Advocate was loathe to fail to secure a conviction in the case, not least in part because of the swell of Edinburgh discontent as the public rage grew by the day. The authorities worked tirelessly on the case for a month before concluding that any hope of securing a successful conviction lay in persuading Hare to turn King's evidence. This would involve Hare admitting his part in the murders and testifying as a witness for the Crown against the very accomplice he had shared ill-gotten riches with. In exchange for this, Hare demanded that he and his wife would both be afforded immunity from prosecution. This offered a release from the difficulty faced by the Lord Advocate who gladly accepted the terms; a single conviction was preferable to a wholesale evasion of justice.

On 8 December 1828, a citation was served on William Burke and Helen MacDougal 'charging them to appear before the High Court of Justiciary, held at Edinburgh on Wednesday 24 December, at 10 am to underlie the law for the crime of murder.' With the day of the trial drawing near, the public excitement grew in its intensity. The feeling against the culprits was stern, perhaps more so with the realisation that Hare and his wife were to be accepted as informers which was received with predictable displeasure. The trial and its possible outcomes were all the talk, its impending revelations keenly anticipated.

In the early hours of Christmas Eve 1828, Burke and MacDougal were conveyed from the Carlton Hill gaol and placed in the cells below the High Court in Parliament Square in preparation for the hearing of the case. The square would play host to this electrifying drama, attracting the elite of the Scottish Bar and Edinburgh's city dwellers, all early afoot to gain admittance to the court room. Indeed, the following day, the *Edinburgh Evening Courant* reported that 'no trial that has taken place for a number of years past has excited such an unusual and intense interest; all the doors and passages to the court were accordingly besieged at an early hour, even before daylight.' At nine o'clock, the court room was bursting at its ceremonial seams, filled with members of the faculty and, of course, the expectant jury, all filing to their seats above the heads of the detestable duo who apprehensively awaited their fate.

Shortly before ten o'clock, the pair were brought up and placed in the dock, with onlookers' necks straining every sinew to glimpse the perceived epitomes of evil. The short and stout figure of Burke was dressed in a shabby blue surtout coat. It was noted that nothing in his physiognomy pertained to a particular predisposition to act with harshness or cruelty, components that certainly made up the crimes he was being tried for. This thinking was a popular one at this time, the belief that criminals could be identified by physical defects which confirmed their savagery. It was thought, for example, that habitual murderers could be identified by their 'bloodshot eyes and big noses', both traits, then, that Burke would be sure to possess. The audience, having eagerly scanned the prisoners, was no doubt surprised by the lack of such indicative features, though this did not stop the glaring eyes training upon them, watching their every movement as though they remained a pertinent threat.

The clock had moved just beyond ten o'clock when the judges ascended the bench and the lordships took their seats. The Crown was represented principally by Sir William Rae, Lord Advocate; while the counsel for William Burke comprised the Dean of Faculty, and Messrs Patrick Robertson, Duncan McNeil and David Milne. For Helen MacDougal, Messrs Henry Cockburn, Mark Napier, Hugh Bruce and George Paton were sided with the female prisoner, who appeared 'more disturbed' than her more composed counterpart. The above roll-call of distinction amalgamated the best men of the Scottish Bar, brought together in this single melting pot of sensationalism.

The Lord Justice Clerk David Boyle as presiding judge then demanded the prisoners paid full attention to the lengthy indictment which was read against them. The indictment caused immediate unsettlement for it bracketed Helen MacDougal with Burke allied to the murders he had committed. Prejudice, therefore, was bound to assert itself, yet no evidence was given in court which supported the charge against her. Burke was charged with 'only' three murders: Mary Paterson, Daft Jamie and finally, Mary Docherty. Of course, the authorities suspected with great certainty that the murder toll far exceeded three, but evidence had been difficult to amass, particularly in virtue of a lack of physical bodies. In respect of justice as a vengeance platform, though, the outcome for the pair if found guilty would amount to the same swinging finale, regardless of figures.

Mindful of the disparities of the indictment, amendments were thus made to the effect that 'the charges be separately proceeded with,' the

Lord Advocate entitled to select which charge was to be first brought to trial. Thereupon he stated his intention to proceed with the third charge in the indictment, the murder of Mary Docherty. Both prisoners were then summoned to plead to the amended indictment, where they both offered the plea of 'not guilty'. With preliminary objections now surpassed, the trial could begin.

A 'cast' list of some depth was attached to the trial of Burke and MacDougal. Fifty-five persons were instructed as witnesses, though not all were used. Perhaps the one whose evidence demanded the most anticipation was that of William Hare, the other half of the murderous pair. As he was brought forward, Hare's appearance brought about quite a sensation. This was an altogether peculiar situation as the evidence provided by both Hare and his wife formed the basis of the Crown's case; 'expectation stood on tiptoe' to hear the account he would portray in which he himself was a prominent actor. His position as an informer required some clarity here, and he was reassuringly cautioned 'that whatever share you may have had in the transaction, if you now speak the truth, you can never afterwards be questioned in a court of justice.' Should he prevaricate, however, then the result shall be the appropriate punishment.

Hare was then put on oath and questioned regarding the death of old Mrs Docherty. Responding to the Lord Advocate, Hare's account of the murder itself is worthy of reproduction, providing an incredible first-hand account of 'burking' in action:

He [Burke] stood on the floor; – he then got stride-legs on top of the woman on the floor, and she cried out a little, and he kept her in breath.

Did he lay himself upon her? Yes; he pressed down her head with his breast.

She gave a kind of cry, did she? Yes.

Did she give that more than once? She moaned a little after the first cry.

How did he apply his hand towards her? He put one hand under the nose, and the other under her chin, under her mouth.

He stopped her breath, do you mean? Yes.

Did he continue this for any length of time? I could not exactly say the time; ten or fifteen minutes.

Did he say anything when this was going on? No, he said nothing.

Did he then come off her? Yes; he got up off her.

Did she appear dead then? Yes; she appeared dead *a wee*.

Did she appear to be quite dead? She was not moving; I could not say whether she was dead or not.

What did he do then? He put his hand across her mouth.

Did he keep it there for any length of time? He kept it two or three minutes.

What were you doing all this time? I was sitting on the chair.

What did he do with the body? He stripped off the clothes. He took it and threw it at the foot of the bed, doubled her up, and threw a sheet over her; he tied her head to her feet.

Hare's evidence caused considerable agitation in court. His offering of a grisly glance into a world unfrequented by most perhaps satisfied the minds of the curious, yet the appearance of his wife was to cause similar levels of excitement. Ushered into the witness box, Mrs Hare held her infant child in her arms, the image adding further tragedy to the scarcely believable situation. Another remarkable aspect of her testimony was that it corroborated with her husband's almost entirely. There can be little doubt they had rehearsed the story prior to their apprehension, suggesting a knowing awareness to their plight.

Following the Hares' evidence, it was then the turn of the police surgeon, who would announce conclusively that Mrs Docherty had died following suffocation or strangulation, and certainly not through intoxication. The prisoners' declarations concluded the prosecution case, whilst no evidence was offered for the defence. Upon the reading of the declarations, the Lord Advocate immediately commenced his address to the fifteen-man jury. The public feeling and horror which had infiltrated Edinburgh was vividly reflected in his opening remarks:

This is one of the most extraordinary and novel subjects of trial that has ever been brought before this or any other court, and has created in the public mind the greatest anxiety and alarm. I am not surprised at this excitement, because the offences charged are of so atrocious a description, that human nature shudders and revolts at it.

Having reviewed the masses of evidence in the case, the Lord Advocate raised the question of admissibility and, of course, reliability of Hare's testimony. He acknowledged that a case against the accused would simply have been impossible to substantiate without the assistance of Hare. The testimony he had provided, his Lordship contended, was thoroughly credible, particularly as it corroborated with other independent evidence.

The trial had now passed into Christmas Day, nothing, however – festivities or otherwise – could derail the intrigue that the case had triggered. The Lord Justice Clerk began to sum up, meticulously poring over the evidence to the jury, who would now be called upon to leave their own enduring mark on proceedings. It was now half past eight on Christmas morning, the trial having begun at ten o'clock the previous morning. The jury retired for consideration of their verdict, the absence lasting 50 minutes – an eternity by the rapid standards of the time. The men of the jury returned to the court, the audience mute and expectant. The foreman, Mr John McFie, offered the verdict: 'The jury find the pannel, William Burke, guilty of the third charge in the indictment; and find the indictment not proven against the pannel, Helen MacDougal.' There was to be no Christmas miracle for William Burke. The news was swiftly conveyed to the enormous crowd outside in Parliament Square, which was met with rapturous cheers.

The law of Scotland, as declared, ensured that 'the man guilty of deliberate and premeditated murder shall suffer death.' The sentence was proposed thus: 'The prisoner be detained in the tollbooth of Edinburgh, till the 28th day of January next, when he shall suffer death on a gibbet by the hands of the common executioner, and his body thereafter given for dissection.' This final recommendation that his body endure the very fate of his victims is, of course, infused with a grim irony, sure to provoke mirth and good humour among the mob. As they dispersed from Parliament Square to enjoy the merriest of Christmases, William Burke could do nothing other than prepare most suitably for his appearance before 'the throne of almighty God'. Indeed, his preparations for death were extensive, meeting with priests of various denominations and praying to God to whom he had long been a stranger.

Burke appeared to regard his approaching doom with composure. He allegedly declared that should he be offered a pardon, he would even refuse it. Though never likely, the very thought would chill the bones of the public, who still harboured a great sense of injustice that Hare and the ladies had evaded punishment. One from four was not ideal, but nevertheless they looked forward to Wednesday, 28 January 1829 with ghastly satisfaction. The preparations at the Lawnmarket execution site were vast, even attracting crowds that pleasured in witnessing the erection of the scaffold, cheering approvingly as the structure took its foreboding shape. The pelting rain did not deter those anxious to see Burke pay for his crimes as they began to take up their places from 'about two o'clock in the morning'. By seven o'clock the immediate area of the scaffold was fully occupied by one of the densest crowds witnessed in Edinburgh, with around 25,000 estimated to be present. Windows offering even a partial view of the site had been bought up days in advance, an entrepreneurial endeavour that perhaps even Burke himself would be proud of.

The condemned man commenced in his final religious exercises before being met by executioner Thomas Williams, who set about pinioning him. Burke, realising his time had now come, expressed his gratitude to the magistrates and prison officials who had administered kindness beyond his deserving during his incarceration. The solemn procession from the jail to the scaffold then began. Supported on either side, he walked up Liberton's Wynd towards the Lawnmarket. Whenever the procession came into view, an almighty and simultaneous shout from the cacophony of voices went up as though rehearsed. Burke was naturally affected by this impassioned display of hatred towards him; had the mob trampled the barriers which herded them so tightly, he would doubtless be torn to pieces. Sensibly then, he hastily ascended the scaffold. His show of fear did not abate any of the crowd's vitriol; his appearance there ramped up the tensions further. 'Burke him, choke him!' yelled the crowd. Reverend Marshall offered short prayers with Burke kneeling at his feet, which only ignited greater animation; in this position, Burke became obscured from view, and this was one execution that could not be missed. The desire to see Burke hang was total, but the other players had not been forgotten.

'Hare, Hare, bring out Hare! Hang Knox too!' they pleaded. But on this day, Burke had to suffice and now was his time.

Williams prepared his man, amid shouts of, 'You'll see Daft Jamie in a minute!', a sobering reminder of his next destination. With the noose around Burke's neck, Williams hesitated. He struggled to loosen Burke's neckerchief, as it seemed the knot was in the wrong place; positioning at the side of the head would result in a clean break of the neck.

'The knot's behind,' uttered Burke instructively; no final words of redemption or solace, merely advice upon administering death – yet who better to advise upon this than the greatest murderer of his time?

The guidance, though, was unwanted – perhaps the executioner had wanted to ensure a lingering and painful death, such was the enormity of Burke's crimes. If this was the case, he succeeded. A witness later claimed that Burke 'struggled a good deal, and put out his legs as if to catch something with his feet; but some of the undertaker's men, who were beneath the drop, took him by the feet, and sent him spinning round – a motion which was continued until he was drawn up above the level of the scaffold.'

The body was cut down, and the man once so active a participant in supplying so many subjects for dissection, now became one himself, but of more than 'ordinary interest' than any before him. On 1 February, his body was publicly dissected by Professor Monro. The infamy of Monro's 'subject' ensured he, rather than the disgraced Knox, finally had a crammed lecture theatre. During the two-hour procedure, Monro dipped his quill pen into Burke's blood and wrote 'This is written with the blood of William Burke, who was hanged at Edinburgh. This blood was taken from his head.' Burke's skeleton was received by the Anatomical Museum of the Edinburgh Medical School, where it remains today, his legacy, it seems, not confined solely to the dictionary.

Chapter 18

William Wilkinson, James Yarwood and William Burgess

As statute has evolved throughout the centuries, the list of crimes punishable by death has also inevitably encompassed much transformation, and a seemingly eternal debate concerning the merits and flaws of capital punishment rages on. Alas, this is not a debate for these pages, but for three men in Georgian Chester, they would feel the full force of punishment available to the authorities, with each man facing his death with a varying disposition.

The three men – William Wilkinson, James Yarwood and William Burgess – were colleagues, each working as a 'flatman', largely on the River Mersey. The men, all from Northwich and with young families, became figures of much contempt – even dubbed 'human wolves' by the local press – not least for their raping of a young woman in Runcorn, but also in their maintaining a perfect indifference through to their very last moments on Earth.

The following account is the one provided by the victim of the assault. On 15 January 1813, a local 22-year-old spinster, Mary Porter, was violently and feloniously assaulted, a horrible prelude to then being 'carnally ravished'. Mary lived with her parents in St Helen's in Lancashire; her father, John Porter, worked as a weaver but was suffering a lack of employment and as such, was unable to offer his daughter a position with himself. With the New Year of 1813 recently heralded in, Mary was keen to secure some work and ensure she began the year well.

She set out to visit a relative in Chester in the hope of gaining employment as a domestic servant, but her admirable intentions would engender consequences which would prove seismic. Her attempts to find work were rebuffed several times before she conceded defeat. Mary cut a sombre figure of dejection as she left Chester to return home. Having reached the town of Frodsham, she was now 15 miles from home and tired, cold and lonely. She was approached by a stranger who, concerned, advised her that her fastest route home would be by a Runcorn ferry, and that she needed to head to Weston Point to catch such a vessel.

At Weston Point, Mary knocked at the door of a small hut, seeking guidance for departure times and advice of where she would need to board the boat. Here she met William Wilkinson, a 32-year-old man with a stout and broad build, standing close to 6 feet tall. Wilkinson pointed out two of his colleagues off in the distance, whom he claimed would be better placed to help her. One of the men, William Burgess, asked Mary where she was intending to go. Mary politely stated that she had hoped to reach St Helen's that same day. However, Burgess informed her that as it was 'not high water till eight at night, and eight in the morning, the journey would not be possible' and she would therefore have to stay the night until it was safe to cross the following morning. Mary was not entirely convinced of Burgess's 'advice', until he swore he was 'telling God's truth', which was apparently sufficient to convince Mary.

The newly-acquainted pair soon passed a public house, and with the jolly encouragement from Burgess ringing in her ears, Mary somewhat reluctantly entered. An apparent gentleman, Burgess ordered Mary rum and water and a glass of ale for himself. Wilkinson and Yarwood soon also entered the inn, and the group of four chatted and sang, making merry until ten o'clock in the evening, the naive girl casting off her inhibitions. She had, by this point, given over all thoughts of crossing, thinking it dangerous at such an hour, so she queried with Burgess if there might be anywhere she could seek lodgings for the night before continuing her journey the following morning. At this point Wilkinson interjected, and keen to assert his dominance and advertise his lofty 'status', offered the use of his 'flat' – as he was its captain, with Burgess and Yarwood merely its 'haulers'. Wilkinson promised supper and breakfast – free of expense – and that her place in the flat cabin would be hers alone. He also professed rather unorthodoxly 'that no one should molest her' – quite the sales pitch indeed.

After much deliberation, Mary finally consented; the men, after all, had appeared pleasant enough and apparently 'talked of nothing indecent nor offensive'. They left the inn, Wilkinson with Yarwood, before Mary, still escorted by Burgess, followed them into the moonlit night. Having walked a bad and rickety road near the shore for 'three or four fields', Burgess was still walking by Mary's side, though she knew not where the other two men had gone. Upon reaching a stile and without warning, Burgess sat himself down and attempted to pull Mary onto him. She resisted resolutely and managed to escape him, but in her panic she ran straight into Wilkinson and Yarwood, who were unscrupulously hiding in wait amongst the flora. Yarwood grabbed the startled girl, refusing to let her pass and restraining her forcefully.

Exactly what the three men subjected Mary Porter to never reached the public eye. The facts were apparently too distressing which, when considering nineteenth-century 'censoring' approaches, we must assume that she was the victim of a truly heinous attack. Indeed, the details of the violation were later described as being of the 'most disgusting and horrid nature, and hoped that [its like] never will again, disgrace a Court of Justice'. She cried out hopelessly for mercy, but her tears were to no avail as the three men unremittingly exhibited their animalistic aggressions on the wretched girl.

When the attack finally ceased, Mary, in fear of being murdered by Wilkinson and Yarwood – the latter having shown particular brutality – agreed to leave the scene with Burgess. The pair reached the town of Runcorn, it now being late into the night with Mary in a horrific state of distress. Burgess had promised to take her to the first light they saw in a cellar window. He knocked to ask for lodgings but when the door opened, the stricken girl bolted immediately downstairs begging for protection, clearly a most 'poor and distressed creature', with Burgess scurrying from the scene. The cellar owner, a Mr Samuel Bennett, was unable to accommodate Mary, but moved by her impassioned state, ensured her lodgings by securing her a bed at a nearby lodging house owned by Mary Gibson.

The following morning, Mary finally returned home to St Helen's. For fear of hurting her parents and the tarnishing it may cause to her own character, she initially kept her ordeal a secret from her parents. However, as a 'great deal of resistance took place' and Mary had been 'very much hurt', it was clear that she had befallen a horrible episode and it was not something she would be able to keep from them. Having heard his daughter narrate her experiences, her father was, of course, horrified. He immediately sent to Runcorn for confirmation that a prosecution may be forthcoming. When the affirmative response was received, he hastily sought out a justice to begin proceedings against the alleged felons.

The three men appeared at the Spring Assizes at Chester on 21 April 1813. The indictment against the men claimed that they had been 'moved and seduced by the instigation of the Devil' throughout their assault of Mary Porter. The trial, before the Honourable Robert Dallas and Francis Burton Esq., excited considerable public interest. The jury were forewarned that the lives of the three men should not be sacrificed on the sole testimony of Mary Porter, but they must attend to *all* of the evidence heard.

The evidence provided by the injured party herself appeared to generate huge swathes of sympathetic feeling from all in the court room; the jury, too, was visibly moved by her three-hour cross-examination. Conducting herself with the greatest propriety, it was reported that her situation attracted as much sympathy from a crowded court as had ever been recollected. In comparison, the defence of the callous trio was limited at best. Yarwood implied a willingness upon Mary's part, to which she refuted but also asserted that, 'I have not always been free from man; I have had sweethearts, but there was no willingness on my part, I was fearful of my life'.

Mary's version of events was corroborated by many witnesses, most of whom confirmed the amiable nature of the young lady. The three men at the bar appeared resigned to their fates – Wilkinson was completely vacant with nothing to say in his defence. Judge Dallas recapitulated the evidence with customary particularity before demonstrating his belief and trust in the jury: 'I shall leave the case entirely to your decision – you have heard the evidence against the prisoners and the defence they themselves have made – and I have no doubt your verdict will be in this case, as it has been in others, perfectly satisfactory to the Court.'

Following a five-minute consultation period, the jury returned a guilty verdict but although recommending the prisoners to mercy, Judge Dallas quashed any hopes that the hangman would not be necessary, declaring that he was fearful that mercy could not be passed in this case. Reprisals culminating in public unrest worried the judge – the appropriate punishment for the awful crime had to be passed, the affable nature of the victim having effected so great a public sympathy that anything less than the ultimate penalty was inconceivable. The death warrants for all three men were then issued.

The date that the triple hanging would be performed was 26 June 1813. The behaviour of the prisoners in gaol in the interim period was reportedly 'highly reprehensible and indecent', much, it appeared, like it had been on the evening on 15 January, which had ultimately brought the men to this unenviable point.

The day prior to their executions, the men were afforded the customary sermon preached by the ordinary (the chaplain) of the gaol, which appeared to have a great impact on Burgess and Yarwood, the latter suffused in a state of tears for most of the service. Wilkinson, however, remained characteristically resolute throughout, completely unmoved by his situation and behaving with a great obduracy. Following the sermon, Yarwood addressed the auditory amid convulsive sobbing: 'Now my dear brothers and sisters, I hope you will all take warning from us'. Burgess was much affected by his accomplice's words and was induced to lean heavily against a pillar just to remain upright. The men were then shown to their respective cells where their last night on Earth lay ahead of them.

Shortly after midday on Saturday, 26 June, officers of the city arrived to perform their stately duties. The three men were led to the site of execution, where their final exchanges – in contrast to the previous evening – would somewhat remarkably be fuelled with bravado and jocularity. Upon surveying the vast assemblage whilst being led to the gallows, Wilkinson spotted several former work colleagues present, all sympathising with the men's fate. Wilkinson, though, apparently unperturbed, yelled buoyantly to them: 'Never mind my lads! Keep up your spirits – we are all of us murdered men! But never heed, I'm just as happy as if I were going to a play!'

Burgess's primary concern was not that of the noose which would soon strangle his youthful life away, but more of who would carry his body afterwards; with a practical clarity of mind, he quickly assigned an acquaintance for the role mere moments before death: 'Jem, I've told 'em to put you down as one of my bearers – mind, don't you forget!'

Even with death so uncomfortably forthcoming, spirits appeared unduly affected. The men each complained of their treatment, and of fate conspiring against them. The public mass which witnessed this ugly show of defiance was doubtless appalled at such behaviour. A refusal to admit guilt was viewed with abject horror in an age when the consensus of opinion was that a person about to go to God should display the grace to admit guilt and beg forgiveness. To counter this protocol with absolute commitment was Wilkinson, who, almost boyishly, bounded up the scaffold steps 'grinning horribly, a ghastly smile'. Whilst the executioner adjusted Wilkinson's halter, he called out for a final time: 'The Lord of heaven be with you – I'm brought here like a bullock to the slaughter through false swearing by a bad man and a bad woman – I'm here like a bullock at a stake to be skewered; but I don't care. I'm just as happy as if I was going to a play! My new handkerchief [alluding to his neck halter] fits me nice and tight!'

The inevitability of Burgess's end had perhaps registered within. Mounting the scaffold far more respectfully than his animated predecessor, his demeanour more reflected the doom which lay only moments away. To an acquaintance, Burgess appealed: 'Give my love to my dear wife and children, and tell them I sent it with my last breath.'

This was perhaps a more typical display of the condemned and their final expressions on Earth, an earnest farewell and reaffirming of where their love was centred.

Yarwood, though grinning broadly as he ascended the steps, felt pronounced to offer stern words of caution: 'Take warning by me, and never have to do with bad women, for they'll bring you to an end like mine – our lives are sworn away by a bad man and woman. The Lord have mercy on us.'

A black cap was then placed over the face of each man, Yarwood suddenly displaying much agitation, his legs faltering and his strength apparently deserting him. The acute trepidation which had swept onto the scaffold was evidenced clearly by William Burgess, the last of the men to speak a word. The fatal signal was offered and amidst the hollering of the hordes, Burgess managed to stammer out, 'My dear lads – we're going.'

And gone they had, Burgess and Wilkinson with merciful speed. However, Yarwood not so, enduring a gruelling four-minute struggle before finally expiring. As the trio hung lifelessly and the crowds dispersed, so concluded the lives of these three miserable men. Despite departing this life, the *Chester Chronicle* continued to encapsulate the public feeling aimed towards the men. Lambasting the criminals for refusing to make a full and open confession, they could, therefore, not 'make atonement to the world', nor could they achieve a 'contrite heart'.

Each of the men suffered the same ultimate fate, yet faced it with contrasting approaches expressed in their parting words. Whether Wilkinson was as carefree as he purported to be, we can never know. A display of such 'gallows humour' is, of course, where the roots of this popular phrase are embedded, and for all those who witnessed the astonishing spectacle, so too surely were the words delivered by the three wretched men upon their premature demise.

Chapter 19

Priscilla Guppy

The recumbent figure on the sickbed devotedly clutching a loved one's hand – a traditional and timeless venue of death, a bedroom transformed into an arena of intense drama where a fate is eternally decided. Final farewells have the capacity, of course, to be decidedly distressing. Yet in the case of a quiet elderly woman, she opted for her final words to help unburden herself of a most startling secret kept for over half a century – a secret that plunged her shocked family into disbelief, and finally untangled an antiquated mystery that had plagued a seaside town for decades.

Priscilla Ryall was the second-born of five children to James Ryall and Bethiah Ridout. The couple were married at Sturminster Newton, Dorset, in 1766, but James was sadly widowed in 1780, Bethiah dying aged only 38, leaving five young children behind. In such trying circumstances, life would be strewn with perils and difficulties for the family. Priscilla, though, met Thomas Guppy and marriage soon followed; on 25 June 1793 at a service in Dorchester, Dorset, she became Priscilla Guppy. The couple wasted little time in starting their own family. In 1794, Priscilla became a mother to James. In the same year, however, her new husband was less interested in paternal duties, instead becoming somewhat magnetic to local disorder and unrest. He was eventually charged with assault, having already been convicted of previous felonies for stealing meat. Prison register details describe Priscilla's husband as a fresh complexioned man stood at 5' 3" with dark hair and a round face but has his 'left eye out'. For his meaty misdemeanours, he suffered the ignominy of being 'privately whipped.'

Following Thomas Guppy's troubles, the family decided to move from Dorchester, settling in nearby Weymouth. The seaside town's popularity had begun to soar from the 1750s, chiefly for its merits as a health resort; sea bathing had become a commonly recommended cure for all manner of ailments by medical men across the United Kingdom. The eminent Georgian doctor, Dr Crane, noted that: 'Weymouth of late years has been much frequented for its commodious Sea-Bathing, which it furnishes, in a manner superior to any other in the United Kingdom…I do not wonder at its being the Resort of many people of the first distinction.'

With such prestigious support attached, the town was soon revelling with royalty when, in 1789, it welcomed King George III, who had chosen Weymouth as a place in which to convalesce from serious illness. Up until 1805, the town continued to receive royal visitations almost every summer. Weymouth became a celebrated town, its residents basking in the groundswell of its new-found affinity with nobility – the words 'God Save The King' were emblazoned unashamedly across the town.

How enthralled the Guppy family were at such processional sojourns is unclear but, in April 1809, their attentions would be diverted elsewhere as they welcomed two new additions to the family: twin boys Thomas and George. Sadly, less than a month following the birth, Thomas died and was buried at Wyke Regis on 14 May.

However, long before this tragedy befell Priscilla and her husband, a close inspection of the Dorchester Prisoner Register of 1792 makes for intriguing and surprising reading. Accompanied by three others, Priscilla is listed as being suspected of the murder of a local man, the outcome revealing that the four were acquitted due to a lack of evidence. With nobody brought to justice for the mysterious crime, the question that reverberated throughout Weymouth was: 'Just who did murder Tillroyd Morgan?'

On the evening of 27 April 1792, 25-year-old Priscilla Ryall was working at a house of 'ill-fame' on the High Street near Boot Lane – now Rodwell Road – in Weymouth. It is supposed that on this night, a local man named Tillroyd Morgan was in attendance at the brothel, accompanied by his friend, William Hardy, who farmed the land at the nearby village of Chickerell. Morgan, 22 years old and, by profession, a jeweller and engraver who 'possessed very promising abilities in the line of his profession', was a popular gentleman in and around Weymouth.

The town descended into despondency and great alarm, however, when, at approximately four o'clock the following morning, a workman happened upon a bundle which was peculiarly wrapped in a muddied sheet. Fuelled by curiosity, he opened up the encased bundle where a most horrid sight presented itself – it was the body of Tillroyd Morgan – his head having been severely smashed in and displaying many other marks of savage violence across his battered body. The alarm was instantly raised and a search instigated. Spots of blood were discovered at the bridge where the corpse had been found, and this trail led directly to the door of the brothel where Morgan had last been seen. Unsurprisingly, suspicion blanketed itself over all who had been within the brothel the previous evening; Morgan's friend, William Hardy, Priscilla and her colleague, Sarah White, and a further acquaintance named William Theddam were viewed as firm suspects for the murder and immediately taken into custody to await trial at the next assizes.

The Dorchester Prison Admissions and Discharge Register for 28 April 1792 reveals that the quartet were admitted and tried at the Summer Assizes of that year. The initial evidence of where Morgan may have met his end was, of course, of much interest, but was ultimately merely circumstantial. The evidence failed to substantiate the charge and the four were consequently acquitted of the murder. William Hardy's servant was a huge contributory factor here, claiming that her master had been at home during the period Morgan was believed to have been killed, and so could not possibly have been guilty of the slaying.

With the acquittals upheld and the trail rapidly running cold, the terrible events of that April evening eventually began to diminish in the minds of Weymouth's locals. As in all such cases though, there was somebody who knew exactly what happened to Tillroyd Morgan that evening, and how he came to meet his brutal end.

The fact that the truth did not emerge for a full sixty-five years following the murder was disturbing enough, but that it should be expressed by a fragile old lady on her deathbed almost defied belief.

In November 1857, 82-year-old Priscilla Guppy was in full realisation that her life was drawing to an end. To all intents and purposes, she had led a fairly conventional life – but rather than choose to express any final declarations of love to her family, or share sentimental notions of her enjoyment of life, she wished instead to make a stunning confession.

With her final words, the enfeebled woman gave a stark account of just what had happened to Tillroyd Morgan all those years previously. She knew the truth better than anybody else – for she had been his killer.

Guppy's confession revealed that Morgan and Hardy had entered into a quarrel between themselves. At some point during the row, Guppy had become involved which resulted in her inflicting an almighty death blow to the head of Morgan, as she crashed an iron into the head of the victim, splintering his skull. After the blow was struck, the limp body of the deceased was wrapped up in a sheet and placed on Hardy's horse, which was standing outside the house of ill-repute. It had been decided that they would take the body through the darkness to the bridge and haul it into the water. In this action, however, their plans were thwarted as several voices were heard in the distance, forcing the unlikely gang to simply drop their burden in the street at the foot of the old Weymouth Bridge.

Following the murderous deed, Hardy had returned home and with all the nous of an accomplished rogue, he set the house clock back two hours. He then retired to rest before waking a short time later and cunningly asking his servant to go downstairs and check the time for him. Returning innocently and unaware that the clock had been tampered with, she told Hardy the 'time'. Whilst Hardy was casually dumping Morgan's body, his servant would be under the impression that he was actually at home with her and therefore could not have been a party to the crime.

As a rather ghoulish aside, Priscilla Guppy also admitted that when she was arraigned before the bar of justice during her trial, she had the gold watch and chain of the murdered man concealed tightly in the hair of her head.

As if to confirm the confession she had just made before her stunned family, in her final death throes the old woman shouted with great animation: 'I beat him in the head with an iron! May God have mercy on my soul!'

Much had changed in the time elapsed since the murder and the murderer's belated confession: the United Kingdom had formally been created, Nelson had defeated France and Spain at the Battle of Trafalgar, handing Britain complete control of the seas, and three changes of monarchy had been overseen. Much occurred during this period on a national scale, and so too, it seems, within the more localised setting of the south coast, as old Priscilla Guppy, the archetypal grandmother, finally admitted that she had lived much of her life as a covert killer.

Tillroyd Morgan's final resting place was the graveyard of St Mary's Church in Weymouth. His tombstone displays an unnerving inscription:

This stone was erected by Public Subscription in remembrance of the cruel murder committed on the body of Tillroyd Morgan, who lies here, on the 27th April, 1792, aged 22…. Here mingling with my fellow clay, I await the awful judgement day, and there my murderer shall appear, although escaped from justice here.

Chapter 20

George Manley

The particulars around George Manley and the crime for which he would pay the ultimate price are limited. What we do know, however, is that moments before his death at the Wicklow gallows in Ireland, Manley delivered an artistic speech of great eloquence and, indeed, defiance.

In 1738, Manley was convicted of the murder of a man named 'Williams'. Confined within the squalor of Wicklow gaol and awaiting the ultimate sentence, Manley appeared little moved at the thought of death. Manacled to the wall of his squalid cell, his confinement was shared by an eclectic mix of fellow law-breakers, increasing the surge of disease as it ravaged its path, leaving a trail of fatalities in its deathly wake. Those who survived the horrors of the gaol had little in the way of an encouraging future, particularly those awaiting execution.

This, though, did little to deter Manley. He behaved with total insensibility to the destiny in wait for him, a resolution he maintained to the last. Having arrived at the place of execution, he was described by onlookers as though he were 'going to a Merry-Meeting'. The crowd could not decide whether Manley was hardened, fearless, or simply mad. When he began his speech, their wonderment was only amplified.

'My Friends,
You look to see – What? – A man take a leap into the abyss of death. Look, and you shall see me go, with as much courage as Curtius, when he leapt into the gulf to save his country from destruction. What then will you see of me! – You say, that no man without virtue can be courageous. You see, I am courageous. You'll say, I have killed a man.

Marlborough killed his thousands, and Alexander his millions: Marlborough and Alexander, and many others who done the like, are famous in history for Great Men. But I killed one solitary man.

Aye, that's the case.

One solitary man. I'm a little murderer, and must be hanged. Marlborough and Alexander plundered countries – They were Great Men. I ran in debt with the ale-wife, I must be hanged.

Now, my friends, I have drawn a parallel between two of the greatest men that ever lived, and myself; but these were men of former days. Now I'll speak a word of some of the present days: How many men were lost in Italy and upon the Rhine, during the last war, for settling a king in Poland?

Both sides could not be in the right; they are Great Men; but I killed a solitary man, I'm a little fellow. The King of Spain takes our ships, plunders our merchants, kills and tortures our men; but what of all that? What he does is good; he's a Great Man, he is clothed in purple, his instruments of murder are bright and shining, mine was, but a rusty gun; and so much for comparison. Now, I would fain know, what authority there is in Scripture for a rich man to murder, to plunder, to torture, and ravage whole countries; and what law it is, that condemns a poor man to death for killing a solitary man, or for stealing a solitary sheep to feed his family. But bring the matter closer to our own country: What is the difference between running in a poor man's debt, and by the power of gold, or any other privilege, preventing him from obtaining his right; and clapping a pistol to a man's breast, and taking from him his purse? Yet the one shall thereby obtain a coach, and honours, and titles. The other – What? – A cart and a rope.

From what I have said, my brethren, you may, perhaps, imagine I am hardened; but believe me, I am fully convinced of my follies, and acknowledge the just judgment of God has overtaken me: I have no hopes, but from the merits of my Redeemer, who I hope will have mercy on me, as he knows that murder was far from my heart, and what I did was through rage and passion, being provoked thereto by the deceased.

Take warning, my dear comrades: Think! O think! what I would now give, that I had lived another life.'

Manley's final words as death beckoned him ever closer caused much excitement to the gathered masses. The *Newgate Calendar* observed at the time that 'as we have never met with a dying speech so satirical and severe upon the general turpitude of mankind, we readily present it to our readers.' His comparisons to Messrs Marlborough and Alexander ensured that the crowds viewed Manley with puzzled awe, his demonstration of a knowledge of mankind was after all 'seldom found in criminals of his description'.

Chapter 21

Frederick Fleet

Frederick Fleet is not a name that instantly conjures sentiments of maritime tragedy. Amidst a gallery of early-twentieth-century 'somebodies', John Jacob Astor IV, Isidor Straus and Benjamin Guggenheim are perhaps more likely to prompt a tearful recognition as some of the more illustrious names who plummeted to the depths of the Atlantic Ocean, having been aboard the majestic, yet doomed, *Titanic*. Fleet, however, was not rubbing shoulders in the dining saloons and smoking-rooms with such captains of industry; indeed, his early life as a literal 'waif and stray' would surely have never even suggested a presence aboard the era's most opulent ship, no matter how unsinkable his optimism may have been.

Frederick Fleet was born on 15 October 1887, the illegitimate son of Alice Fleet and a father never known to him, Frederick Laurence. The parental bond, not exclusively a natural thing it would appear, certainly lacked a nurturing quality in the case of Fred Fleet, and he was placed into care very early. In December 1889, Fleet was a little over 2 years old and was admitted to the Liverpool Foundling Hospital, where he would remain for three years. During his time there, it would appear that his mother, though irregularly, did contribute small payments to young Fred's upkeep. Just as importantly, she also managed to maintain a regular correspondence with the hospital matron. However, regardless of the origin of these intentions, Fred could not have failed to feel the shroud of neglectful loneliness envelop him following his mother's next movements. Alice departed for America, joined by her sister in October 1890, the hopeful pair seeking their own personal American dreams, eventually settling in Springfield, Massachusetts.

As Alice lived out her optimistic pilgrimage, her young son remained parentless within the Foundling Hospital. During this period, the hospital began to encounter its own issues. Inadequate funding hindered its prospects and an enforced closure appeared certain. In such an instance, the most likely fate for Fred was a referral to the local workhouse, though this was averted by an application to the Church of England requesting assistance. The application reads as a woefully sad document which chronicles Fred Fleet's early stages of abandonment. The application to the 'Church of England Central Society for Providing Homes for Waifs and Strays' perhaps reveals enough in its title alone. Yet its contents clarify the turgid situation he was dumped into during his earliest years.

Fred's transfer was arranged to the newly-opened Liverpool Diocesan Boys' Home, Elm Lodge, Seaforth in March 1893, where he was most likely accepted amongst the first cohort of residents. Its capacity was for thirty boys aged between 7 and 14 years old, and whilst there is little corroborative evidence relating to Fred's time here, surviving testimonies would suggest that the home would have offered him the relatively stable and safe environment he had yet to experience. A former resident of the lodge wrote a nostalgic letter to his former matron recounting the joyous Christmases he had enjoyed there. He wistfully wrote of memories of 'liberal supplies of apples, oranges and biscuits, turkey and plum-pudding, and perhaps a threepenny bit!' Fred's general role in the home would, of course, involve chores; cleaning dormitories and communal areas, and tending to the outside spaces whilst also attending the local school.

It would seem, however, that life in the home did not provide a positive reaffirming for all of its residents. It should perhaps not be too great a surprise that the young man's splintered and shunned early years led to behavioural concerns within Elm Lodge. It is with ironic foresight now that these troubling years unintentionally formulated Fred's future destiny. He became of much concern to the Society shortly after his twelfth birthday in November 1899. A flurry of correspondence followed between senior staff of Elm Lodge and other homes, during desperate attempts to have Fred rehoused.

Towards the end of 1899, the founder and secretary of the Waifs and Strays Society, Mr Edward Rudolf, contacted the Tattenhall Home, Cheshire, with the hope that they might be able to receive Fred. Secretary Adela Joyce's reply from Tattenhall is telling. She advised that whilst 'there is a vacancy at Tattenhall we can therefore receive this boy on trial; but if he is as troublesome as he has apparently been at Seaforth, we shall not be able to keep him.' Although his reputation was a youthful one, it was already beginning to obstruct Fred's opportunities. His trial period at Tattenhall never materialised, despite the arrangements having seemingly been cemented.

Rudolf's efforts on Fred's behalf were exhaustive, but it transpired that the Seaforth Home Committee had vastly different plans for the young man. Beatrice Lockett of the Seaforth Committee wrote to Rudolf explaining that the planned move would no longer be in Fred's interests and that her husband had written to the commander of the industrial school ship *Clio* to enquire if they could 'get Freddy on that ship.' The *Clio* was a former Royal Navy corvette moored off Bangor in the Menai Straits. These vessels were intended to provide young boys with skills in seamanship and help prepare them for a life at sea.

Lockett's motives for the hasty rescheduling of Fred's immediate future are unclear. They were made with some urgency certainly, and garnered no apparent opposition, but whatever the foundations of the U-turn, the actions of Mrs Lockett and her colleagues realigned Fred's future towards a previously unanticipated voyage.

Despite receiving valuable training and skills in seamanship, accounts of life on board reflect a rather draconian and uncompromising reality. The boys were subject to arbitrary discipline, beatings and merciless bullying, all of which were common facets they had to endure. Details relating to Fred's life aboard the *Clio* are sketchy, though he commendably incurred *Clio*'s rigours for four years, honing the skills which would later be called upon in such desperate circumstances.

During his tutelage, Fred remained in touch with one member of the Home Committee at Elm Lodge, George Killey, the man who ultimately may well have secured Fred's future with the esteemed White Star Line. In a letter to Edward Rudolf in 1910, Killey adopts an almost fatherly tone of triumph, commenting on his one-time despair of Fred, but, in consequence of his training aboard the *Clio*, he has 'grown a fine young fellow', and is now a 'lookout man on the White Star Liner, *Oceanic*'.

Thomas Henry Ismay was the founder of the White Star Line when, in January 1868, he paid the princely sum of £1,000 to acquire its trade name, flag, and goodwill of the company, which had originally been created by John Pilkington and Henry Threlfall Wilson. The business, however, could not achieve financial parity, and, weighed down by heavy debts to the Royal Bank of Liverpool – some £527,000 – the shipping line was forced into bankruptcy, upon which Ismay, ever the opportunist, turned an original failure into a lucrative prospect.

Fleet's naval teeth were cut following four years aboard the *Oceanic*. As a seaman, he earned the monthly sum of £5, which was supplemented by a further 5 shillings for lookout duty. It was in this occupation that he would leave the *Oceanic* and take up a permanent observational role aboard the most luxurious vessel ever built: the much-heralded *Titanic*.

The maiden voyage of *Titanic* was scheduled to begin on Wednesday, 10 April 1912, departing from Southampton. To have been a part of her embryonic life on the water was a thrill for crewmen as well as the expectant passengers, for although Fred Fleet would not be afforded the glittering experience reserved for those in the upper echelons of the distinct class structure onboard, the prestige of the occasion was something he, too, could revel in.

The crew began to stream aboard early on the morning of departure, prior to the arrival of the ship's foremost in authority, Captain Smith, who stepped aboard at half past seven. The massive vessel was now alive with the frantic scampering of crew undertaking final inspections before the embarkation of passengers. A final part of the safety inspection involved the crew lowering two of the lifeboats to ensure functionality, and prove their capability in handling them, though it was, of course, hoped these vessels would remain redundant.

By midday, *Titanic* was ready to depart Southampton. Some 900 passengers had embarked here with additional passengers to be collected at Cherbourg – 142 first-class, 30 second- and 102 third-class passengers came on board in the French port, before setting course for Queenstown, County Cork in Ireland. Prior to the ship reaching the Irish port on the morning of 11 April, Captain Smith ordered an emergency drill, where safety equipment, emergency doors and exits were subject to scrutiny; alas, no record exists as to whether the lifeboats were again tested. Nonetheless, a further 240 enthused passengers boarded at Queenstown before *Titanic* headed out towards the immensity of the Atlantic.

During *Titanic*'s initial 24 hours at sea, progress was good; 386 nautical miles had been covered and the ship's grandiose trappings and furnishings were completely in keeping with the early hyperbole of its magnificence. Far removed from the lavish trellised walls and sprawling staircases, however, there was an abundance of messages in the wireless room regarding dangerous navigational conditions ahead. Plentiful warnings of ice were received from several ships, though potential danger was certainly not perceived as imminent, the ship still being some way from hazardous zones.

The morning of Sunday, 14 April dawned cold and clear. A slight haze accompanied the crisp early hours – remarkably, this raw climate was deemed reason enough to abandon the regulatory lifeboat drill, despite the fact that *Titanic* had already received further ice warnings. These notifications continued into the afternoon, passengers blissfully unaware of any impending obstacle from within the plush confines of the brimming libraries and steaming Turkish baths.

The outside temperature was rapidly plummeting, a chilling indication of the presence of bouldering icebergs. The job of the lookout crew was of particular importance on the night of 14 April, and notes made within the night order book confirmed the necessity of remaining vigilant for these glacial masses. At eight o'clock, Fred Fleet's colleagues, Archie Jewel and George Symons, replaced George Hogg and Frank Evans as the eyes of the ship. The lookout crew comprised of six men who worked in pairs during shifts of two hours. A period of four hours off would then be followed again by a reinstatement of duty.

The men were stationed high up the mast in the crow's nest, some 50 feet above the forecastle deck. The role of those in the crow's nest was an overtly simplistic one, yet in practice it required unwavering concentration, relentlessly observing the expanse ahead of them for looming hazards. An apparently tame ocean could very quickly become one of uninhibited rage and an ongoing wariness was necessary, though on this evening the sea was calm and still, the sky moonless, and the stars overhead were lucid and clear.

Captain Smith retired to his cabin at nine o'clock, having expressed orders that he be roused immediately in the wake of any untoward occurrences. Smith was, of course, aware of the multitude of ice warnings received during the voyage, another of which, issued shortly following his retirement for the evening, warned of ice which lay directly ahead of the ship's path.

Fred Fleet climbed the ladder to the crow's nest at ten o'clock. His duty was to concentrate on the port side (left) with colleague Reginald Lee minding the starboard (right). The two men huddled vigilantly in their confines high above the liner. Initially, only the men's intermittent misty exhalations were visible in the numbness of the night. Something, however, of a far more sinister nature was about to present itself.

At twenty to midnight, Fleet's shift was nearing its end when he spotted a dark object, high above the water, dead ahead. Coiling into immediate action, Fleet rang the brass bell three times and phoned the bridge, reaching First Officer William Murdoch. Fleet yelled the now infamous words 'iceberg right ahead,' – the three words securing Fleet's immortal status in *Titanic*'s ever-enduring narrative.

The warning resulted in immediate action by the ship's crew in desperate attempts to avoid colliding with the mass. The ship began to swing away from the iceberg, but not far enough. Fleet watched with horror as the looming unearthly object drew ever nearer. Willing the mighty vessel to veer past the iceberg, however futile, was now his only remaining recourse. It would not be enough.

Deep below the waterline, the hull collided intensely against the ice, popping rivets and opening a fatal gash penetrating the ship's under-belly. The severity of the impact was largely unknown amongst the passengers, although those upon deck would witness large fragments of ice tumbling down around them. Quite how much fear this instigated in those aboard an 'unsinkable' ship is impossible to gauge, though it soon became apparent that the greatest ship of its time was mortally wounded and, along with its many passengers, would soon be in its final death throes.

The stoic heroism and indeed – though infrequent – bouts of cowardice demonstrated by those aboard *Titanic* during her final death plunge to the depths of the icy Atlantic have rightly been well-documented and as such, require no further recounting here. The human tragedy was immense. Evocatively captured by the *Evening News* poster announcing 'Titanic Disaster Great Loss of Life', this epitomises the fact that just over 1,500 souls perished that evening. 705 people survived the disaster, Fred Fleet amongst them.

Such an extensive death toll would, of course, attract the inevitable inquiries, from which possible causes would emerge and lessons gleaned from the atrocity. The first inquiry held at the Waldorf-Astoria Hotel, New York, resulted in over 1,000 pages of testimony from a total of eighty-two witnesses. Fred Fleet's testimony is ensconced within its pages, the reading of which reveals an endearing naivety within Fleet's responses as he faced the questioning of a dogged Senator William Alden Smith. Following Fleet's revelation that there were no binoculars for the lookout crew – a thoroughly bizarre notion – Smith queried the extent in which their usage would have helped up in the crow's nest on the night of the tragedy. 'We could have seen it a bit sooner,' Fleet remarked. 'How much sooner?' Smith enquired. 'Well, enough to get out of the way,' Fleet quipped simply.

However likely or otherwise that Fleet's uncomplicated 'solution' to a possible averting of disaster was, the thorough inquiry did lead to alterations in policy and legislation, and to this end at least, was a force for good. For those who survived the dreadful events on the Atlantic though, whilst initially considered 'fortunate', many existed in a state of purgatory. Fleet became one of surely many 'insomniacs of the *Titanic*', the cumbersome advance of that 'black thing' etched painfully into his beleaguered mind.

A mere two months following the sinking of *Titanic* though, Frederick Fleet was back on the ocean, serving briefly as a seaman on the White Star liner *Olympic*. This was a short-lived venture, however, and by August 1912, he had severed ties with the company. For the next twenty-four years, Fleet sailed with Union-Castle and a smattering of similar companies before retiring from the sea in 1936. His links with the sea were not wholly dismantled, however, choosing to work for Harland and Wolff shipbuilders, which ironically had built the *Titanic* and indeed the *Olympic*.

Away from the seas, in 1917, Fleet married 26-year-old Eva Le Gros from Jersey. A year later, they had their only child, Dorothy, on 24 November 1918. Fleet spoke reluctantly about his experiences, yet they continued to haunt his life. One such instance when Fred Fleet did speak about the fateful evening was with *Titanic* researcher Leslie Reade in 1964. It is with heart-rending emotion that Fleet described to Reade the trauma that had encircled his life following the *Titanic* experience, haunting him ever more. He did seek medical intervention, but to little avail. The extent of psychological trauma and its surrounding concepts were, if identified, generally in their infancy. 'Survivor guilt', for instance, was originally termed in 1961 and would feasibly have affected Fleet, though any treatment or indeed recognition of it would have been unlikely at this time.

Physically, severe blackouts were becoming a frequent and concerning ailment for Fleet, and one which required admittance to the Royal South Hampshire Hospital for a short period. He and his wife Eva were residing at Norman Road in Southampton, lodging with Eva's brother, Philip Le Gros. Fleet was at this time engaged in part-time employment as a street vendor for the *Echo* newspaper in Southampton, but was leading a life much depressed. Tragically, this depression peaked when, shortly after Christmas 1964, Eva passed away. Fred was alone once more.

Following Eva's death, Fred was urged to seek alternative lodgings. It is thought that both Fred and Eva's brother mutually understood that in the wake of Eva's death, Fred should move out; he had, after all, only advocated the arrangement for his sister. Fred had, in fact, already approached the welfare department but with little success. Fred's state of mind was now in chaotic disarray, his life unravelling around him. His wife's passing and the prospect of homelessness would culminate in exhaustive stresses for even the most centred individual; paired with the ceaseless emotions and unshakeably distressing recollections from *Titanic*'s final evening, it is little wonder that the 77-year-old's disposition was permeated with immeasurable grief.

Fred's grief was now manifesting itself in recurrent fashion. On 4 January 1965, his daughter Dorothy was visited by the police. Her father had been found in a distressed condition, threatening suicide. This, though, was not a course of action Dorothy believed her father would take.

On the morning of Saturday, 9 January, Dorothy saw her father alive for the last time. He visited her at her home, hugely dejected and tearful. He remained gravely despondent for the duration of the visit, which lasted almost an hour. He handed Dorothy a wallet containing £5, asking her to look after it for him. As he left his daughter, he informed her that she would shortly receive a letter. She assumed it would be from the welfare department.

Later on Saturday evening, Le Gros noticed that Fred had packed his cases and stripped his bed. He assumed Fred was staying with friends, so retired to bed. The next morning, Le Gros stepped outside towards the coal house. Fred was leaning against the clothes post at the end of the garden. He appeared to be meditating. Le Gros called out to his brother-in-law, but Fred did not reply. Moving closer, Le Gros was horrified to realise that Fred was hanging. The man whose eyes had first set upon the cause of the greatest maritime tragedy of its day was dead.

Le Gros wasted no time in summoning the police. At forty-seven minutes past nine, Constable Beasley arrived at the scene. The rope was not part of the garden's clothes line, and appeared to have been specifically purchased for this tragic purpose. The rope had been woven around the clothes post several times, while a handkerchief, having been tied loosely around Fred's mouth, remained in place. His feet were almost touching the ground, and nearby, a set of small wooden steps stood – a mere 2 feet high – from which Frederick Fleet had evidently jumped and thus ended his internal torment forever.

A shopping bag lay close to the body. PC Beasley found inside a sealed envelope addressed to his daughter, Dorothy. Written in Fred's handwriting, the heartbreaking letter read:

My Dear Dorrie

I am sorry what I am going to do I can't stick it any longer, tonight I am hanging myself. Now the stuff in the bedroom is yours two cases, clock, carpet, the carrier by the clothes post outside, the lamp on the floor and wiring I don't know weather [sic] it belongs to me or Phil you must ask him the bed clothes you please yourself if you want them don't forget the small case also the chamber I don't know about the bed I am not interesting myself about it I hope to be dead.

Well my dear this is goodbye love to all from your broken hearted father what an end another Titanic man gone. I have left the Photos in the small case don't forget the basin under the sink, now Dorrie I am giving you a big thing to do I have always worried about being buried alive do you know anybody that would help you to have my body taken to the hospital to do what they like with it. I know its not nice to ask a thing like this to be done. Dear Dorrie a new pair of shoes upstairs if you know anybody would like them well this is all I have to say goodbye to all my friends.

Dad xxxxxxx

At the inquest into Fred's death, the coroner reported that, 'It was known by the deceased that after her [Eva's] death he would have to find other accommodation and these two things may have played upon his mind.' A verdict of suicide was recorded.

Fred's tragic end was entered almost with incidental purpose to the story of the *Titanic*. In woeful accordance with his lived anonymity, Fred was buried in a pauper's grave in Hollybrook Cemetery in Southampton. His final resting place appeared to be a sad reflection of his life, positioned in a lonely and desolate area that received little attention.

In 1993, however, Fred was afforded a headstone befitting of his legacy. The Titanic Historical Society was created in 1963 in America. The organisation wished to pay Fred the respect that many felt he had not received at the time of his death. Funded through donations from the society, a new headstone was erected at Fred's grave. Finally, a just monument now serves as an infinite reminder to one of the *Titanic*'s forgotten men – Fred had received the attention and recognition that so painfully eluded him in life.

Chapter 22

William Shaw

'I am innocent of my daughter's murder!'

These were the final desperate words of William Shaw immediately before his appointment with the hangman in 1721. The words reverberated around the execution spectacle, prompting whispered deliberations among the riveted commentators. Shaw had always been a man on the right side of the law, an able upholsterer with fine tradition, yet his words were, without exception, not believed by those who clamoured to witness his life ebb away at the end of a rope at Leith Walk, Edinburgh. The evidence and reasoning for this certainty presents as follows.

William Shaw lived with his daughter, Catherine, in Edinburgh. Of Catherine's mother, there appears no record, though father and daughter resided in general amicability, until the ageless wrangle regarding appropriate suitors for a father's daughter reared its loathsome head. The dispute had created much tension and a downturn in domestic civility within the household. Catherine cherished the attentions of a young jeweller, John Lawson, but he was deemed of vast inadequacy to even contemplate Catherine's hand in marriage. The old man Shaw was unrelenting in his opinions of Lawson, alleging his lifestyle to be entrenched with profligacy and addicted to every kind of depravity – a far cry from the simple living soul Shaw preferred and envisaged for his daughter. The ideal specimen of suitability to the father's eyes was a son of Alexander Robertson, a friend and neighbour, who thoroughly convinced in his gentlemanly and refined conduct.

Shaw risked a prodigious wrath when opting to banish Lawson from his home. His unyielding objections against the man were ever-increasing and he was adamant that his daughter should have no base in which to tangle herself with such a rogue. Yet many an impish nature has proved lustfully magnetic, and so it was that Catherine, now irretrievably intoxicated by the jeweller, continued to clandestinely rendezvous with her forbidden lover.

A secretive tryst of this nature, however, had little chance of remaining veiled on Edinburgh's teeming alleyways and cobbled streets. The eighteenth century had witnessed a significant surge in numbers on the city's streets and the rumour mill passed through its residents as speedily as disease and dysentery. Upon the inevitable discovery of his daughter's disobedience, the father grew into a state of considerable rage, a tempestuous quarrel ensuing with passionate expressions exploding from both sides.

An unfortunate neighbour, James Morrison, dwelt in the adjoining property to the Shaws, a mere single partition providing the only division from the bellowing bombardment between the pair. Morrison could not help but overhear the bickering couple, and was particularly struck by the daughter's repeated pronouncement of such words as 'barbarity, cruelty and death'. The father eventually removed himself from the hostilities, fleeing into the street outside and locking the door behind him. For some time after, the house fell silent, the expletives and resentment having dissipated into the night. Abruptly though, the neighbour Morrison was once more inclined to lend a curious ear to events within the Shaw house when the apparent calm was replaced by something far more disturbing. Morrison could hear a succession of groans and minacious murmuring from Catherine, her sounds almost deathly. Having heard the earlier quarrelling, it was with much alarm that Morrison ran from his property baying for the help of other neighbours. A small group of hastily assembled tenants initially entered Morrison's room and listened here attentively for a time. As earlier, a strange gurgling and groaning sound was audible. Suddenly, Catherine was then distinctly heard to exclaim, 'Cruel father, thou art the cause of my death!'

Struck by this, they hastened to the door of William Shaw, frantically banging it and demanding entry. The frenzied knocking was repeated again and again, but to no reply. Morrison and the other neighbours had, to their minds, clearly overheard a sensational occurrence, their suspicions fully formed and unequivocally decided that William Shaw had slain his daughter in a fit of frenzied rage. A constable was sought and entry was forced into the house, upon which a dire sight greeted their entry. There lay Catherine, weltering in a congealing pool of her own blood, the fateful knife lay at her side, the blade clotted with evidence of its wrongdoing. The girl was alive, barely, though it was clear to all that her passing would be an expeditious inevitability. Sensing that Catherine's worldly position would soon be obsolete, Morrison hastily asked the girl if her father had been responsible for the butchery. In an expiring and speechless state, Catherine listlessly motioned with her head – in the affirmative – before slipping away to her death.

At this mortal moment, William Shaw returned to his property and entered the room. All eyes were instantly upon the startled man, Shaw himself utterly befuddled at the presence of such a random conglomeration in his home. His confusion then turned to despair at the sight of his daughter lying slaughtered on the floor, the man instantly becoming a pale imitation of himself, a trembling ruin sunken to his knees amid the deplorable horror before him. His explicit display of anguished grief, however, was viewed as no more than a smoke-screen, a point which garnered further belief when the constable discovered bloodstains smattered across the shirt of the distressed father. There was now little doubt of Shaw's guilt in the minds of the beholders, so the man was instantly hurried off before a magistrate.

The grieving father had no time to contemplate the grave position in which he had so rapidly become embroiled. He was immediately committed to prison on suspicion of the murder of his daughter. He was shortly brought to trial, acutely aware of the shadow of suspicion that lingered all around him. His defence acknowledged the confinement imposed upon Catherine in order to prevent intercourse with Lawson. Shaw, though, went further, stating that he frequently insisted upon her marrying Robertson and it was indeed this subject over which the pair had locked horns on the evening she was found murdered. Morrison attested to this, but Shaw insisted that when he left his daughter in a fit of rage on the night of the murder, he had left her 'unarmed and untouched'. Attempts to explain the presence of blood on his shirt were of great significance, Shaw claiming it to be a consequence of having bled himself some days prior and the bandage becoming untied.

The jury predictably viewed Shaw's version of events as fanciful; his assertions completely weightless, the jury was fully convinced that such a criminative fact had merely been created by the accused. Certainly, the circumstantial evidence before the jury was formidable – its reliability, perhaps not so – but for the means of reaching a just verdict, the jury ignored any discrepancies and upon the several concurring circumstances, found William Shaw guilty of his daughter's murder.

With his declaration of innocence upon his lips as he died, William Shaw's execution took place in November 1721, at Leith Walk. The Shrubhill area of Leith Walk was the site of a gibbet known as the Gallows Lee: 'the field with the gallows.' The hung bodies were generally buried at the base of the gallows, but Shaw was sentenced to further discredit and following his death at the rope, he was then to be hung in chains, or 'gibbetted'. When this rare sentence was pronounced, the offending body would be cut down from the scaffold after hanging for the usual hour. It would then be hung up once more, this time inside the gibbet cage, designed for exposing the criminal corpse. This punishment had a multitudinous impact; placing the body in full public view acted as a striking deterrent to the living, and denied the corpse a burial, instead becoming nourishment for the boisterous carrion crows. The gibbet was engineered for effecting maximum horror. The pungent odours of the rotting body – which could remain caged inside for several years – would contaminate the air for miles around, as the gibbet eerily creaked and swayed in the wind, ensuring the body would never be at eternal rest.

Shaw's body had been hanging in chains for almost a year when an extraordinary occurrence further affected the sorrowful tale. In August 1722, the possessor of the late William Shaw's house was, by chance, rummaging around near the chamber area where Catherine's dying body had been found. He stumbled upon a paper which had fallen into a cavity on one side of the chimney. It was folded as a letter, which upon opening, was found to contain the wretched girl's final earthly act – a written confession of self-murder.

Barbarous Father,
Your cruelty in having put it out of my power ever to join my fate to that of the only man I could love, and tyrannically insisting upon my marrying one whom I always hated, has made me form a resolution to put an end to an existence which is become a burden to me. I

doubt not I shall find mercy in another world; for sure no benevolent being can require that I should any longer live in torment to myself in this! My death I lay to your charge; when you read this, consider yourself as the inhuman wretch that plunged the murderous knife in the bosom of the unhappy CATHERINE SHAW.

Tragically, it is thought that the unhappy girl, having authored the letter in her irksome state had placed it on the mantelpiece for her father to find upon his return home. Unwittingly, the letter dropped into a cavity abreast of the chimney and there it remained until the cruel hand of fate and 'justice' had already tragically prevailed.

The letter was shown to many of Catherine's relations and friends, of whom each avowed its authenticity of her having penned it. The sensational nature of the tale became much talked of in the locality, and the magistracy of Edinburgh were fiercely scrutinised. Being convinced in the genuine nature of the letter, law enforcement officials had little choice but to beat a hasty retreat and order the emaciated remains of William Shaw be removed from the gibbet and given to his family for posthumous interment. In a further reparation to the innocent man's memory and the honour of his surviving relations, a pair of colours were ordered to be waved over his grave, in token of his innocence. The merest of consolations which Shaw himself, at the right hand of God, surely scoffed at.

Those of a particularly suspicious disposition may, of course, be tempted to flirt with the notion that Catherine had hidden the letter very knowingly, fully aware that her father would be the prime suspect in her murder which would see him vengefully punished by the full weight of the law. Whatever the case in this respect, we will forever remain in wonder. What is certain, however, is that through the final written words of an anguished and woeful girl, William Shaw's sufferings were discovered to have been hopelessly misaligned with justice, becoming one of the saddest cases of its day.

Chapter 23

Ernest Brown

Northumberland's rugged and rural expanses are well-championed. Yet amid the vast and scenic landscapes lie a littering of bygone-century fortifications and bastles (fortified farmhouses) which still proudly stand, serving as stark reminders that this once-lawless frontier demanded resilient efforts by locals to protect themselves and their possessions from the Border Reivers. England's northernmost county is steeped in a bloody and intense history; a busy theatre of battles, depredations and continued agitations. Its proximity to the Scottish Borders provides the glaring rationale here, for paradoxically, this is a county of majestic beauty, far removed – one would think – from harbouring scenes of extreme and dramatic bloodshed. One such occasion played out here was the Battle of Otterburn, fought in 1388 between the House of Douglas and the English Percys. Several chroniclers have described the course of the battle, though none of the accounts are sufficiently precise in their topographical references to identify the precise location of the battlefield, though general consensus agree that the fighting occurred to the west of Otterburn.

More than 500 years later, the village of Otterburn, suitably named by the Otter Burn that dissects the village, would experience a trauma of such intrigue that the village was unmercifully catapulted into the grateful arms of the world's print press. The fusion of mystique and murder has an enduring capacity, evident even today, and the events of the evening of 6 January 1931 in cosy Otterburn continue to ignite debate. Furthermore, the final spoken words of a man apparently unconnected to the village have ensured that the tragic tale of Evelyn Foster has lingered on in the minds of the genial and diligent Northumbrian folk, and beyond.

In the early 1930s, the Foster family name was of some importance in rural Northumberland. Joseph Foster was born in 1874 in Haltwhistle near Hexham, to the west of the county. He met Margaret, who would soon become Foster, subsequent to the pair's marriage on 10 February 1900. The Foster family began to grow soon after the marriage; first-born John quickly being followed by Evelyn, who was born on 20 November 1901. It was not until 1909 and 1911 respectively, that Dorothy Edith and Margaret Elizabeth completed the Foster family, who were by now a distinguished family unit in the heart of a close-knit community in Otterburn. The family chose to settle in a large stone-built house to the west of the village known as the 'Kennels'. Such a name would perhaps suggest a prior association with dogs at some point, though this is unconfirmed. Joseph Foster had the property converted into one dwelling, presumably to house his sizeable family.

Directly opposite the house was the Foster family business, a garage from where Joseph was the proprietor of a small bus and taxi company and where he would perform repairs as a competent motor engineer. Joseph Foster was a crucial component in keeping local people moving, providing services to Newcastle and Hexham, and maintaining the motors of the fortunate few with their own means of travel.

With his business expanding, Joseph required assistance which came in the form of his second-born, Evelyn. She had not been particularly enamoured with school but had an adept understanding of mechanical procedures; having left school, she secured employment within her father's business, initially serving the fuel pumps and gaining valuable 'unofficial' driving practice from an early age over the quiet Northumbrian roads and tracks, where she would disturb no more than a clutch of birds or the occasional crossing farm animal.

Evelyn's reaching of legal age to drive happily coincided with a rise in popularity of travelling by taxi, and with all aspects of the enterprise flourishing, her father soon handed her the sole responsibility of the taxi service. As the business continued to grow, Evelyn began to purchase more cars to meet the increasing demand. Locals were fast becoming more adventurous and socially conscious, willing to seek new experiences further afield – mundane whist-drives at local village halls were regularly being replaced by trips to picture houses and theatres in Newcastle.

One of Evelyn's more-favoured cars was a Hudson Super Six, which she had bought in 1930 for the princely sum of £200. She had made many previous journeys in the Hudson, and would have no reason to suspect that the one she made on 6 January would be her last.

Shortly before half past six in the evening, bus driver Cecil Johnstone and his conductor Tommy Rutherford arrived in Otterburn as part of the regular service from Hexham. There were three passengers still aboard as they approached the final stop at the Foster garage. One of them was Esther Murray, who was heading on to Cottonshopeburnfoot, a tiny hamlet in nearby Redesdale. Evelyn took Mrs Murray to her destination and having dropped her off, she began the journey back to Otterburn. As she approached Elishaw Road Ends, she noticed a car parked and then a man wandering across the road trying to flag her down.

He explained that he had been in the Border town of Jedburgh and from there, he had missed the bus to Newcastle. He made clear to Evelyn that the parked car at the side of the road had given him a lift to Elishaw Road Ends, from where he could make the short walk to catch a bus from Otterburn to Newcastle. Evelyn told the man that the bus to Newcastle had already left, but that she could take him into Otterburn and from there he might be able to arrange a lift to Ponteland, where he could then get an onward bus to Newcastle.

During the short journey into the village, Evelyn agreed with the man that should he fail to secure a lift in the village, then she would pick him up at the bridge and take him on to Ponteland herself. She parked outside the Kennels and the man went into the village seeking the lift, whilst Evelyn went into the house to relay the story to her mother Margaret, and also to get an idea of the fare she ought to charge the man should she end up taking him to Ponteland. She had already quoted around the £2 mark, but thought this may have been on the expensive side so she sought clarity from her father. Margaret Foster, however, was less concerned with the fare cost but apprehensive at the thought of her daughter ferrying an unknown man across the dark and sultry moors. With concern, she quizzed Evelyn about the apparent decorum of the man, who Evelyn reassuringly asserted was 'very respectable and gentlemanly like'. With that, she proceeded to the pumps to refuel the car in anticipation of the possible journey with the mystery man. In the meantime, Joseph Foster had worked out the fare if the journey was to go ahead – £1 16 shillings.

Evelyn's younger sister, Margaret, had by now joined the family exchange and suggested that if Evelyn was to make the journey with the man, then she should take family friend George Philipson with her, if for no other reason than to reassure the family. Concurring that the instruction was an appropriate one, Evelyn took hold of a torch and departed the house, stepping out into the raw and wintry evening. She did, however, make the journey alone; George Philipson was not sought to accompany her as her sister had suggested.

Exactly what happened next is open to some postulation, but what follows is based exclusively on Evelyn's statement as would be later described to police.

It would appear that the mystery man so central to this case was indeed unable to arrange a ride so he had, as arranged, met Evelyn at the bridge by the Percy Arms. The pair then headed out of the village and off towards Ponteland. They would never arrive there though, instead reaching as far as Belsay before the man decided he wished to return to Otterburn, and that he should now drive the car. The bemused Evelyn declined and was immediately punched in the face, presumably as a form of restraint, the man climbing into the driver's position and driving on towards Wolf's Nick. The car then came to an abrupt halt before the terrified girl was thrust into the rear of the car and dowsed in liquid from a bottle. The Hudson then careered over a verge and plunged downwards onto the moor before halting in a ditch. The car was then set on fire – with Evelyn still lying prone on the back seat.

It was now a little beyond nine o'clock and the final bus towards Otterburn had left Newcastle's Haymarket bus station. Aboard were only a few passengers and the familiar pair of bus conductor Tommy Rutherford and driver Cecil Johnstone. It was perhaps with good fortune that none of the evening's passengers were travelling as far as Otterburn, for what they would have seen would doubtless have remained with them forever, as was the case for the two Foster employees.

As they passed through Wolf's Nick, it was Cecil Johnstone who first saw it.

An unmistakeable glow of isolated fire on the otherwise barren and icy moor caught his unbelieving eye. The bus halted abruptly with initially only Johnstone running towards the fire, his colleague remaining with the bus. Soon though, Rutherford too was scrambling across the crisply-set moor as the realisation dawned that something was desperately amiss. Interspersed between the crackling of flames, a faint and slight groaning sound could be heard near the front of the car. The two men, by now filled with a curious trepidation, were surveying the burning mass with stringent scrutiny when Rutherford noticed a dark object lying between the car and road. Recognising it as Evelyn, Johnstone knelt down beside her and she was heard to utter, 'Oh, that awful man.' She was lying on her side, naked from the waist down, and her head was turned away as her trauma-ravaged body convulsed rhythmically on the frozen moor. Distressingly, she was using any remaining energy to lick the droplets of ice that were encrusted on the moor all around her, in a desperately vain attempt at rehydration. Johnstone removed his overcoat and wrapped it around Evelyn, and as he did so, he noticed that her left palm was almost completely burned away.

As he manoeuvred her gently into his coat, Evelyn's full range of injuries were not apparent, though it was plainly clear that she was suffering from extensive burns. In efforts to comfort her, Johnstone told Evelyn who he was, but she offered no evidence of recognition. He gently picked Evelyn up from the moor and headed towards the bus, with Tommy Rutherford guiding the way across the darkened landscape. The agonised Evelyn was lain down in the bus before the three raced back to Otterburn for assistance. Arriving back in the village at half past ten, another employee of the Foster garage, Thomas Vasey, heard the bus arrive and curious of its appearance at such a time, hurried across towards it. The journey to Otterburn had presumably led to a subsidence of the shock Evelyn had been in, as she recognised the motor mechanic and asked that he 'lift her up'. Vasey asked Evelyn who had committed such a barbarous act, to which she unknowingly replied: 'He threw something over me and set fire to the car'. Johnstone and Vasey together, doubtlessly struggling to digest what they were seeing and hearing, then carried the young girl to her home and upstairs to her bedroom before lying her on the bed. Having settled Evelyn into some modicum of comfort, the formalities of phone calls to the police and doctor were made. Vasey then made the short journey to the village of Elsdon to fetch District Nurse Lawson. Sadly, upon viewing Evelyn's wounds, the district nurse was rather ineffective in how much she could help the patient, limited only to the treatment of the facial burns. What Evelyn desperately required was strong medication to help cope with the pain.

The local police had now descended upon the Kennels and before them lay a complete puzzle of a case, of which they would scarcely be accustomed. The established caricature of the village bobby entangled in mere poaching disputes and incidents of sheep rustling suited comfortably with Otterburn, yet here they were with a badly burned young lady before them and an apparent case of attempted and unprovoked murder. Upon arrival, however, the police were informed that the offence could very well soon be upgraded to one of murder as it was appearing increasingly likely that Evelyn would succumb fatally to her injuries.

Sergeant Shanks and Constable Fergusson hurried to Evelyn's bedside in the hope that she could offer up any vital information which would assist the investigation. Around her bedside formed a conglomeration of police and doctors, alongside Evelyn's mother, Margaret, who rather oddly, the police allowed to take the lead in questioning her daughter, whilst Constable Fergusson hastily took notes. Evelyn explained that whilst lying on the moor, she heard the petrol tank of the Hudson explode, before hearing a car approach and stop at the scene then proceed on its way again. Margaret Foster then asked her daughter if she had been 'indecently attacked' to which Evelyn answered in the affirmative. She was also able to assert that the man wore a hard hat and a dark (probably blue) overcoat, but could not accurately gauge his accent. Following the statement made to the police to which her replies had been 'lucid and sensible', Evelyn lapsed in and out of consciousness for several hours and appeared mercifully unaware that death was at hand, until she turned to her mother for a final time and whispered, 'Mother…I have been murdered.' Evelyn Foster died in her bed at five to nine on the morning after her horrifying ordeal.

The story of the murder soon became headline news. The tried and tested concoction of a murdered young girl upon some bleak and desolate place, by a perpetrator who apparently simply melted away without trace, appeared to capture the public's imagination in the same unrelenting fashion as we still grimly see today. Otterburn suddenly became a hub of activity – the collective belief that Evelyn had been murdered caused an inevitable panic among residents throughout the parish. But police were unconvinced that she had been murdered at all, persisting instead with the alternative theory that Evelyn had started the fire herself in an elaborate insurance plot.

The burned-out Hudson was ordered to be removed from the moor and admitted for the inspection of a motor expert, performed by William Jennings of Morpeth. On Thursday, 8 January, Jennings performed his inspection and returned with some rather unexpected conclusions. The engine, he found, revealed no sign of severe fire and, despite the apparent intense heat, the petrol tank had not ignited and still held its contents within. He confirmed that the fire had begun in the rear of the car as Evelyn had said, but could not clearly confirm by whom it was started.

The idea that the incident was a staged scam understandably caused much furore in the village, particularly to the Foster family; her father was insistent that 'the murder was a well planned plot' but the police could not identify a motive. Yet the insurance theory itself was hardly underpinned by robust thinking; the car was not inordinately insured, and furthermore, neither Evelyn or the Foster family appeared to be in any financial difficulties.

As if to epitomise the haste at which life had suddenly altered in the village, the Village Memorial Hall was now the focus of attention. Only a week earlier, Evelyn had attended the hall in celebration of the Christmas festivities, yet in mournful comparison, the building was now receiving her lifeless body for the inquest into her death. The coroner for the South District of Northumberland was Philip Mark Dodds, and the pathologist was Professor McDonald. The inquest would, however, prove short as the pathologist declared that he could find no physical marks of the punch to the face that Evelyn had apparently suffered – perhaps the most prominent point of the inquest – before the coroner adjourned proceedings until 2 February.

Regardless of the police's attempts to establish the truth behind Evelyn's death, the heart-rending and inescapable prospect of the Fosters burying their daughter arrived, on a most gloomy and misty January day. The miserable weather did little to deter mourners; hundreds of people from outlying villages and towns descended on Otterburn and would witness, as the local press described, 'One of the saddest ceremonies'. Evelyn was laid to rest in the grounds of the Church of St John the Evangelist, only yards from her family home.

On the morning of Monday, 2 February, the inquest into Evelyn's death resumed. The jury of nine men – all known to Evelyn – were tasked with deciding whether Evelyn's death was murder or accidental; the notion of suicide was not an option in the case. Margaret Foster was the first witness called, to which coroner Dodds raised the painful prospect that Evelyn had committed the act herself. Mrs Foster denied the allegation whole-heartedly. Asked why her daughter had not taken George Philipson with her on the night she picked up the mystery man as she was advised to do, Mrs Foster claimed that Evelyn had simply not seen him to ask. The mournful mother was finally asked to identify some pieces of clothing that were suspected of being Evelyn's. At this, she lost control and amidst her tears she was led back to her seat.

On the final day of the inquest, things would not be any less difficult for the family to endure. The first witness called was Dr Edward McEachran who confirmed that the cause of death was due to shock caused by severe burning. It was the second witness of the day, however, who garnered the most intrigue. The pathologist, Professor Stuart McDonald, was the man who would provide the answers to the mounting speculation that shrouded the case, not least the prevailing question of whether Evelyn had been the victim of murder or some form of self-inflicted scheme.

As the room hushed, Professor McDonald began by describing the extent of the burns that Evelyn suffered throughout her body.

The most severe burns were situated on the front of the middle portion of the body, on the front and inner aspect of the upper part of both thighs and, to a lesser extent over the lower portion of the flanks on both sides. There was superficial diffuse burning of the face from the chin to the middle of the forehead and at each side to the front of the ears. The eyelids were swollen, the eyelashes and eyebrows were charred, but the eyeballs had escaped. There was extensive removal of the superficial skin about the chin, mouth and nose. The hair of the head had practically escaped the burning.

The subsequent part of the pathology report focused upon the possibility that Evelyn Foster had suffered any sexual interference. The post-mortem stated that, 'The hymen was roughly oval in shape and admitted the tips of the right fore and middle fingers. Its edges were fimbriated but there was no laceration or signs of recent injury.' McDonald confirmed the lack of a sexual element to the attack, commenting that he 'examined the deceased for evidence of sexual interference but came to the conclusion that she was virgo intact; there was no evidence of violation'. The professor continued by confirming that he could find no evidence of any facial injury or bruising, which, of course, Evelyn had claimed occurred. The Fosters sat throughout this period impassively, Mr Foster, though, demonstrating intermittent moments of anxiety.

Following the statement made by Mr Jennings and his motor engineering report, Mr Dodds commenced his appraisal of the inquest and left the jury in no doubt as to what their aim was. 'The doctors are quite agreed that death has been caused by shock due to burns. It is your duty to find out how these burns were sustained.' He concluded his summing up by offering his personal view on the events: 'My opinion, I must say, is that I do not think there is sufficient evidence to say that these burns were caused by another person'.

If Dodds's mind was clear on what happened on the moor, the jury was not quite so convinced. Taking just over two hours to arrive at their conclusion, Mr McDougal, the jury foreman, finally announced the collective decision: 'The verdict is wilful murder against some person unknown'. Mr Dodds, doubtlessly somewhat irked at the decision, wrote down the official statement: 'We, the jury, find that Evelyn Foster died on the 7th day of January, 1931, at the Kennels, Otterburn, from shock due to burns caused by petrol being wilfully thrown over her and ignited by some person or persons unknown'.

From this point onwards, much bitterness enveloped the case; the police disagreed with the decision of the jury and maintained their stance that whatever had happened to Evelyn Foster on 6 January, she was certainly not the victim of a murder. The Foster family, and particularly Evelyn's father, painstakingly continued to seek the answers that the police were unable to find. However, even he, Evelyn's staunchest believer, was eventually forced to admit defeat, stating: 'I have not given up hope entirely, but, I am afraid, the end of a fruitless quest is in sight'.

To this day, absolute proof of what occurred on that fateful freezing night has yet to be established. One interesting theory, however, involves the final word spoken by a man immediately prior to his death some 150 miles away in Armley Prison, Leeds.

Shortly before four o'clock in the morning on 6 September 1933, another small village was rocked by unfamiliarly mysterious events, this time in Towton, North Yorkshire, when an almighty explosion erupted from Saxton Grange and its garage. The Grange's residents quickly realised where the flames were emanating from and swiftly vacated the property, immediately calling the emergency services for assistance. Firefighters were then able to reduce the inferno sufficiently for the police to inspect the garages. Principally, the remnants of two burnt-out cars remained, but chillingly, in the back of one of the cars, a Chrysler, sat the blackened corpse of Mr Freddy Morton, owner of the property. In the first instance, it was naturally believed that Mr Morton had perished in the fire, but the following morning, subsequent to a post-mortem, it was discovered that the victim had been killed from a gunshot wound to his abdomen. Had the gunshot wound struck the upper part of Mr Morton's body, it would never have been discovered because that part of his body had completely burned in the fire. Yet, as the finest of judicial margins sometimes dictate, the unlikely discovery now yielded the hunt for a murder suspect.

Suspicion quickly fell upon an unlikely source – groom and chauffeur to the family, Ernest Brown. It rapidly transpired that the apparent ageless motive of infidelity was the basis for the killing, Brown having indulged in several intimate liaisons with Mrs Dorothy Morton, the wife of the victim. Brown had, on the night of the murder, been seen carrying a gun. In the statement he made to police attempting to explain this, he insisted that he had been out shooting rats in the grounds of the house, yet upon a police search of the specific areas in question, no signs of any shots, pellets, or indeed dead rats were found – it was clear that Ernest Brown had a case to answer.

The ensuing trial opened at Leeds Assizes on Monday, 11 December before Mr Justice Humphreys. Following a trial lasting four days, the jury of ten men and two women returned a verdict of guilty, ensuring that Brown's final appointment on Earth would be with the hangman.

On 6 February 1934 at Armley Prison, Ernest Brown met his fate. Yet when stood on the top of the gallows, he was asked if he wished to confess anything. Brown, with his dying breath is alleged to have said 'ought to burn', just as the trap was sprung, killing him instantly.

Was Brown perhaps referring in some way to his preferred method of murder, or was his final word 'Otterburn' and therefore a knowing nod to a previous, as yet unsolved, murder deep within the bleak and inhospitable moors of Northumberland?

Whether the final murmurings of Ernest Brown are viewed as a conclusion to one of Northumberland's more sensational cases, or if it simply perpetuates a myth now inhabited in folklore, opinion is divided. Yet almost ninety years have elapsed since Evelyn Foster's death, and the fact that there is still opinion on the case confirms its durability in the public consciousness. The Foster family grave remains a stark reminder of the bygone tragedy that once rocked the village of Otterburn, its power to intrigue and captivate appearing to endure for ever more.

Bibliography

Anderson, M., *Executions and Hangings in Newcastle & Morpeth* (Wharncliffe Books, 2005)

Aries, P., *The Hour of our Death* (Allen Lane, 1981)

Bailey, B., *Burke and Hare: The Year of the Ghouls* (Edinburgh: Mainstream Publishing, 2002)

Baillie, J., *An Impartial History of Newcastle upon Tyne* (Vint & Anderson, 1801)

Barnes, Justyn, *The Official Manchester United History* (Carlton Books, 2001)

Bartlett, D.W., *The Life of Lady Jane Grey* (Miller, Orton & Mulligan, 1885)

Bleackley, H., *Some Distinguished Victims of the Scaffold* (1905, reissued by Project Gutenberg, 2016)

Cawthorne, N., *Witch Hunt: History of a Persecution* (Arcturus Publishing Limited, 2003)

Coote, S., *A Play of Passion* (Macmillan London Limited, 1993)

Dixon, R., *Evelyn Foster: Murder or Fraud on the Northumberland Moors* (Wolf's Nick Publishing, 2011)

Douglas, M., *Witchcraft Confessions and Accusations* (Tavistock Publications Limited, 1970)

Edwards, O.D., *The True Story of the Infamous…Burke and Hare* (Polygon Books, 1980)

Fuller, T., *The History of the Worthies of England* (1663)

Gardenier, B., *The New York Reporter Containing Reports of Trials and Decisions* (New York, 1820)

Glinert, E., *London's Dead: A Guided Tour of the Capital's Dead* (Collins, 2008)

Harris, N., *Memoirs and Literary Remains of Lady Jane Grey* (1832)

Haynes, A., *The Gunpowder Plot* (The History Press, 1994)

Holmes, R., *Witchcraft in British History* (Frederick Muller Limited, 1974)

Hone, W., *The Everyday Book and Table Book: Volume I* (London, 1837)

Houlbrooke, R., *Death, Religion and the Family in England 1480-1750* (Oxford University Press, 1998)

Hunt, A., & Whitelock, A., (eds.), *Tudor Queenship: The Reigns of Mary and Elizabeth* (Palgrave MacMillan, 2010)

Ives, E., *Lady Jane Grey: A Tudor Mystery* (John Wiley & Sons, 2011)

John, J., *Dark History of the Tudors – England's Most Infamous Royal Dynasty* (Amber Books, 2017)

Jupp, P.C., and Gittings, C., *Death in England – An Illustrated History* (Manchester University Press, 1999)

Kingsley, C., *Sir Walter Raleigh and his Time* (reissued by Project Gutenberg, 2014)

Levack, B.P., T*he Witch-Hunt in Early Modern Europe* (Routledge, 2016)

Linebaugh, P., *The London Hanged: Crime and Civil Society in the Eighteenth Century* (Verso, 2003)

Lisle, L.D., *The Sisters Who Would Be Queen – The Tragedy of Mary, Katherine and Lady Jane Grey* (Harper Press, 2008)

MacGregor, G., *The History of Burke and Hare and of the Resurrectionist Times* (1884, reissued by Project Gutenberg, 2004)

Mackenzie, E., *History of Northumberland: Volume 1* (Mackenzie and Dent, St Nicholas' Churchyard, 1825)

Marsden, J.I., 'Sex, Politics, and She-Tragedy: Reconfiguring Lady Jane Grey', *Studies in English Literature, 1500-1900* Vol. 42, No. 3 (2002)

Mathias, J., 'Victorian Attitudes Towards Self-Murder', *Curious Histories* (blog on oldoperatingtheatre.com) 11 November 2016 *(http://oldoperatingtheatre. com/blog/victorian-attitudes-towards-self-murder)*

Morgan, M., *Victorian Scandals* (Robinson Publishing, 2018)

Oldham, J., *Informal Law-Making in England by the Twelve Judges in the Late 18th and Early 19th Centuries* (Georgetown University Law Center, 2011)

Pickering, D. & A., *Witch Hunt – The Persecution of Witches in England* (Amberley Publishing, 2013)

Ponting, N., Carter, G., Bevan, F., et al., '*Double Tragedy at Kingsdown' in Swindon Heritage, Issue 18, Summer 2017*

Raleigh, W., *The Discovery of Guiana* (reissued by Project Gutenberg, 2006)

Riffenburgh, B., *Titanic – The Story of the Unsinkable Ship* (Andre Deutsch Publishing, 2008)

Rimmer, S., 'Victorian Parlour Maid's Tragic Suicide Letter to her Sister, 1900', *Abroad in the Yard* blog in Ancestry section of abroadintheyard.com (https://www.abroadintheyard.com/victorian-parlour-maids-tragic-suicide-letter-to-her-sister-1900/)

Roughead, W., (ed.), *Trial of Mary Blandy* (1914, reissued by Project Gutenberg, 2004)

Sharpe, J.A., 'Last Dying Speeches: Religion, Ideology and Public Execution in Seventeenth-Century England', *Past and Present, No. 107* (May 1985)

Smith Fussner, F., *The Historical Revolution: English Historical Writing and Thought 1580-1640* (Routledge & Kegan Paul Limited, 1962)

Strevens, S., *The First Forensic Hanging: The Toxic Truth That Killed Mary Blandy* (Pen & Sword Books, 2018)

Swift, M., *The Titanic: The Memorabilia Collection* (Igloo Books, 2013)

Tallis, N., *Crown of Blood – The Deadly Inheritance of Lady Jane Grey* (Michael O'Mara Books Ltd, 2016)

Thomas, K. & Gunnell, D., 'Suicide in England and Wales 1861–2007: A Time Trends Analysis', *International Journal of Epidemiology*, Vol 39, Issue 6 (December 2010)

Walker, M., 'Fatal Affair at Saxton Grange' in *Master Detective* (True Crime Library, 2016)

Weber, F.P., *Aspects of Death and Correlated Aspects of Life in Art, Epigram and Poetry* (T. Fisher Unwin, Ltd, 1922)

Wilding, R., *Death in Chester* (Gordon Emery, 2003)

Wilson, D., *Pain and Retribution – A Short History of British Prisons, 1066 to the Present* (Reaktion Books, 2014)

Wilson, P., *Murderess* (Michael Joseph Ltd, 1971)

Young, A.F., *The Encyclopaedia of Scottish Executions 1750-1963* (Dobby Publishing, 1998)

Archival Sources

AD2/1/3 – Indictment; JC4/18 – High Court Book; JC8/23 – High Court Minute Book; HH21/8/1 – Register of Criminal Prisoners (relating to Chapter 17, all deposited in National Records of Scotland)

AD2/24 – Indictment; AD14/53/448 – Precognition; JC8/61 – Minute Book; JC26/1853/525 – Case Papers (relating to Chapter 8, all deposited in National Records of Scotland)

Board of Trade – Civil Aircraft Accident Report of the Second Independent Review appointed to consider the accident to Elizabethan Aircraft G-ALZU at Munich on 6 February 1958 and to report whether blame for the accident is to be imputed to Captain Thain (London: Her Majesty's Stationery Office, 1969) https://assets.publishing.service.gov.uk/media/5422f6c3e5274a13140005db/CAP_318_G-ALZU_6_Feb_1958_Elizabethan_Munich_1969_2nd_UK_Acc_Report.pdf

COS/3/54/1 – Police Report, Statements, Autopsy, Examination of Exhibits (relating to Chapter 23, deposited in Woodhorn Museum, Northumberland Archives)

DDHD/39/3 – Suicide Letter; DDHD/CR/39/3 – Inquest Report (relating to Chapter 9, deposited in Lancashire Record Office)

The Remarkable Confession and Last Dying Words of Thomas Colley, executed on Saturday, August 24th 1751…for the cruel murder of Ruth Osborne, etc. Thomas Colley, Malefactor. London: R. Walker, [1751] (P.P.1349.a.42.(12.) (Pamphlet courtesy of the British Library)

Trial and Execution of Charles Smith 1817 (deposited in Newcastle Library)

Online Sources

British Newspaper Archive	www.britishnewspaperarchive.co.uk
Capital Punishment UK	www.capitalpunishmentuk.org/blandy.html
Hidden Lives Revealed	https://www.hiddenlives.org.uk/homes/SEAFO01.html
Jim Batten's British Explorers	http://www.britishexplorers.com/woodbury/raleigh.html

Old Royal Naval College, Greenwich	https://ornc.org/our-story/royal-hospital/life-as-a-greenwich-pensioner/
Peter Higginbotham's 'The Workhouse'	http://www.workhouses.org.uk/
The Ex-Classics Website	www.exclassics.com
The Proceedings of the Old Bailey	www.oldbaileyonline.org
Titanic Historical Society, Inc.	https://titanichistoricalsociety.org
Titanic Inquiry Project (US)	https://www.titanicinquiry.org/USInq2/AmInq04Fleet02.php
Wilstone: A Short History	https://wilstonesticks.com/wilstone---a-short-history.html#

Podcasts

Helen Castor, 'The Tragedy of Lady Jane Grey' [podcast], History Extra (8 January 2018)
https://www.historyextra.com/period/tudor/the-tragedy-of-lady-jane-grey/

Anna Beer, 'Walter Raleigh: Enemy of the State' [podcast], History Extra (29 November 2018)
https://www.historyextra.com/period/elizabethan/walter-ralegh-raleigh-enemy-of-the-state/

Index